QUESTIONS AND ANSWERS

QUESTIONS AND ANSWERS

FIRST AND SECOND SUPPLEMENT
TO
TOWARD THE LIGHT

PUBLISHED BY
MICHAEL AGERSKOV
TOWARD THE LIGHT PUBLISHING HOUSE, ApS.
COPENHAGEN, DENMARK
1979

The original editions were published as separate books in Copenhagen, Denmark, in 1929 and 1930, both under the title
"Spørgsmål og Svar"

TOWARD THE LIGHT PUBLISHING HOUSE, ApS.
"Vandrer mod Lyset"s Forlag, ApS.
22 Købmagergade, 1150 Copenhagen K,
Denmark

Copyright© 1979
All rights reserved.

No part of this work covered by the copyrights hereon may be translated, reproduced or copied in any form or by any means – graphic, electronic or mechanical, including photocopying, recording or taping – without the written permission of the Publisher.

ISBN 87-87871-52-1

Library of Congress Catalog Card Number:
79-9594

Published under the auspices
of
The International Foundation for "Toward the Light",
Copenhagen, Denmark.

PRINTED IN DENMARK by DYVA BOGTRYK-OFFSET GLOSTRUP

PREFACE

Since the publication in 1920 of "Toward the Light" and its addendum, "The Doctrine of Atonement and the Shorter Road", my wife and I have received numerous written and oral questions from people in all walks of life concerning the interpretation of specific details in these books.

The great majority of these questions have been of such a nature that we were able to answer most of them in a few words, or refer the questioner to a closer study of the books; but there were others that required not only a fuller, but also a completely *authoritative* explanation.

In such cases my wife addressed herself to the author of the Commentary in "Toward the Light", her deceased father, and asked him to give the answers. She then received these answers through inspiration and intuition, in the way that has been explained in detail in the Postscript to "Toward the Light".

The resulting seventy-one answers are collected in this book. However, the form of some of the answers differs from that in which they were expressed in the letters sent to the questioners; some are expanded, others abbreviated, but the informal style of a personal letter has been modified. These changes owe their origin, of course, to my wife's transcendental informant.

It was furthermore the wish of the transcendental world that human beings should be given authentic guidance in the important area of sexual matters. This guidance has been included as a special Appendix to this book, since it was not occasioned by questions from the earthly world.

We know that many of these answers will arouse astonishment and opposition. To this I can only say that the answers are presented exactly as received and that all of them are approved and authorized by God, our Father. It will then be for human beings to decide whether to accept or reject them, in accordance with the dictates of their *conscience*.

1st June, 1929
The Publisher

CONTENTS

Question	Subject	Page
1.	Communication with spirits of Light. Telepathy between human beings	11
2.	The preparatory work for the production of "Toward the Light"	12
3.	Definition of "medium" and mediumistic talents	17
4.	Messages from spirits of Light to specially chosen people	18
5.	Spontaneous phenomena and spiritualists	20
6.	The removal of earthbound spirits from the plane of the Earth	21
7.	Life-span of the Eldest incarnated by Ardor	23
8.	Possession by spirits	23
9.	Influence of Light and Darkness on human beings	23
10.	Evaluation of spiritual truths	24
11.	Why the work of producing "Toward the Light" was given to a woman	25
12.	Advocates of "Toward the Light"	29
13.	Attitude of Danish Church leaders to "Toward the Light"	30
14.	Mormonism, Theosophy, Christian Science and Anthroposophy	33
15.	"The Shorter Road"	35
16.	The necessity for reincarnation	36
17.	Forgiveness of sin through prayers to Christ	40
18.	Prayers for those suffering under the Law of Retribution	40
19.	Possible injustice through prayers of intercession	43
20.	Prayers to saints and prayers to heathen "gods"	44
21.	Prayers to God by human beings	44
22.	Primal cosmos: Darkness, Light, Thought and Will	46
23.	The hot vapours of the Earth and the immaterial bodies of the Eldest	47
24.	Forms of transportation in the spheres	47
25.	Attachment of the spirit to the foetus	48
26.	Time of death of the human body	48
27.	Formation of the Mother Suns	49
28.	The Mother Sun of our galactic system	50
29.	The Central Sun: God's Kingdom	50

30. The invisibility of God's Kingdom 51
31. The astronomical dimensions of the Milky Way 51
32. The distant nebulae 51
33. Luther's "vision" at Wartburg 52
34. Luther's bodily sufferings 52
35. Luther's spiritual sufferings 52
36. The total time for the incarnations of a human being 53
37. Ties of friendship and kinship 54
38. Meeting of man and wife in the beyond 55
39. The concept of love 56
40. Love between duals and neighbourly love 57
41. Primal prototypes of earthly plant life and God's
    love for human beings 59
42. Blasphemy against the "Holy Ghost" 59
43. The human urge to make offerings 61
44. The Jewish people and human sacrifice 62
45. The Messianic Hope of the Jewish People 63
46. Joseph, the father of Jesus 63
47. Conception of Jesus by the "Holy Ghost" 64
48. The 24th December as the birthday of Jesus 65
49. The humility of Jesus 66
50. Crucifixion of Jesus, the Council in Jerusalem 68
51. Crucifixion of Jesus, guilt of Pilate and the Council 69
52. The release of Barabbas 70
53. The words: "Eloi, Eloi, lama sabachthani" 71
54. The death of atonement of Jesus 72
55. The robber on the cross 73
56. An attack on "The Doctrine of Atonement and
    the Shorter Road" 74
57. The doctrine of Jesus' death of atonement 76
58. The divine trinity in ancient religions 77
59. The concept of the Messiah 78
60. Human beings in the presence of God 79
61. God's existence through all eternity 80
62. God and the natural laws 80
63. God and human suffering 83
64. A Deity of Darkness in a cosmos of Darkness 86
65. The annihilated "kingdom" around the Earth 89
66. The Apocalypse 90
67. Ardor's ether-recordings 91
68. The point in time for Satan's – Ardor's – return
    to God 93
69. God's continued creation of human spirits 93

70. Biblical evidence for the forgiveness of Ardor by God
    and human beings 94
71. Sins and crimes of humanity after Ardor's return
    to God 96

APPENDIX

Marriage, birth control and abortion 101

SECOND SUPPLEMENT to "Toward the Light"
follows after page 115

1.

Is it possible in earthly terms to explain how the spirits of Light can make contact with human beings, and how telepathic communication between human beings can arise?

These forms of communication can best be illustrated by reference to radio transmission and reception.

The spirits of Light send their messages, admonitions, warnings and so on by thought through *the waves of the Light-ether,* so that they can be received by the *psychic brain* of human beings. In the same way that various "wave-lengths" are used in radio transmission, the spirits of Light also employ shorter or longer wave-lengths in the Light-ether, attuning their thought-vibrations exactly to the ether waves that can be received by the psychic brain of the particular human being with whom they wish to communicate.

Telepathic communication between human beings is similar to this, but with the difference that the thoughts sent out by human beings are only very rarely received by the person for whom the message is intended, because the *internal structures* of the sender's and the recipient's psychic brains are not *attuned to each other.* No instructions will, of course, be given here on how human beings during life on Earth can themselves attune their psychic brain exactly to that of the person with whom they wish to make contact by the difficult means of telepathy. (See "Toward the Light" p. 310:2,3).

Transmission and reception of *thought* by means of earthly radio definitely cannot occur. Where individual human beings apparently can receive messages in this way the connection is not made through earthly radio but between the psychic brains of the sender and the recipient. These are in mutual correspondence because they happen to be attuned to the same "thought-wave" at that moment.

No one in this age of radio who knows from personal experience how clear and sonorous radio communication can be should for a moment doubt the reality of the "spiritual", the psychic communication between the leaders of mankind – the spirits of Light, the Youngest – and human beings, especially since earthly radio stems from "spiritual radiophony", and therefore *is no more than an imitation, a mere reflection of the original.* Neither should anyone doubt that "spiritual" communication can be *pure and clear and unaffected by Darkness,* provided *that the psychic brains of the sender and the recipient respond similarly to the same wave-length in the Light-ether.*

All inspiration and intuition belong to the area of "spiritual radiophony", but the ether waves of both Darkness and Light can be employed – *by the spirits of Darkness and by the spirits of Light* respectively.

2.

Why was the introductory work of producing "Toward the Light" based on spiritualism in view of the fact that spiritualism as a whole is not recognized according to the Divine Laws?

The first occurrence of so-called occult or spiritualistic phenomena in the earthly world was due to the Eldest, who sought by countless means to gain dominion over the weaker human souls. Generation after generation has known and recognized these phenomena. Accounts can be found in the ancient Scriptures from the earliest times – *and to a great extent also in the Bible* – of various kinds of event that all fall into the category of occultism, or – to use the more modern term – spiritualism. But it is clear that God has never in any way desired or sanctioned occurrences that were intended to constitute proof of transcendental intervention in the earthly world, since the procedure for such proof *had been given by the Eldest on the basis of the powers of Darkness.*

Communication between God and human beings, or the spirits of Light and human beings, has always, ever since the time that God endowed human beings with spiritual life, been based on inspiration and intuition, as well as on spontaneous thought-impulses and spontaneous appearances by the spirits of Light before the eyes of human beings.

In the nineteenth century, when renewed interest in communication with the transcendental world arose, God considered the possibility that by establishing a more direct connection than hitherto between the spirits of Light and a small number of chosen human beings, He could in this way more quickly redeem Ardor and the earthbound spirits. He could also, through this more direct communication, clear the astral environment of the Earth of much of its incumbent Darkness. The basis for God's decision was that *the spirit of the times* had now matured to the extent that at least some thousands of human beings should be capable of understanding and rejoicing in the establishment of such communication.

The course taken by God until then had been the following: from time to time and with longer or shorter intervals to incarnate some of the Youngest with the task of becoming founders of religion or religious reformers. This was done in order to bring human beings knowledge of the transcendental world and its laws and to lead them to a truer and deeper understanding of the nature of God and His relationship to mankind. But since the Eldest continually sought to lead the incarnated Youngest astray, continually sought to defile and distort the truths which the Youngest taught humanity, and since the Eldest during their incarnations also appeared as institutors of new religious movements, or even outrightly denied the existence of God, these countermoves created additional confusion in human religious perception of God, of the beyond and of life on Earth; for numerous different sects and creeds thereby appeared, whose adherents to this day oppose one another, all trying to win proselytes for their own postulates and dogmas. But despite all countermoves on the part of the Eldest, the course previously taken by God would still at some point in the future, when the human spirit had grown more mature and more rational, have led to the desired goal: namely, *the rejection of all existing beliefs in favour of a true and deep acknowledgement of God as the Creator and Father of the human spirit.*

However, since God always tries to make the best of the evil onslaughts of Darkness, He therefore decided to oppose the Eldest with their own weapons – but by the methods of the Light. God chose this way because, among other reasons, it had been proved time and again that it was impossible for the incarnated Youngest – because of the Darkness on Earth – to remember their pledge to their Father: *during their lives on Earth to take pity on their eldest fallen brother, to forgive him and to pray for him.* For so long as this promise had not been fulfilled and Ardor therefore remained Prince of the Earth and of mankind, the steps forward in the cause of the Light with respect to religion could only be few and infinitely small. God therefore decided to try the *"Shorter Road"*,[1] so as to bring order to the religious chaos on Earth more quickly through a more direct and more comprehensive guidance, and at the same time to redeem Ardor. And God gave the eldest of the Youngest – Christ – instructions[1] on the way in which this could be accomplished.

---

[1]) See "Toward the Light" pp. 94-98.

The Youngest chosen for this work had to live on the astral plane of the Earth as disincarnated beings – that is, invisible to human beings – amid dense accumulations of Darkness, surrounded by earthbound spirits and the images and recordings of human sin and crime – *an existence so dismal and enervating as to defy description.* But God had chosen not to employ this method earlier in the history of humanity for the very reason that the life which the Youngest would have to endure would be so trying and full of horror; for it could be employed only if the Youngest themselves would exert *all* their energy to overcome Darkness. And since *the time* had now arrived when the Youngest expressed a deep and sincere yearning to attain an effective and early solution with respect to Ardor and the fallen Eldest, God knew that in all likelihood *the difficult mission could now succeed.*

Since the spirits of Darkness were thus to be opposed by their own weapons – occult and spiritualistic phenomena – it was essential to find human beings who could serve as intermediaries between humanity and Christ and his helpers. With a view to this goal God incarnated in the course of time a number of the Youngest and certain highly advanced human spirits who were suitable for this purpose.

The many disappointments and difficulties of the "Shorter Road" are described in "Toward the Light", pp. 98–100; however, the goal was still reached within the time allotted by God despite all the countermoves of the Eldest. But it was not reached before the disincarnated Eldest and the disincarnated Youngest had fought a long and hard struggle.[1] For while the Youngest sought to influence the so-called mediums to work for the cause of the Light, the Eldest tried at the same time in every possible way to obstruct these mediums and to draw them deeper into Darkness. Only too often did the Eldest succeed, and every time this happened Christ and his helpers had to turn to other mediums. But this struggle back and forth between the disincarnated Eldest and Youngest created among the human beings on Earth a steadily rising interest in occultism, spiritualism and psychic research. When Christ and his helpers finally found a truly suitable intermediary, they had of course to impart to their earthly helper full insight not only into *the fallacies and falsehoods,* but also into *the truths of spiritualism.* Their assistant was also made fully aware of the *sinister influence* from *the spirits of Darkness* to which human beings expose themselves when they submit to trances and physical manifestations, that is to say, materialization phenomena. Not until this had been achieved, and all possibility thereby elim-

---

[1] See also "Some Psychic Experiences" p. 36 – "the powers of Light and Darkness" – to p. 39 regarding this struggle between the Eldest and the Youngest.

inated that the earthly intermediary might be brought under the direct influence of Darkness, could the actual task begin – the task that consisted of winning back the Elder – Ardor – and the brothers and sisters who fell with him, as well as of persuading the earthbound spirits to leave the plane of the Earth of their own accord. Besides showing their earthly helper the proper way of assisting them, this also achieved the purpose of showing her how mistaken the teachings of spiritualism were, and necessarily had to be. In this way the spirits of Light also struck a blow at the spiritualist movement, so that they were able during the transference of "Toward the Light" *to include a solemn warning to all involved with spiritualistic phenomena and to enjoin them to cease these communications, which are not permitted* **under the laws of God.**

When Christ and his helpers finally won complete victory over Darkness and thus achieved the goal that their Father had set them, they all returned to their abodes. And from that moment *none of the spirits of Light has participated in any spiritualistic séance in any manner whatsoever, for which reason the only connection that so-called mediums have with the spirits of Light is through their guardian spirit – their conscience – in the same way as any other human being. Any assertion to the contrary on the part of spiritualists has no connection whatsoever with the truth.* Let this be emphatically repeated: *such is the situation and not otherwise,* for among the spiritualists' mediums there are many who are *self-appointed* intermediaries between this world and that which they claim to be the world of Light. But their assertion *is untrue!* Their messages and religious views are thus quite worthless. There is no further basis for the existence of spiritualism, and the sooner spiritualists understand this and accept the consequences, the better it will be both for themselves and for the fellow human beings whom they lead astray.

The "Shorter Road" was thus shown to be feasible, the goal was reached and the struggle between the disincarnated Eldest and Youngest is over – *and will never again be resumed!*

Although spiritualism and its various precursors[1] originally stemmed from the influence of the Eldest upon human beings, and thus have their origin in Darkness, these communications with the transcendental have brought mankind certain benefits that should not be underestimated. For many people have thereby come to understand that earthly life does not end with the death of the body, but continues beyond death and the grave; that human spirits must again and again be incarnated in order to be capable of finally reaching God's

---

[1] Swedenborgianism, among others.

Kingdom; that the spirits of Darkness have in many ways led human beings astray; and that many psychic and physical powers exist whose use remains a mystery to human beings, because they do not perceive them in the proper manner. And since God permitted the Youngest for a time, and under the laws of the Light, to establish communication with certain human beings who were chosen for that purpose, the following results have been achieved: Ardor – Satan – has returned to God; all future incarnations of the fallen Eldest have been brought under God's leadership; all earthbound spirits have been removed from the plane of the Earth; all visual ether-recordings of human sins and transgressions – recorded while the earthbound spirits lived as human beings on Earth – have been obliterated and can never reappear, since Ardor is no longer the Prince of Darkness.

Mankind has also received "Toward the Light" and "The Doctrine of Atonement and the Shorter Road"[1] as visible results of the work of the Youngest. But it will of course be a very long time before mankind fully understands the worth of these gifts and benefits, even though many people are already aware of their unique value. The time will come, however, when human beings with gratitude and understanding *will recognize the work that has been done to facilitate their journey toward the distant Fatherly Home.*

Many will perhaps object that the spirits of Light, by employing the aspects of the Light that exist in spiritualism as a means of attaining their goal, are themselves to blame for the extensive spread of spiritualism. The only answer to this is that it was done in accordance with *God's wish,* in *the manner indicated by Him* and under *His guidance,* because God knew that human beings would one day become *so spiritually mature* that they *would understand both the procedure employed and the results produced.* And God also knew that although the teachings of spiritualism would have many followers for a long time to come, the dominion over human beings exercised by the spirits of Darkness through the various manifestations of spiritualism *would in reality be broken on Ardor's return to His Kingdom.* It would therefore only be a question of a longer or shorter period of time before it would completely lose its hold on the human mind. And to assist in the early achievement of this aim, clear and solemn warnings and instructions have been given in "Toward the Light". *May this work soon be understood!*

---

[1]) "Greetings to Denmark" is not included here since it is a special gift to the Danish people.

3.

**1) How should the term "medium" be correctly understood?
2) Are mediumistic talents to be found exclusively among the so-called spiritualists?**

1) "Medium" or "intermediary" is the term used to describe people who are in some way suited to serve as a connecting link between the visible and the invisible worlds. These people can be employed by the spirits of Light as well as by the spirits of Darkness – the incarnated "Eldest" and human spirits who visit the plane of the Earth without permission.

Spirits of Light no longer appear at spiritualistic séances, neither as leaders nor as religious speakers,[1] as claimed by spiritualists. They act only through spontaneous phenomena at God's request and according to His directions. When Christ searched for helpers on Earth in order to redeem Ardor, he was accompanied by several of the Youngest. During this period they and Christ often visited small, private circles in order to influence the members so that they might possibly become suitable for the work. But since this work has ceased long ago there is no longer any reason for the spirits of Light to appear at either public or private spiritualistic séances. However, the spirits of Darkness act both through spontaneous phenomena as well as through the spiritualistic séances arranged by human beings. But communication through spiritualistic séances is not permitted under God's laws, nor are spontaneous communications such as, for instance, thought-impulses, visions and various other types of phenomena that are caused by the spirits of Darkness.

Anyone who experiences occult phenomena should be able to determine whether a spirit of Darkness or a spirit of Light has produced them. But in either case *a fervent prayer to God will* bring the necessary help and clarify the issue. The only direct daily communication a spiritualistic medium has with the spirits of Light is with the guardian spirit, or conscience, who always tries to guide its charge away from the influence of spiritualism. However, if the charge does not pay heed, or if he or she does not follow the admonitions given, more and more Darkness will be attracted until finally the voice of conscience can no longer be heard – it is absorbed by and cannot penetrate the dense wall of Darkness. This leaves the spirits of Darkness at liberty to deliver their false messages, fantasies devoid of meaning and religious sermons, whose substance conflicts with that

---

[1]) See "Toward the Light" p. 244:1. See also the answer to the preceding Question.

which is stated in "Toward the Light" and its Supplements.

2) No! Since all communication with the invisible world takes place through *inspiration, intuition* and various *spontaneous thought-impulses,* it is a matter of course that people of mediumistic talent do not have to be, and preferably should not be, spiritualists in order to act as intermediaries between human beings and the world beyond.

All who in the cause of the Light have something to offer humanity within the fields of invention, science, art or religion, are mediums, i.e., intermediaries, between the visible and the invisible worlds. They are the interpreters who must necessarily be the connecting link between humanity and the Light's eternally flowing sources of spiritual life. Through inspiration and through their own intuition they receive assistance in bringing such innovations and improvements to mankind as the spirit of the times is ready to accept. But since the spirits of Light very often work with *long term objectives,* that which they bring to mankind in this way often lies far beyond the aims *that the spirit of the times can comprehend.* These messengers of the Light are therefore often denounced and misunderstood by their contemporaries. But *no one has the right to call such people "spiritualists", regardless of the area in which they serve as the earthly assistants of God and of the Light.*

4.

Since "Toward the Light" so strongly dissociates itself from spiritualism, should not the section on transcendental communication on page 253 of that work have been omitted? Or do these circumstances have nothing to do with "spiritualism"?

The circumstances referred to have only a very indirect bearing on spiritualism.

This passage must first and foremost be read in context with the preceding paragraph on p. 252:2, which is introduced as follows: "Should God need human beings as helpers or intermediaries in the future there are numerous ways in which the spirits of Light can call upon human beings and communicate with them whenever this may be desired". This refers to the spirits of Light, and to the guardian spirits in particular, which emerges clearly from the next paragraph. Since it is further stated on p. 253 that people who receive messages from the transcendental world without having requested them will always, directly or indirectly, receive at the same time such proof that they can never doubt the identity of the originator, it is apparent that it refers to identification in connection with the spirits of Light rather than in connection with deceased human beings. Proofs can be given in many different ways, for example through the recipient's intuitive understanding, through visions, or through the logical, clear and concise presentation of the messages.

It is furthermore stated on p. 253 that: "When communication with human beings is established on the initiative of the transcendental world, this is normally because they were selected to assist in spreading knowledge and understanding of life after death through writings, lectures and the like, before their life on Earth began." These forms of communication therefore belong to the category of *"psychic research"*, which is only indirectly related to spiritualism. People can thus very well be engaged in psychic research and still dissociate themselves entirely from spiritualism. Those who for some reason have been chosen to gather information, partly through their own experiences and partly through those of others, in order to enable them by various means - written or oral - to document to their fellow human beings the close relationship between the invisible world and the visible, should therefore never, as it is also stated on p. 253, allow themselves to be intimidated by the lack of judgment or insight into these matters on the part of their fellow human beings. Indeed, be they even called "spiritualists", which in reality they are not, this term is meaningless if in everything they do they follow the way that they are shown by their guardian spirit - their conscience.

Therefore, the paragraph mentioned can never be of direct benefit to spiritualism, since it does not refer to communication with spirits of the "deceased". Reference is made only to people who are not already bound by the often deficient, false and misleading explanations and postulates of spiritualism. It refers only to the chosen ones who are able to collect, sort out and judge if not all, then at least some of the matter brought to light through occult phenomena. But unfortunately, only a few people are fully able to classify and judge occult phenomena and experiences, even though they have been chosen for this purpose. For even if they are not bound by the postulates of spiritualism, they can be bound by so many other commitments in life on Earth, such as the dogmas, doctrines and postulates of Christianity, Theosophy, Anthroposophy or various other creeds. Only those who are completely unprejudiced and who do not pay the least attention to what has already been accepted and established will be able to undertake such a task properly and with any prospect of producing results that are in accordance with the truth. And since the so-called spiritualistic mediums usually come from the general populace, it should be obvious that they cannot be entrusted with a task such as the educational work mentioned above. Only truly cultured, enlightened and well-educated people, to whose body one of the Youngest or a spiritually highly advanced human spirit is bound, can be entrusted with such an assignment.

It should also be remembered that the spiritualists cannot adopt the term "medium" or "intermediary" to apply only to *their own intermediaries* between the invisible and the visible worlds. This term applies in the broadest sense to *all people* who in one way or another can be employed by the spirits of Light in their inspirational activities on Earth. (See also the answer to the preceding Question).

5.

Cannot spiritualists experience spontaneous phenomena that are due to the spirits of Light?

Spiritualists are of course also able to experience spontaneous communications with the spirits of Light in the form of visions, dreams of warning, admonitions or visions of death. But this occurs only if this is the wish of the transcendental world – *not because of demands or special preparations on the part of human beings, and it occurs without the intervention of spiritualistic mediums and* will therefore *never* take place at *spiritualistic séances.*

However, such spontaneous phenomena may also be due to the incarnated Eldest and can be experienced both by spiritualists and by non-spiritualists. Anyone who experiences occult phenomena should therefore try to decide to which category these belong and from within the self carefully consider the occurrence in order to achieve the proper understanding of whether the originator can be identified as a spirit of Darkness or a spirit of Light. Hideous visions, loud knocks, explosive sounds,[1] calls of mockery, malicious or obscure thought-impulses and similar spontaneous phenomena are always due to the Eldest, who during their nocturnal sleep release unlawfully try to influence unstable souls. A prayer to God for help to prevent such eerie experiences will always be answered, and thus make recurrence impossible. *But the prayer must come from deep in the heart, or it will be of no avail.*

However, other phenomena such as visions of a certain beauty,

---

[1] These can also be due to negative and positive attractions and discharges of Darkness.

the appearance of differently coloured light-formations, religious inspirations, pre-warnings of death and the like, might appear to the recipient to have derived from the spirits of Light. In such cases the recipient should also seek enlightenment on the phenomena through a prayer to God. If his mind is then filled with calm and peace, a spirit of Light was the originator. But if he has an uneasy feeling and is unpleasantly preoccupied with the experience, then he will know that it was due to a spirit of Darkness, who produced these phenomena thinking that through such demonstrations it could more easily gain dominance over that human being.

6.

Is the statement in "Toward the Light" on pages 238 and 247, regarding the removal from the Earth of the earthbound spirits, more than a postulate?

This statement is not a postulate but *an absolute truth.*

Stern warnings are given on pages 250 and 253 to all kinds of spiritualistic mediums against involvement with the spirits of the "dead", since mediums can only hamper and delay them in every way rather than bring them any kind of help.

But while the warning on this subject given in "Toward the Light" remains generally unknown there will apparently be no improvement in this respect in relation to human spirits from the fifth sphere and from the lower planes of the sixth sphere. (Spirits who dwell in the first four spheres are prevented from descending to the plane of the Earth by the Light-Barrier, unless they have permission, and are assisted by their guardian spirit. See "Toward the Light", p. 249:1,2, regarding the Light-Barrier).

The reason why earthbound spirits apparently still exist is that spiritualistic mediums continue to hold séances and thus tempt weak-willed human spirits to leave their dwellings in the spheres in order to appear at these séances. But spirits who visit the plane of the Earth without permission, drawn by the demanding thoughts and desires on the part of mediums, friends and relatives that they should produce manifestations, always feel confused, wretched and desperate amid the Earth's accumulations of Darkness. And when they find themselves in earthly surroundings their earthly memories immediately awake, and in most cases they forget their existence in the sphere from which they came. They feel rather as human beings *who are beset by agonizing and confusing dreams.* But in the same way that sleeping human beings can act and think sensibly in their dreams, human spirits who are unlawfully present at séances on the plane of the Earth can make statements concerning their earthly lives that are *in accordance with fact,* or *which touch upon factual circumstances.* When these spirits return once again to their dwellings in the spheres they recall their stay upon the plane of the Earth as if they had awakened from *a nightmare* or from *some weird dream.* Thousands of human spirits are drawn to the Earth *every day,* and *every day* the spirits of Light guide the disobedient back to their dwellings in the spheres.

Apart from the aforementioned human spirits, many of the Eldest – the incarnated – can also attend spiritualistic séances during nocturnal sleep release.[1] These Eldest can in many ways exert a disturbing and spiritually destructive influence wherever they appear by giving false information – for example of a religious nature – and by seeking to instil evil, wicked or sinful thoughts in the minds of those present. The Youngest cannot always prevent this, even though they try to protect human beings by accompanying the Eldest on their unlawful excursions. (See "Toward the Light" p. 293:3). Human beings must themselves seek to avoid the influence of the Eldest, firstly by not attending séances, secondly by always paying heed to their conscience and thirdly by praying to God for help and protection. For only God can build *a protective wall of Light* between human beings and *those* of the Eldest who are still able to influence them in evil and sinful ways.

The Eldest incarnated by Ardor can thus continue for a long time to exercise an adverse influence upon mankind; but they are no longer able to take possession of human beings, not even during nocturnal sleep release, since they remain bound to their sleeping bodies at such times. Only disincarnated spirits have been able to possess human beings. And since the Eldest upon the death of the body are now brought to distant globes from which they cannot return to the Earth, *the occurrence of such possessions now or in the future is entirely precluded.*

---

[1]) See "Toward the Light" p. 293:2.

7.

Since the Eldest incarnated by Ardor cause so much harm among human beings, why does God not call them back from earthly life? Why must they remain here for another fifty to sixty years?[1]

Ardor has determined the time of death for all the Eldest incarnated by him. If this predetermination should be changed, so that God might recall these Eldest before the time determined by Ardor, then each one of them would have to consent to this. God has, however, spoken to all of them during one of their nocturnal sleep releases, but only a few of them would comply with His wish that they should depart from life on Earth. *And since God never opposes the free will of the individual He cannot cause the others to "die" before the time appointed by Ardor.*

8.

Can human beings be possessed by the disincarnated human spirits who unlawfully visit the Earth?

No, this is absolutely impossible. Human spirits do not have the power of will required to cling to – or rather adhere closely to – a human body.

The possessions which occurred before 1911, when the earthbound spirits still lived on the plane of the Earth, took place only because there were thousands upon thousands of the disincarnated Eldest among these earthbound spirits.

Concerning apparent possessions see "Toward the Light" p. 312:3-6, and p. 313:1,2.

9.

How can human beings determine whether they are under the influence of the powers of Darkness or those of the Light?

Light and Darkness, the two powerful magnetically acting forces, influence the human world each in its own way. The Light is guided by God's Thought and Will, whereas Darkness acts partly under

---

[1] See "Toward the Light" p. 322:1.

guidance, partly blindly and aimlessly. If Darkness at present[1] exerts a guiding influence on human beings, it stems from the incarnated Eldest during their nocturnal sleep release or from spirits of deceased human beings who unlawfully visit the plane of the Earth. This form of influence of Darkness will always manifest itself in the human world in such a way that it leaves the affected individual with a distinct feeling of spiritual coercion. If the influence is without guidance – that is, exclusively through radiations of accumulated Darkness – the feeling of constraint is less pronounced, but still present.

On the other hand, the influence of the Light never imparts any feeling of coercion. Slowly and calmly, almost imperceptibly, the guardian spirit – the conscience – brings the individual under the influence of the Light, and this influence grows stronger and stronger as the individual submits to its guidance without offering resistance. But if a human being begins to *question* his or her conscience, or to place *demands* on the invisible guide or to doubt that this guidance *is based on the Thought and Will of God,* such demands and such doubts will automatically attract Darkness, since any doubt in the reality of an absolutely just and logical divine intervention in earthly life is rooted in the confusing and degenerative power of Darkness. The same holds true for any *demands* which human beings place upon God.

Therefore, if one has a feeling of being under *strong spiritual duress* in any way, either the powers of Darkness or the spirits of Darkness are behind this feeling of constraint. In contrast, the influence of the Light is felt as *a profound calm and peace of mind.*

10.

Do human beings have a definite criterion for evaluating "spiritual truths"?

The standard for evaluating the spiritual truths will for any spiritually advanced human being be the perfect calm and peace which fills the mind of the individual when whatever he or she is searching for has been found and intuitively recognized as the truth. *For calm and peace in the recognition of the truth will always stand in contrast to the uneasy feeling of uncertainty and falsehood.*

---

[1]) Before Ardor's return to God, the influence af Darkness was exercised mainly through his guidance and that of the disincarnated Eldest.

It is extremely rare for people to whose physical bodies young and undeveloped spirits are bound to be able to feel this, the exalted calm and peace of the eternal truths. As these people are so dependent on the world of Darkness in which they live, it is very difficult for the thought of their undeveloped spirit to distinguish between truth and falsehood. Therefore, they rarely search for spiritual truths *themselves* but are content to follow the herd along *the beaten* and *familiar paths*. Blindly they follow in the footsteps of their leaders and firmly believe everything that these leaders uphold to be eternal divine truths – even if these postulates have *nothing* whatsover to do with the truth.

For it requires great spiritual maturity to be able from one's innermost self to weigh, measure and recognize the proper value of the spiritual truths.

11.

Why was a woman entrusted with the work of producing "Toward the Light" in the earthly world? Why did God not choose a clergyman, for example a high-ranking prelate or a Doctor of Theology? Should not a man have been chosen for this task?

Let us look more closely at this question, for there are several reasons why God especially chose a woman for this work.

Imagine the situation in which God knew that Ardor's return was imminent. It was imperative for God, when this return was an accomplished fact, *to inform mankind of what had happened.* But how could this be done in the clearest and most convincing manner? The inquirer suggests that a clergyman, a high prelate or a Doctor of Theology would have been better suited to the purpose of communicating with humanity at large. In this the inquirer is *in profound disagreement with God,* as the following will show.

The work would have to be carried out through *inspiration* – thought-impulses from the Youngest – and through the chosen prelate's *intuition*. However, a man's intuition is normally never as strong, pure and clear as a woman's. This would therefore have constituted the first difficulty to be overcome. God could have strengthened this man's intuition, but He would then have been obliged to strengthen his male will as well, since a strong and clear intuition unaccompanied by an equally strong will to reproduce and comply with the received impulses could never lead to a really good result. But a strengthened male will could also very easily lead to sheer *obstinacy,* which could in no way be expected to meet with the Will of God. The prelate would perhaps have complied to some extent with the received impulses, but in view of his religious and clerical ties, his wilfulness would have drawn its own conclusions from what he received from the transcendental world. The result would be that the facts God wished to bring to the knowledge of mankind would become more or less distorted and obscured through the innate tendency of human beings to adapt received information to their own opinions. If a Doctor of Theology had been chosen a further difficulty would probably have arisen in addition to those already mentioned: a theologian would certainly have organized the material as a highly scientific study in comparative religious history. Such a work might well be justified, but would not in this case be the appropriate means for conveying what God wished to be emphasized.

However, God intended not only to give mankind knowledge of Ardor's return, his fall and his creation of the human body. He desired not only to provide the many main religions, the various religious creeds and the numerous sects with a common basis in truth, but also to teach human beings to understand the truth in transcendental[1] communications and to teach them the danger of uncritical involvement with occult or spiritualistic manifestations. And even though it is conceivable that a high prelate or a Doctor of Theology could have been guided by the Youngest to develop an interest in these phenomena, such an individual would hardly become personally involved in thorough psychic research for any length of time. He would hardly have studied the truths and dangers of occult and spiritualistic phenomena by conducting experiments personally, even if these took place under the guidance of God and the Youngest. At best he would have collected material relating to various other people's experiences and on this basis drawn his own conclusions. Because of such a person's religious and clerical allegiance the result would have been a condemnation of these phenomena as the work of demons, of evil spirits. In this way the truth concerning occultism and spiritualism would not have emerged in the way desired by God; for then the communications of the Light with human beings – through the Youngest – would also have been denounced. This would have been yet another difficulty for God to consider.

However, God had considered these problems some years before Ardor's return, since He foresaw that this was about to happen, and He very quickly reached the conclusion *that He could employ nei-*

---

[1]) See also Question No. 2.

ther prelates nor professors for this imminent and difficult task. He therefore had to find a solution. For not until prelates[1] and professors[1] were presented with an accomplished fact would there be any possibility – and then only a faint one – that a work which from beginning to end was clearly and logically structured, and furthermore *bore the stamp of truth,* would awaken their interest and understanding. But how could such a solution be found? For God knew that no human being during earthly life would be capable of creating a religious, ethical and philosophical work that would in all respects be in full accordance with the truth, even though the disincarnated Youngest did their utmost to guide and direct. Such a task would demand more than human beings and human thought could accomplish. God therefore decided to cause this work to be created by "spiritual intelligences" from the transcendental world, and when all preparations for its appearance in the human world had been completed, to employ the help of the woman who had previously been of assistance to Christ in his work with the earthbound spirits. For at that time God foresaw that she would also be of assistance to Christ in the redemption of Ardor. And since, through the guidance[2] she had been given over a longer period of time[2] by Christ and his helpers, she had learnt both what was true and what was false in spiritualism, had learnt in every way to follow the guidance to which she had freely submitted, this was *in God's view the best and the proper solution.*

According to God's wish and under His supreme leadership "Toward the Light" was thus created by disincarnated spiritual intelligences – when Ardor had returned – but the text was compiled from questions *asked by human beings.*[3] Ardor was personally entrusted with the task of answering the questions pertaining directly to his own fall and that of the other Eldest, to their creation of the human body, to their fight against God and the Youngest and to their attempts to draw mankind deeper into Darkness and under their dominion, as well as conveying the message of his own redemption and return. He was also given the assignment to describe the dormant state of Darkness, the Light, primal Thought and primal Will, as far as this was possible. The remainder was entrusted to Christ, to the "spiritual guide"[4] of the female helper on Earth as

---

[1]) Among the clergy there are many who before their present incarnation promised God to speak in support of any book about Ardor and his acts, if it were possible to produce it in the human world. See "The Doctrine of Atonement and the Shorter Road" pp. 29-31.
[2]) See "Some Psychic Experiences", in which this guidance is described.
[3]) See Postscript to "Toward the Light".
[4]) See Postscript to "Toward the Light".

well as to others of the Youngest who had been chosen by God to assist in this extensive and very difficult task. Under this arrangement, the message to mankind would not suffer *the shortcomings of the works of human beings* but would be a work for which its transcendental creators *could accept full responsibility both before God and before humanity.* The task of the earthly helper was then to act as an *interpreter,* that is to say, through intuition to translate the thought-language of the transcendental intelligences into a language which could be understood by human beings. Thus she was fully aware of the fact that nothing was due to her own thoughts or opinions, she understood that she was to exclude her own self, that she was merely a *useful interpreter,* an *available translator.* If for instance a book on Earth is translated from one language into another, the translator would never place *his or her name on the title page, claiming authorship,* unless that person was prepared to risk exposure as *a fraud.* Nor would anyone who interprets a speech delivered to an audience in a foreign language pose as *the author of the speech.* The same holds true in this case. The female interpreter and translator on Earth has no right to present herself as the "author" of "Toward the Light", or of the other works which have been presented to humanity through her. The responsibility for these "messages from the transcendental world" therefore rests also *with all the spiritual intelligences* who created them according to God's wish and under His guidance. But the shortcomings of a very few passages in the Commentary in "Toward the Light" would have to be ascribed to the interpreter, who in her earthly existence had no knowledge of the vast majority of the subjects presented and discussed. However, also this part of the work was concluded and brought to the result desired by the transcendental world[1] so that all is in exact agreement with the truth.

The foregoing should therefore suffice to explain why God chose to entrust this earthly part of the work to *a female helper* and did not prefer to assign it either to *a high-ranking prelate of the Church* or to *a theologian.*

A collection of works such as "Greetings to Denmark", "Toward the Light" with its Supplement[2] and "The Doctrine of Atonement and the Shorter Road" will never again be presented to mankind by this means; *for the spiritual intelligences of the transcendental world are fully responsible only for these works, and for this reason the collection is and will remain* **unique in the history of humanity!**

---

[1] See Postscript to "Toward the Light".
[2] There is a possibility that a further Supplement will be forthcoming if a sufficient number of questions are asked while the female helper still lives on Earth.

12.

Since God has limited His foreknowledge, how could many of the Youngest presently embodied on Earth have been incarnated with the purpose of becoming advocates[1] of "Toward the Light", when God at the time of their incarnation could not have known the time when Ardor would return?

Ever since the Youngest were incarnated among human beings for the first time their main objective was *to win Ardor back*. Time and again God laid the plan for this work; time and again the Youngest were sent to Earth by the thousand to work together according to the plans given by God. But if the chosen Youngest failed to carry out their main objective, it should be obvious that the others would also fail in carrying out their part of the plan. This was for example the case with Zarathustra, Jesus, Mani, Mohammed, Luther, Calvin and Zwingli. And this is what happened a great many times both before and after their time. They failed in their main objective of winning Ardor back, and consequently their assistants could not carry out the work which they had promised to complete. In all those cases where these historically well known men could have won Ardor back, the plan for the work had been given by God, who from each of those Youngest who had pledged themselves to serve either as leaders or assistants in the earthly world had received their promise to let themselves be guided by their guardian spirit – their conscience – in order for the mission *to succeed*. But God could *not know beforehand* whether or not the work would succeed. Not until He saw that the person charged with the main task was unable to gain victory over Darkness, *was not able to pray for Ardor,* did He know that a further attempt would be required, that new incarnations would be necessary.

When Christ promised to attempt the "Shorter Road" (see "Toward the Light" p. 94:6 to p. 97:3) a large number of the Youngest were incarnated both at the same time and later in order to provide help and support so that a good result could be achieved.

This time a prayer was said for Ardor, and grief-stricken and remorseful he returned to God.

And since the appearance of "Toward the Light" was a natural consequence[2] of his return to God, *those* of the Youngest who before the commencement of their present incarnations had promised

---

[1] See "The Doctrine of Atonement and the Shorter Road" pp. 29–31.
[2] See Answers to Questions Nos. 11 and 68 in this Supplement.

God to act as spokesmen for this work, if efforts to produce it in the earthly world succeeded, must now keep their promise *or else take the responsibility that follows from the breaking of this pledge* **without good reason.**

13.[1]

If the leaders of the Danish Church continue to reject "Toward the Light", how can this work become the true religious foundation for mankind's belief in God?

The ways of God are many, but they all lead to the same goal: a common acknowledgement by all mankind of God as Father and Creator of the human spirit; a common acknowledgement of the origin and basis of transcendental and earthly life; a common acknowledgement that the only true and proper communication with God the Father is through *direct approach to Him in prayer and in thought* with no *intercessors* – be they Christ, "The Mother of God", the saints or others; a unanimous rejection of baptism *as a precondition for salvation;* and a unanimous rejection of *Communion* and all other *Sacraments*.

Even though the Danish clergy instead of advocating "Toward the Light" maintain a highly sceptical attitude toward the truths of this work, or seeк to oppose its promulgation, there are other ways in which the false doctrines of the Church can be countered and finally destroyed so as to make way for *the true teachings*.

How this can be brought about is explained in the following:

Since the time in a prehistoric age when human spirits had become so spiritually developed that they were able to conceive an interest in and an understanding of divine values, they have while residing in the spheres during their time of learning received instruction from the disincarnated Youngest regarding God and His relationship to mankind. This instruction was given in outline and without particular detail but sufficed to bring forth in the mind and thought of every human spirit during life on Earth a yearning for God and a yearning to strive toward greater knowledge and clarity. This yearning was the basis upon which the incarnated Youngest should build during their earthly lives when they assumed the role of religious founders or reformers. But, as explained so many times, Ardor and with him the Eldest sought in every way not only to lead the in-

---

[1]) The Answer to this Question pertains only to the religious part of "Toward the Light".

carnated Youngest astray but also to distort, obscure and defile all that the Youngest taught mankind. But despite all the distortions and all the falsehoods of Darkness the human spirit retained its longing for God, for knowledge and clarity. *And this longing is the basis of all human religious needs and feelings.*

When Ardor was finally won back to God through the love and patience of Christ, the way was open for a uniform and true religious teaching for all humanity, for Ardor – the great stumbling block who had hitherto obstructed the way – was now removed for ever. And when "Toward the Light" with the help of an earthly interpreter was introduced to the earthly world, the disincarnated Youngest who direct the instruction of the human spirits in the various spheres received a message from God enjoining them in the future not only to give the human spirits the usual outlined knowledge of Him and His relationship to mankind, but also to instruct them in detail, in other words *to acquaint them in every particular with what is taught in "Toward the Light"*. The human spirits born to life on Earth since this teaching began will therefore not only carry in mind and in thought a deep yearning for God but will also possess a knowledge and clarity of thought that reaches far beyond that which any religion developed and accepted by human beings can offer them. They will therefore more or less consciously, more or less rapidly, react to the various religious dogmas, doctrines and postulates that are taught in homes, schools, churches and temples all over the world. In particular they will quickly reject the gruesome doctrines of Christianity and its various sects concerning Christ's "death of atonement", eternal perdition and eternal suffering in an everlasting Hell, as well as the doctrines of Baptism, Communion and other Sacraments and intercession by the "Mother of God" and by the saints, as being irreconcilable with their religious feelings and their innermost yearning for God. As time passes and new generations grow up the many and different authorities or leaders of Christendom throughout the world will then meet with ever growing opposition from laymen who cannot feel satisfied with what is taught by the Church, because its teachings are not in accordance with the innermost feelings in the mind and thought of the individual. Slowly the Christian teaching in its main religions as well as its numerous older and newer denominations will disintegrate and finally meet with extinction. And the message which is presented in "Toward the Light" will then be accepted with joy and gratitude, since it in every respect reflects that *which is innermost in the human spirit and which the spirit longs to meet in life on Earth.*

But also those among the Danish people who with their innermost being now feel in harmony with what is presented and taught in "Toward the Light" will to the best of their ability seek individually to pass on the knowledge and understanding of this work to their fellow human beings. This is taking place and will continue to take place through writings, lectures and discussions. In this way more and more people will be won for the eternal truths. However, all who unite under "Toward the Light" will *remain in the Danish Church;* for the intention is not to create a new sect, the intention is to let the thoughts and information of this Message *penetrate and infuse the Danish Church,* which through this work slowly but inevitably *will face its dissolution.*

But it goes without saying that if the leaders and authorities of the Danish Church had understood the opportunity, all at once *a fully dignified and glorious Church reformation* would have emerged, a reformation which would have resounded far beyond the borders of the land and given the Danish people a unique place in history. But this was not achieved; **the clergy did not recognize the propitious moment!**

But perhaps the coming reformation in a not too distant future will be carried forward by the demanding sentiment and will of the people, and in that case it will not be for the clergy *to carry the palms of victory.*

Whether the movement which has now been initiated in order to adopt a true, uniform and lasting foundation for humanity's perception of God and the beyond will be of longer or shorter duration before it succeeds cannot be said with certainty. For it depends on human beings themselves, it depends on *whether they will accept or reject God's Message.*

But one thing can be said with certainty: "Toward the Light" has gained a foothold in the human world, its thoughts and its message can never be cancelled out and can never disappear; *for what has been given rests upon the rock of truth, and is borne forward by the wish of God and under His guidance.*

Even though all the clergies of the world should turn out in full force to stem the progress of "Toward the Light" they would never succeed. The work will nonetheless advance and its thoughts will spread from man to man, for *"Though the mills of God grind slowly* **nothing in the world can stop them!"**

14.

Why are Mormonism, Theosophy, Christian Science and Anthroposophy not mentioned in "Toward the Light"? Each of these religious movements has a great many followers all over the world.

Although neither these particular religious movements nor many other religious sects and denominations are mentioned directly in "Toward the Light", Christ does say in his Speech to the servants of the Most High or of the Church (p. 122:5): *"... to whichever nation, to whichever faith you may belong ..."*. Christ thus addresses the leaders and teachers of all religious beliefs, and since the aforementioned sects are all of comparatively recent origin they do not play a role of any significance in the astral world – that is, in the six spheres around the Earth to which human spirits are brought after the death of the earthly body – and there was therefore no particular reason why they should be mentioned separately.

These "modern" religions have only been known among mankind for a relatively short time, so that the handing down of these teachings from generation to generation through the astral brain of the individual has not yet formed a solid basis for the religious conceptions and memories of the human spirit from its lives on Earth.

The situation is completely different in respect of the ancient religions such as Shintoism, Buddhism, Christianity (with its numerous derivatives) and Mohammedanism. Through the many centuries that have passed since these religions were introduced at various times in the earthly world, generation after generation has identified itself with these beliefs. A firm foundation for these religious beliefs has thus been created, not only on Earth but also in the astral world of the human spirits – a foundation that is difficult to shake, however deficient and erroneous it may be in many respects. Numerous generations – individual after individual – have during their lives on Earth acquired the dogmas, postulates and teachings of these religions concerning the divine and have through the astral brain[1] passed them on as an inheritance to their descendants, in whose astral brain[1] these doctrines lie dormant until they are called forth, for example through religious influence in homes, schools or institutions. When the human spirit is released after the death of the body, its religious perception will therefore have been strengthened through *the religious beliefs of its earthly "forefathers"*.

---

[1]) See "Toward the Light" p. 274:1 to p. 281:2, regarding the interaction between the astral, psychic and physical brains.

Because of the religious basis formed in this way in the memory of the human spirit, it is inexpressibly difficult for teachers and educators – the disincarnated Youngest – in the schools and institutes of higher learning of the astral spheres to reason with these human spirits, to explain to them the religious delusions which they have lived by and believed in during their lives on Earth. But it is most difficult of all to influence those human spirits who through numerous incarnations have embraced Christianity in its various main denominations and older sects. For they all more or less cling to the main dogma of Christianity: *salvation through belief in the death of atonement of Jesus.* This false dogma has caused boundless grief and suffering, since all who sincerely and in complete trust have accepted it will in no way depart from their firm belief *that with his blood Jesus Christ has atoned for their guilt of sin.* Only after repeated incarnations in countries where for example Mohammedanism, Buddhism or still more ancient religions predominate, has it been possible to reason with the human spirits released at death and make them recognize the truth and justice of this single most important point in the upbringing of humanity: *that what human beings have sinned in the earthly world against God or against their fellow human beings they themselves must fully atone or obtain forgiveness for under the leadership of God. For Christ is not and never has been a sacrifice of atonement for mankind's guilt of sin!*

Thus, "Toward the Light" addresses itself primarily to the followers of the main religions, for even though Buddhism and Mohammedanism, for instance, do not profess the teaching of Christ's death of atonement, these religions are still beset with so many misconceptions that they cannot form the true religious foundation which determines the education and progress of humanity toward the Light and the Kingdom of God.

But one thing should not be forgotten, be the subject the ancient or the more recent religious beliefs: *a few truths or glimpses of truths can be found in them all.*

However, the chaos which now prevails in the many different earthly religions – (see the Answer to the preceding Question) – will at some time in the future be superseded by the truths presented in "Toward the Light", so that all mankind's religious understanding and perception of God and the beyond will rest upon one common foundation. In order to be able to attain this goal, the human spirits in the various spheres have been instructed on the basis of these books ever since "Toward the Light" appeared on Earth, and they are not incarnated until they are fully acquainted in every detail with the religious truths of this work. Endowed with this knowledge the future generations will ever more strongly reject the dogmas of the prevailing religions, and thus religious life will gradually – although possibly very slowly – be guided onto the proper path, **the path that leads directly to God, to His profound and boundless Fatherly love.**

15.

Does the designation "The Shorter Road"[1] apply to the road which Christ and the disincarnated Youngest followed in order to win back Ardor – Satan – as well as to the road to God through human forgiveness of Ardor?

Yes, the expression applies to both.

God showed Christ the road which he and his helpers could follow in order for them through patient and intensive work to win Ardor back to God's Kingdom more quickly. And since Christ fully succeeded in overcoming Ardor and winning him back by the means indicated[1], a "Shorter Road" has been laid open for all humanity through this victory of Christ, whereby the individual human being can more quickly attain the proper childlike relationship to God, namely by *the road of forgiveness.* For that human being who from deep in the heart has compassion for Ardor, and is therefore fully able to forgive him, will at once clearly understand *that the belief in the death of atonement of Jesus is but a meaningless, longer road to God and His Fatherly love.*

But those who believe that this detour is the only proper path will of course in every way insist that theirs is the right perception, since Jesus said: "I am the way!" To this there is but the following answer: Christ taught *nothing* of *"belief in the death of atonement", nothing* of the *"Mystery of the Cross", and never* that *his blood cleansed or redeemed the guilt of sin of human beings.* All this was *the work of human beings* at later times; *it sprang from heathenism and Darkness and is infinitely far removed from truth and reality.*

The sooner human beings abandon the *quagmire* of the long detour and seek the *firm ground* of the Shorter Road, the sooner will they achieve the proper understanding of God and His relationship to humanity.

---

[1] See "Toward the Light" p. 94:6 to p. 97:3.

16.

Is reincarnation absolutely necessary? And how is the Law of Retribution applied?

The purpose of reincarnation is this: through a many-sided but slowly advancing spiritual development to bring the human spirit to such maturity that by virtue of its own thought and will it is able in every circumstance of life to reject the influence of Darkness.

When a newly created human spirit undergoes its first earthly life its spiritual self, represented by thought and will, can only be compared with an imperceptibly faint spark of light. The first lives on Earth are therefore little more than a form of vegetating, an acclimatization to human life. After some initial incarnations the spiritual self begins to respond to the guidance of conscience – the guardian spirit. But it is clear that a human being of very low spiritual development cannot have as sensitive a "conscience" as can a more spiritually advanced individual. And since the newly created and very young human spirits exist mainly among the human races that are at the lowest or lower stages of development, the "spiritual laws" by which, for example, a "savage" must be judged cannot correspond exactly to the laws that apply to a member of a civilized society. A savage – to whom a newly created or very young human spirit is bound – who has not learnt to respect human life or the possessions of others, cannot be spiritually judged in the same way as a human being who through spiritual and worldly upbringing has learnt to respect these things, and despite greater spiritual resource yet kills, robs and steals. Not until the "self" has learnt to distinguish between its own possessions and those of others and has learnt the value of human life will it be held responsible for its wicked and sinful actions, of whose consequences it is then spiritually aware. For any violation of conscience will necessarily bring punishment – that is, atonement – in its wake. When the spiritual self knows that it commits an act that by nature must be punishable, thus of its own free will becoming a lawbreaker, then the individual through the abuse of the free will becomes subject to the Law of Retribution and cannot evade the consequences brought upon the self. Only if the individual fully repents of a sin committed can forgiveness be achieved through a prayer to God, and only through an appeal to the fellow human being that was wronged can forgiveness possibly be achieved and the hard blows of retribution thereby avoided.

The transgressions of mankind can be divided into two main categories:

1) Sins against God and against the divine within the self. These

transgressions can be forgiven only by God, and when His forgiveness is achieved the guilt of sin is annulled for ever.

2) Sins of various kinds that human beings commit against one another. These are clearly also sins against God, but in these cases the transgressor must also obtain the forgiveness of those who have been wronged before the guilt can be annulled, even if the sinner has been forgiven by God.

God's forgiveness of sin that is committed against God or against the holy, the divine[1], within the self *can be obtained while the transgressor still lives on Earth if the sinner before death can fully understand his or her guilt and fully repent of the wicked, evil and unlawful thoughts and actions.* **Belief in the death of atonement of Jesus in no way alters the human guilt of sin, and gives no remission of sin to any human being.**

If a human being during life on Earth has neither been able nor willing to admit and repent of its sin and guilt, this must be done after the earthly life has ended, since every human spirit is confronted upon awakening in the astral spheres with a recapitulation of its life on Earth. But as soon as repentance occurs the repentant receives God's forgiveness at the same moment, and the matter is expunged for ever and without any demand for atonement; *for God's mercy and compassion,* which are manifestations of His love, *transcend the Law of Retribution.* (See "Toward the Light" p. 306:3).

If a person sins against a fellow human being and during life on Earth admits the wicked deed or evil design and thus fully repents, and if he or she seeks in every way to obtain the forgiveness of the person wronged but meets only with determined rejection, then the transgressor can be spared the repercussions of the evil or wicked actions through the power of God's love and compassion. But in such a case the transgressor must in a new life on Earth perform some act of love toward the person who suffered under the original transgression. However, the moment the transgressor obtains forgiveness from a fellow human being, the guilt is annulled without any demand for future atonement; *for also the mercy and compassion of human beings transcend the Law of Retribution.*

But if a person has sinned against a fellow human being and will neither admit to any guilt of sin nor seek to obtain the victim's forgiveness while both still live on Earth, the transgressor will upon awakening in the beyond after death be confronted with the wicked, evil or unlawful act. The deed must be carefully considered over and over again, until an understanding of its sinful nature has been

---

[1]) See Question No. 42.

reached, and with this understanding grief and remorse awaken. But in this case it is usually too late for the sinner to obtain the victim's forgiveness: a) because he or she may not return from *life on Earth* within the time allotted the transgressor for rest and learning; b) because the victim belongs in a higher sphere to which the transgressor does not have access; c) because the victim returns to the sphere but will not in any way forgive. In such cases the transgressor must *submit to the full severity of the Law of Retribution* and must then in a future life on Earth atone for the sin, that is to say, endure the self-inflicted spiritual or physical suffering. But through the suffering endured the transgressor will learn to be more careful so that the next time he is about to commit an evil deed, like the one for which he has just atoned, it becomes easier for him to *resist the temptation to act against the guidance of his conscience.*

If the Youngest during their life on Earth in some way transgress against one another, they too must submit to the Law of Retribution. But in this case the transgressor acknowledges a sin much sooner than does a human spirit, consequently it is easier for the Youngest to repent and forgive one another and therefore in most cases avoid the Law of Retribution. But despite the deep remorse of the transgressor it can happen that the victim for a long time refuses to forgive, both in life on Earth and in the astral world. Whenever this has been the case, the Youngest who refused to forgive has then been incarnated without any mission to carry out, without being one of the pioneers of mankind, in other words to a life on Earth like that of any other human being. And the transgressor – likewise one of the Youngest – has then become the guardian spirit of the victim during the subsequent incarnations until the person wronged has overcome all anger and hatred. For persons who nurture their hatred, persons who are irreconcilable are of no use to God in the work of love that the Youngest are carrying out on behalf of humanity's journey toward the Light.

Therefore, all should in their present lives on Earth seek *to repent* of their errors, their sinful and criminal thoughts and acts and through remorse try *to obtain forgiveness from God as well as from their fellow human beings* before their earthly lives have ended. Much grief and many sufferings will be prevented by such a course of action. Every individual should therefore in all aspects of life adhere closely to *the guidance of his conscience,* for the more often a human being transgresses against his or her conscience, the more difficult it gradually becomes to follow its advice, admonitions and warnings. *By yielding to their own lusts, their own base inclinations,* **human beings increase the number of their incarnations.**

There is one provision under the Law of Retribution which no one can escape whether the transgressor's spiritual self is a human spirit, one of the Youngest or one of the Eldest. However, it is not applied to the very youngest of human spirits until they are able on this point *to respond to their conscience*. The statute referred to is the provision which states that all who kill a person or who in some way cause the death of their fellow human beings must in coming incarnations save as many people from sudden death as they have killed or caused to die. (See "Toward the Light" p. 114:6).

However, exceptions are made in the application of this statute. For the person who commits a crime and subsequently during life on Earth accepts and suffers the penalty allotted according to the laws of earthly society, that person *has nothing more to atone*. But since the law of God demands that every individual who has killed a fellow human being in a subsequent incarnation must save a human being from death, that person who by earthly laws has atoned for his or her crime will comply with this statute through *an act of love*. By virtue of God's protection, this transgressor will therefore *always* emerge safely and unscathed from the dangerous task. Whereas the person who has evaded the penalty of earthly justice will be protected neither by the guardian spirit nor by God during the attempt to save the life of a fellow human being, for which reason that person will *never* escape unharmed from such an action, and death, maiming, prolonged illness, burns or the like will be the result. In other words, he must atone for his past crimes with his own life or with bodily suffering. Thus God's Law of Retribution may in certain cases demand a life for a life; however, *the earthly courts of law have no right to make such demands.* (See "Toward the Light", Speech of Christ, p. 125:3).

Persons who during their existence as earthly rulers, commanders or leaders of the people are indirectly responsible for the loss of thousands of human lives during wars and uprisings or through death sentence can expiate the guilt of the many abruptly terminated human lives by: 1) saving a large number of people from some impending catastrophe in various subsequent incarnations, such as through resolute action averting, for example, a train, ship, mine or fire disaster; or 2) as inventors in the service of mankind by bringing safety to otherwise dangerous occupations; or 3) as scientists by finding means for the effective prevention or control of one or more of the diseases that in so many ways afflict mankind. *God Himself* ensures through this provision that a proper balance is maintained between the human lives that are lost and those that in compensation are to be saved from premature or painful death.

The two last named methods of atonement can only be employed in respect of the Youngest and partly in respect of the Eldest, since human spirits clearly do not possess sufficient spiritual powers to act as *inventors* or *scientists* in life on Earth.

17.

Can Christians who according to the doctrines of the Church worship Christ as the second member of the Holy Trinity obtain forgiveness of sin through prayers to him?

No, definitely not. For what human beings have sinned against God *only God*[1] *can forgive.* And what human beings have sinned against one another *they must seek to forgive one another*[1]. (See "Toward the Light" p. 101:3).

Christians who equate or identify Christ with God do not obtain forgiveness for their sins merely by addressing themselves in prayer to Christ. But they can often feel significant relief when their remorse is deep and sincere; for sincere remorse will always draw the Light to the repentant. Yet they will continue to feel *as sinners in their relationship to God.*

If, on the other hand, God forgives a human being who has turned to Him in grief and remorse, then *all burden of sin vanishes* immediately. The same occurs when human beings forgive one another. **For the love and compassion of God and of human beings transcend the Law of Retribution.**

18.

If one considers the possibility here on Earth that the spiritual or bodily sufferings of a relative, friend or other fellow human being are due to the individual's subjection to the Law of Retribution, can one through prayer to God annul or perhaps alleviate these sufferings? For God's compassion transcends the Law of Retribution.[2]

People who have brought sufferings – spiritual or physical – upon themselves under the Law of Retribution *have forfeited God's forgiving compassion* by failing to repent of their sins or transgressions

---

[1]) See answer to preceding Question.
[2]) See "Toward the Light" p. 306:3.

during the time allotted to everyone after each earthly life is ended.[1] For God's compassionate forgiveness *depends* upon the human being's or the human spirit's *grief and remorse.*

As stated so many times before, the human spirit upon its awakening in its dwelling in the spheres is confronted with the errors, sins and transgressions of which it has been guilty during its incarnation. But very many spirits who during their incarnation have adhered to one of the main denominations of Christianity will neither consider nor repent of the sinful actions of their lives. They invoke *the death of atonement of Jesus Christ,* they claim that all is forgiven and annulled through *the Eucharist* – while partaking of **"the flesh and blood of Christ".** Usually nothing can be done with these spirits; they continue stubbornly and unyieldingly to cite the dogmas of the Church, even though many of them at times have doubted the reality of these dogmas during their incarnation on Earth. When these spirits will not repent, because they maintain that Jesus has atoned for their sins, they obviously can neither obtain the forgiveness of God nor of their fellow human beings, which is a condition for the annulment of sin **without atonement under the Law of Retribution.** Not until the spirit returns from a new incarnation,[2] during which it has suffered as a human being for its guilt of sin and thereby atoned for it, will it understand *that the death of Jesus Christ upon the cross was no death of atonement for the sins of humanity.*

But the inquirer asks whether those who see their fellow human beings suffer under the severity of the Law of Retribution can through prayer to God suspend this retributive punishment or at least alleviate it. *No! No prayer to God can terminate these sufferings, not even prayers that spring from the deepest feelings of love or compassion.* For the individual who suffers thus would not repent in time, and must now learn through suffering that obstinacy and defiance are of no avail, whereas grief and repentance will bring about the proper relationship between God and human beings. However, prayers for help by human beings can also in these cases alleviate the sufferings of a fellow human; for every prayer for help brings the power of the Light to the one for whom the prayer is said, and this addition of Light can bring so much spiritual strength that the person who suffers will feel the pain less strongly and therefore endure it with greater patience. But no human being can during life on Earth determine how helpful these prayers of intercession are, since

---

[1]) See "Toward the Light" p. 186 and Question 16 in this Supplement.
[2]) This kind of incarnation is exceptional, however. See "Toward the Light" p. 113:2, regarding the repentance of human beings.

no one knows how severely the "penalty of expiation" has been meted out in each case. Not until the life on Earth has ended will the intercessor learn how severe the sufferings were intended to be and how much they were alleviated by the intercession. Therefore, anyone who sees a fellow human being suffer spiritually or bodily should out of a feeling of love or compassion intercede for that person with God. **Likewise, the prayer for those departed should never be forgotten, since such a prayer can bring Light to the darkened minds and thereby overcome the human spirit's defiance during the difficult time of self-searching.**[1]

The belief in the death of atonement of Jesus, in the element of forgiveness in the Eucharist pervades the Christian part of humanity as **a mighty curse.** But these false teachings derive from Ardor, and these doctrines have delayed and will for long periods of time continue to delay a numerous host of human beings in their journeying toward the distant Fatherly Home. This situation cannot improve so long as there are men and women among the mentors and leaders of the Church, as well as in the congregations, in whose sermons or religious pronouncements God is given prominence as the stern, avenging divinity to whom human beings dare only address themselves in humble and trembling "fear of God", nor so long as Christians will continue to regard Christ as the one who has atoned for the sins of mankind. Not until all teaching, all talk of this tyrannical, fickle and avenging "human god" has ceased for ever, not until baptism has been rejected as a condition for salvation and it is acknowledged that the Eucharist and all other Sacraments are without any significance, not until people cease to condemn their fellow human beings to "eternal torments" in an "eternal Hell", not until then can those who profess the faith of the main Christian denominations and their various sects expect to progress more quickly on their toilsome journey. However – *and this cannot be said too often* – it is for the individual human being to decide whether he or she will continue to follow the ancient, false doctrines and thereby delay[2] the progress toward the Light and toward God – or whether that person will reject all of this and turn to the truths which God has made known to humanity through "Toward the Light" and "The Doctrine of Atonement and the Shorter Road" – **For God compels no one to do that which is right, and no one must compel his neighbour!**

---

[1]) See Speech of Christ in "Toward the Light" p. 118:5.
[2]) See Speech of God's Servant in "Toward the Light" p. 136:13 to p. 137:1.

19.

Prayers of intercession by humans for suffering and unhappy fellow human beings draw the Light to those for whom the prayers are said and bring them help. – Do our prayers therefore not create injustice by bringing Light and help to some and not to others?

In the Speech of Christ, p. 118, on the subject of prayer and the power of prayer, he says: ". . . Be not selfish in your prayer . . . but pray for all human beings on Earth. And forget not those who at death are delivered from their earthly bodies! . . ."

By this Christ calls upon human beings to advance so far in compassion and love for their fellow human beings that in their prayer to God they can include *all* and ask for help for those who are in need of it. Therefore, when you pray, think of all who suffer, both spiritually and bodily; think of all who grieve and of all lawbreakers, no one should be forgotten, all should be remembered in the prayer. The expression "no one should be forgotten" does not mean, of course, that numerous names should be recited, on the contrary, it means that the individual during prayer should try to include *within the thought* that part of humanity which grieves and suffers. If the desire to bring help to those who suffer is sincere and deeply felt, help will be forthcoming in one form or another even though the person praying may not know of this[1] during life on Earth.

But not only does Christ urge human beings not to be selfish in their prayer, he also states *that he will be the spokesman – that is, he will pray – for those who are in need of his help.* Out of his deep love Christ takes upon *his shoulders* that which human beings in their selfishness, in their blindness and in their lack of compassion leave undone, as something with which they do not wish to concern themselves or something which they do not understand can be of any use. If people forget their fellow human beings *he* will remember them; *he* forgets no one – not even *those* among "the deceased" whose remembrance soon fades from the memory of the living.

Therefore, because of the love of Christ, no human being is excluded from the Light-giving power of prayer. And the prayers of human beings create no injustice.

---

[1] See the preceding Question.

20.

Since the prayers of human beings to the so-called saints are of no avail (see "Toward the Light" page 84) and therefore are not heard by God, are the prayers of the heathen to their "gods" also in vain?

In those cases where human beings worship many gods they perceive their idols as representations of divinity. Many heathens also believe – and especially in the past did believe – that a part of the divine soul, or the spirit, is enclosed within the "image", thus imbuing it with life. Although they are idolators, worshippers of many gods often find it easier through prayer – however childish in form – to meet with God and with His Thought because their idols, or images, are expressions of the "great spirit", the deity – father, creator and ruler – whom they believe to be the guide and leader and to whom they turn in prayer.

Since most saint-worshippers pray directly to individual saints instead of praying to them to intercede with God, and since the so-called saints do not exist in the manner understood by Catholic believers, they pray in fact to completely imaginary beings. The "great spirit", or deity, that for the heathen exists "behind" the idol does not exist "behind" the image of the saint. Saint-worshippers are thus often much further removed from the divine than the heathen. But if human beings regard their saint *merely as a link between themselves and God,* and consciously or otherwise *discern the Divinity behind the saint* during prayer, then their prayers will reach God – but otherwise they will not reach Him. But then they are no longer prayers to an imaginary saint, then they are prayers to the Divinity. However, the crux of the matter is that the prayer that is addressed to God, by whichever name He is known to the human being, should come from a *trusting heart;* for there are clearly "idolators" who pray to their idols and images in the same thoughtless manner in which many Catholic believers pray to their saints.

21.

Why does God so seldom hear our prayers? Do we not pray long enough on each matter? Should we be more insistent than we are? (See Luke 11: 5–9).

As is well known, it was common practice at the time of Jesus to speak in parables. Several of the parables ascribed to Jesus therefore did not originate with him but were well known among the people. The parable in *Luke 11: 5-8 did not originate with Jesus,* and therefore cannot be considered here, especially since it expresses *merely human thoughts and actions.* However, the words of verse 9 were spoken by Jesus, but they have been inserted and applied in a place *where they do not belong.*

Jesus has never suggested that human beings should be importunate in their prayers, nor that they should pray any given number of times on a single matter so as possibly to tire God so much with their persistence that He would temper justice with "mercy". These human notions stem not from Jesus but from the Evangelists. (See, for example, also the parable in Luke 18: 1-8 which did not originate with Jesus either).

The reasons why God does not grant the prayers of human beings in every case are, for example, 1) that many pray without thought – quite automatically; 2) that many pray without trust that their prayer will be heard or granted; 3) that many pray for help to avenge insults and reverses that they have suffered; 4) that many pray for help where they are able to help themselves, God's help thus being unnecessary; and 5) that many pray in such a way that their prayer becomes a *demand* and is therefore no longer a prayer. Such forms of request are of no avail, for *they will not be heard by God.* All should pray in the trust that God will help at the proper time and in the proper manner, and that He will only help *if He judges that help is necessary.* (See also the Speech of Christ in "Toward the Light" p. 117:3 to p. 119).

Yet another thing must be considered, namely, that the present earthly life of a human spirit is *always based upon its previous lives.* For this reason – because of the retribution[1] that the human being has brought upon itself – God is in many cases both unable and unwilling to change the existing state. In such cases human beings *must* endure life's many and various griefs and hardships, however difficult this may be; for they must remember that *they are always in one way or another themselves to blame for their lives developing as they do.* But those who in complete trust in God's guidance, love and justice turn to him for help in finding their way out of difficult and oppressive situations, or in finding the proper solution to intractable problems, *will always receive the necessary help and the necessary strength.*

Therefore, even if people pray for help of the kind *they* wish, *and help comes in some other form than was expected or desired,* it will nevertheless transpire that God always chooses to help in the way **that He knows is best and proper.**

---

[1] See Answer to Question No. 18.

22.

On page 3 in "Toward the Light", it is stated: "In the Darkness was the Light; in the Light were Thought and Will. But Thought and Will were not in the Darkness." How are we to understand this? When the Light is in the Darkness and Thought and Will are in the Light, must they not also be in the Darkness?

No! At the time referred to on page 3 Thought and Will were *only in the Light,* but not in the Darkness.

On page 160:5 it is clearly stated: "This picture of the inert state and struggle of Light, Darkness, Thought and Will must be understood as an abstraction and not interpreted in terms of concrete, earthly concepts of space, measure, time, and so forth." However since it appears difficult for many to understand the fact that primal Thought and primal Will were only in the Light and not in the Darkness, a further explanation will be given here based on conditions known on Earth; although such an explanation should be unnecessary, since anyone who is familiar with abstractions should be able to understand the description on page 3.

Thus, Darkness, Light, Thought and Will should be understood as the then existing *primal cosmos,* the basis for *the present cosmos.* In order to illustrate the appearance of primal cosmos in earthly terms, one can think of a fruit, an apple for example, since the shape and inner structure of that fruit conform approximately to the shape and structure of the primal cosmos.

Primal cosmos is .... the apple
Darkness is .... the skin and meat of the apple
Light is .... the core
Thought and Will are .... the seeds

We all know that the seeds of the apple are in *the core,* so no one would say that they are in *the meat of the apple* or in *the skin.* And so it was with Thought and Will (the seeds). They were in *the Light* (the core), but not in *the Darkness* (the meat and skin of the apple).

Thus, one can rightfully say that Thought and Will were in the *primal cosmos.* One cannot dispute this. Similarly, one can rightfully say that the fruit seeds are in *the apple.* One cannot dispute this either.

The error many have made in their perception of the message given on p. 3 in "Toward the Light" stems from the fact that these people have not understood that Darkness, Light, Thought and Will together constituted the *primal cosmos.*

23.

How could the hot vapours of the Earth (see "Toward the Light" page 10) have any effect at all upon the immaterial bodies of the Eldest?

The Darkness that had taken the Kingdom of the Eldest and the Earth into its possession also flowed[1] through the "immaterial" bodies of the Eldest. The Eldest were thus in contact with the streams of Darkness that had produced the hot vapours during the period in question (the Earth's cooling-off period).

Had the Youngest visited the Earth at that time their "immaterial" bodies would not have felt the hot vapours, because no Darkness flowed through them. The vapours could only have affected them in the same way that all Darkness affects the beings of Light – as though they were in an atmosphere deficient in oxygen. (See "Toward the Light" p. 187).

24.

According to "Toward the Light", page 182, the means of transportation in the spheres resemble those on Earth, whereas it is stated elsewhere on the same page that human spirits can move about within their own sphere by means of thought and will. How can these two statements be reconciled?

It is indeed stated in the passage referred to that human spirits can move about within their own sphere by means of thought and will, but no statement is made to the effect that this is *an invariable rule.* If this were the case then all other "means of transportation" would clearly be superfluous. Each human spirit is free, however, either to use the means of transportation available in the spheres, or employ its thought and will for this purpose. But since it always requires some exertion for human spirits to move from place to place by means of thought and will, it is easiest for them to make use of the means with which they are familiar from life on Earth, especially for beings

---

[1] See "Toward the Light" p. 9:7-9.

who were accustomed to comfort in their previous incarnation. Most human spirits therefore make use of the means of transportation available within each of the spheres.

Gradually as the human spirit develops, the capacity for concentration of the self also increases; it thereby becomes easier for it to employ thought and will as means of transportation. But the transportation otherwise employed will not cease to operate for that reason – as it cannot be expected that everyone *at all times* will confine themselves to using the power of thought and will.

25.

In "Toward the Light", page 190:1, it is stated: "Once bound to the foetus, the spirit remains in close proximity to the pregnant woman." Is the spirit in question fully conscious? Can it not resist and thus, for example, disrupt the bond? Does the spirit later have any recollection of this period?

The moment the spirit is brought to its future "mother", it is lulled into a state of semi-sleep so that as an appendage without power and will it follows the pregnant woman wherever she goes. As the formation of the foetus progresses and the shape of the spirit-body becomes more and more indistinct, this sleep becomes deeper. The spirit is thus quite oblivious of what takes place while it is bound to the foetus, and consequently it will later have no recollection of this period of time.

26.

In "Toward the Light", page 215:3, it is stated that the cord which binds the spirit to the body severs the moment death occurs. Does it take place when the heartbeat stops? – Or when does it happen?

The cessation of the heartbeat is one of the stages in the "death-process" of the body. The real and absolute death takes place the moment all connection between the molecular particles of the body and the astral particles of the counterpart has slackened completely, and the stage of separation of the body and the counterpart sets in.

A weakening, a slackening in the interweaving of the molecular and astral particles therefore takes place after the heartbeat has stopped, but before absolute death occurs. And when this process is so far advanced that it is completely impossible through stimulants or other means to strengthen the weakened interweaving and thereby revive the heartbeat, the cord that binds the spirit to the body severs – i.e., *at the moment of death*. When the cord has severed and death has truly occurred, the astral connection to the soft tissues of the body is loosened – that is to say, the molecular and astral particles drift apart – and the counterpart is released and separated. (See "Toward the Light" p. 189:1).

No standard can be given for how long the weakening process takes, as this process varies considerably and partly[1] depends on the condition of the body when the heartbeat stops. If "death" has occurred through, for example, an accident, under narcosis, in shock, or under similar conditions, and the body is otherwise healthy, the process can be very slow, whereas it can be concluded within a very short time if "death" is due to a long and wasting illness. The reason for this is that a considerable reduction in the elasticity of the molecular and astral particles has set in during the course of the illness, and that this weakens the mutual interweaving.

The separation and the release of the counterpart from the earthly body also takes longer to complete if the body is healthy at the time of death. (See "Toward the Light" p. 189:2

27.

How can the two descriptions of the formation of the mother suns in "Toward the Light" on page 167 and page 260 be in agreement? The first description states that the inner core is a core of Darkness, the other that the inner core of each mother sun was formed by the slower vibrations of the Light.

The two descriptions are in complete agreement as the following comparison will show:

1) In the first description it is stated: "Since the Darkness precipitated in the ether has a lower oscillation frequency than the Light, the rotation around the centres of force caused it to collect as a core – a core of Darkness".

2) But in order to make the formation of mother suns at all possible, God had to draw the ether over the given centres and bring it into a rotating motion. And since the less rapid oscillations of the Light

---

[1] If death occurs in a very warm climate, for example in the South, the high temperature will accelerate the weakening of the particles even if the body is otherwise healthy.

would necessarily be closest to the centres, the core was from *the beginning* created from these oscillations. Since the Darkness that was enclosed within these slowest oscillations of the Light was incapable of keeping pace with the rotating ether and steadily sank more and more, it collected into a coherent core around the centres, thereby releasing the slowest oscillations of the Light. Freed from the inhibiting Darkness the Light-ether spread around the centres and cores of Darkness and outward with steadily faster oscillations, until the formation of the mother suns was completed. This is given in the second and more detailed description, which is thus only an expansion of what was first described. Both passages must therefore be read together so that a clear picture can emerge.

To summarize: the cores of the mother suns were initially formed of the slowest oscillations of the Light, which enclosed the Darkness that with its even slower oscillations necessarily had to collect around the centres and ultimately form a solid cohesive core – *a core of Darkness*.

28.

It is stated in "Toward the Light" on page 170 that the mother sun of our star system "may some day be seen from the Earth". How must this be understood? Is the mother sun not visible?

The mother sun is visible to the naked eye; but only through very powerful instruments of observation will it be possible at some future time to "see" or *show* which is the right star.

The expressions *"be shown"* or *"be pointed out"* from the Earth would in this case have given a more precise idea of the factual situation than the expression "be seen", since the form of the sentence can give the impression that the mother sun is not visible to the unaided eye, which it definitely is. (See the information regarding the synonyms and the vocabulary of intermediaries, or mediums, given in the Postscript to "Toward the Light", p. 342).

29.

Is the Central Sun (God's Kingdom) in motion, or does it remain at rest in the same place?

The Central Sun is in motion, but since it is the mid-point for the four mother sun systems (or galactic systems) it does not move in orbit around any other body but remains in its place *eternally rotating about its own axis.* It is borne by God's Thought and secured by His Will – **the basis for all cosmic laws.**

30.

Shall we at some future time be able to see the Central Globe – God's Kingdom – through very powerful telescopes?

No, this will never happen; for God's Kingdom has *no "core of Darkness".* It is in fact *the cores of Darkness* of the star globes that human beings see in space.

31.

The enormous numbers that astronomers deal with in connection with the size of our galactic system and the distances between its globes appear to be at variance with the picture of the star universe that is given in "Toward the Light".

These disproportionately large numbers arise from the fact that astronomers have omitted *a highly significant factor* from their calculations. When this as yet unknown factor is discovered – which human beings must do for themselves – it will transpire that the correctly computed numbers are much lower than the present estimates, and will thus approach the values given in "Toward the Light", page 168:3 to page 169:3.

32.

What is the situation regarding the distant nebulae, such as the Nebula of Orion, which astronomers believe to be independent galactic systems?

Human beings must themselves find the answer to this Question. When the factor mentioned in the answer to the preceding Question is found, the "riddle" of the stellar nebulae should soon be solved.

33.

Is Luther's "vision" at Wartburg more than legend? Besides his task as reformer, was he also assigned the task of praying for Satan?

Luther's "vision" of Satan was real. Luther was one of *those* Youngest who had pledged to remember the prayer for Ardor while they were incarnated. But also he[1] misunderstood the promptings of the guardian spirit, and instead of praying for Satan, he *cursed* him. *And Ardor thereby gained greater power over him.*

34.

Were Luther's bodily sufferings of his own making? That is to say, were they an atonement for transgressions in previous incarnations? (See "Toward the Light" page 306:2).

In Luther's time, children were brought up with far greater severity than they are today. The work demanded of them – partly as punishment for various offences, and partly to keep them occupied so that Satan would not gain a hold over them – was often far too strenuous for children.

Luther's physical weakness stemmed partly from over-exertion in childhood, but mainly from his ascetic monastic life, since the severe self-torments brought him various bodily sufferings. They were therefore of his own making,[2] *but they were no atonement for the guilt of sin from previous incarnations.* The weaknesses that could be ascribed solely to his childhood could have been remedied in adolescence. But instead of hardening his body, Luther weakened it still further through the fasting and self-torments of monastic life.

35.

Why did Luther endure so much spiritual suffering? Surely he was one of God's emissaries and must have carried out his mission under the leadership of God?

The emissaries who during their earthly lives carried out their

---

[1]) See "Toward the Light" regarding Jesus' vision of Satan, pp. 39–40.
[2]) See "Toward the Light", p. 306, footnote 2.

work while Ardor was still the "Prince of Darkness" were always in many different ways led astray by him and his helpers, the disincarnated "Eldest". And Luther was no exception. Ardor also misled him in a great many things, especially in that which concerned the main points of his mission. Luther built upon, rather than repudiated, the teaching of Paul, for example, and the result was the dogma of Justification by Faith. Thus, he often found himself in opposition to his spiritual leader (his guardian spirit, or conscience), a situation that will always create division, confusion and anxiety of mind and thought, and therefore cause spiritual suffering. The feeling of guilt of sin that weighed so heavily upon Luther sprang from the anxiety and discord in his mind, but this anxiety and discord was mainly due to the influence and promptings of Ardor, who also incited him to take his monastic vow against the warnings of his conscience. This inner voice of opposition finally brought him to break his vow and find peace of mind on that point. But if Luther had in *every way* followed his conscience, he would never have become the spiritually troubled and divided being he in fact was; *for a close contact with the guidance and admonitions of the "conscience"* **will always bring spiritual peace, calmness and clarity of mind and of thought.**

36.

In "Toward the Light", page 322:3, it is stated that about three million earthly years is the longest time that a human spirit has been bound to the Earth and its spheres.
1) Does the expression "has been" indicate that this hitherto longest time has been exceeded? 2) Did the incarnations of the Eldest possibly have any bearing on this figure? 3) If so, is it possible to indicate the time of incarnations for each individual in the future?

1) It is correct that the expression *"has been"* refers to conditions that prevailed in the past *but no longer do so.* Had this not been the case the formulation would have been the following: about three million earthly years is the longest time that a human spirit *is* bound to the Earth ...

2) Yes, the incarnation of the Eldest which began around 12,000 B.C. have brought *disorder* to the calm and steady progress of the human spirits.

3) Nothing definite can be said concerning this question. It can only be stated that the figure of approximately three million years will at worst *be doubled or redoubled many times over,* but how

many times no one knows – not even God. For human beings themselves have *to a large extent an influence* on how long this period of time will be. The sooner they learn to follow the directions given in "Toward the Light", the shorter will be the series of incarnations required. However, even at best, the time will extend far beyond the three million years.

The interval between incarnations – the sojourn in the spheres – will not be changed for the young human spirits, whereas the intervals will become progressively longer for those that are more advanced or very advanced.

Since God always maintains a balance in all that happens, and since the sequence of incarnations of human spirits will be longer in the future than hitherto, the period of development in the worlds of Light will *be of shorter duration for these spirits* than for those who have already been released from earthly life and now live in the worlds of Light.

37.

Why can we human beings not unravel in every detail the ties of friendship and kinship that bind us to one another? Much would thereby become comprehensible to us while we are still on Earth.

For human beings to be able to unravel the ties of friendship and kinship relating to their previous incarnations, they would not only require a clear memory of their own previous existences but would also need to remember those of their friends and relatives. Since God by His Will, and in accordance with His laws, withholds the incarnated spirit's memories of previous lives on Earth, human beings normally have no recollection of previous incarnations. (See "Toward the Light" p. 279:3).

Such memories would only create spiritual suffering and confusion in the lives of human beings. Such memories would make life unendurable for everyone.

Those who have had enemies, persecutors and opponents in previous incarnations, and those who have hated, murdered, plundered and impoverished their fellow human beings will always in future incarnations be reborn in close kinship with these enemies, persecutors and opponents, and with the victims of their transgressions. Alternatively they will meet one another during their incarnations in such a manner and under such circumstances that possible friendships can arise. And when through imposed kinship or through possible friendship people have learnt to love where they had formerly hated and cursed, and learnt to do good where they had formerly caused grief, harm and suffering, they will on meeting former adversaries or victims in future incarnations experience a mutual – though inexplicable – sympathy. For those who have once learnt truly to love one another or have once conceived true friendship for one another will have overcome the hate, enmity and sin of the past for ever. In this way God brings human beings to love and to respect one another, so that at some future time they may in spirit and in truth become *as brothers and sisters.*

The struggle of each human spirit out of the Darkness of earthly life and toward the Light, from the first incarnation on Earth to the last, is as one single great reckoning. Each rebirth on Earth adds a figure to the account, and when all the figures are in proper order *they will show the total result that God had in view.* However much human beings may wish to disentangle the threads that bind them during earthly life to friends and kin, they will never be able to do this. But God – the Father of the human spirit – keeps close account of relationships among human beings, keeps close account of their friendships and enmities, and of their sins and their good deeds. Only He is able to unravel the ties that bind human beings to one another; only He is able to gather together the individual figures of the many reckonings so that they are brought into the proper order and give the proper value, whereby the true result can be achieved. And this result is: *mutual love and harmony among His beloved children.*

"For the ways of God are many, and they are past finding out."

38.

In the Speech of Christ on page 128 it is implied that husband and wife will meet in the heavenly dwellings; but is this not an erroneous supposition in view of the fact that husband and wife most often belong spiritually to very different spheres, especially in the case of the Youngest and the Eldest?

Husbands and wives who wish to see each other again in the beyond will always have this wish granted – and thousands upon thousands have rejoiced in such reunions.

But if the partner left behind on Earth does not return to his or her sphere before the other's time of rest and learning has expired, they will meet after a later incarnation – but only *if they so desire.*

But should one of the marriage partners be of the Youngest and the other be a human spirit, then the Youngest will always be able to seek out the human spirit in his or her own sphere. If the partners are human spirits from different spheres, then the one dwelling in the higher sphere will come to the one in the lower sphere – not the reverse.[1] In cases where a human spirit and one of the "Eldest" have been bound to human beings who have lived as man and wife on Earth, the human spirit has in most cases not desired any reunion – for very obvious reasons. If married life has been "hell on Earth", there will of course be no desire by either party to meet after death. But husband and wife who do not wish to meet in the beyond will always in a later incarnation be confronted with each other *in order to forgive by learning to love each other anew.*

In those very rare cases in which the human spirit did wish to meet the spouse – when the person in question had been one of the Eldest – because he or she felt that their marriage could have been more successful if they had only demonstrated greater love and patience, the human spirit has been accompanied to the Hell-Sphere by one of the Youngest to be confronted with the former spouse. What took place at these meetings concerns only those involved. Since the Hell-Sphere (the "ravaged Kingdom") is now obliterated, husbands and wives will in the future *meet only in the spheres or in a new life on Earth.*

If one of the Youngest and one of the Eldest had lived as man and wife on Earth, the Youngest would in most cases have sought out the Eldest in the Hell-Sphere. The result of those meetings would often be that the Eldest was delivered from the Darkness of Hell, submitted to the Law of Retribution, was incarnated under the leadership of God – in other words, returned to God – and thereby *became willing to strive forward through the many incarnations in order to restore his or her personality.*

39.

Can the concept of love be explained?

The concept or abstraction that human thought tries to express by the word "love" is in itself indefinable; the only forms of expression or metaphors that can be found in earthly languages are approximations that more or less adequately convey the meaning.

---

[1]) In a few individual cases a human spirit has been brought to a higher sphere accompanied by its guardian spirit, so that the desired meeting could take place. But the rule is given above.

Compared to Thought and Will the concept of love is *the nerve fibre of the Light*.

Thought and Will are the highest concentration of Light, but love is the *essence* of Light, a *power* that penetrates and infuses Thought and Will. One can therefore say that love is an *almighty* or *all-conquering power*, and this power finds its ultimate, sublime expression in God's Fatherly love, since the life nerve of the Light issues from Him and through numerous filaments extends to all beings created by Him, so that the essence of love eternally streaming from God, the Father, will in the course of time penetrate and infuse all His children. The further the spiritual self progresses toward God, the greater will be its *fulness of love* and the easier it will be for the self, in being and in action, to display and practise love.

In this way, through the life nerve of Light, God is connected with all His created beings, and through His love that flows through all of them, He brings His children to the Fatherly Home, to life eternal. Even into the most deeply fallen spirits does the nerve of life extend its filaments, and in due time love in one of its numerous forms will manifest itself and despite inner or outer resistance infuse the self; and when all resistance is broken *God, the Father, will have won back His child.*

Love is *the ideal* for human perfection.
Love is *the weft* of human life.
Love is *the prism* of the heart.
Love is *the mainspring* in the work of the Youngest for humanity.
Love is *the bond* between the male and the female dual.
Love is *the energy* of life.
Love is *the source of life* in God.

40.

Can the love between duals be set up as an ideal of neighbourly love?

No! Love between duals can definitely not be set up as an ideal *of neighbourly love.*

1) Because the former by far transcends the latter; 2) because earthly marriages are rarely based on a "spiritual dual bond", for which reason the vast majority of human beings will not be able to understand the concept "dual love"; 3) because love between the duals among God's first created children – the Eldest and the Youngest – is so infinitely far above a corresponding love between God's very youngest children, the human spirits, since the foundation for

their love is developed slowly through the many incarnations during which the human spirits in various ways learn to understand and to love one another.

But the duals' form of love will gradually become more comprehensible to the human spirit as it progresses in spiritual maturity. However, no human spirit will fully be able to comprehend this love until the earthly incarnations have ceased. For the duals' form of love between human spirits can only unfold in harmony of perfect beauty during their spiritual life partnership on the globes in the distant star universes. But in order to understand this, one must bear in mind that God's first created children – the Eldest and the Youngest – were created as far *greater spiritual individualities* than were the human spirits. The bond, the bond of love, that unites the male and the female parts to each other, was thus already *very strongly developed* at the creation of the dual pairs. But when God creates human spirits, these dual spirits are only *faint "sparks" of the spiritual Light* of God's Being, and for this reason the bond of love between them *is only very weak*. But these pairs, who are created simultaneously, will always and for time eternal belong together, *nothing can separate them*. And the bond between these pairs will grow stronger and stronger as their spiritual development progresses.

As the human spirits are as yet so infinitely far behind the Youngest in spiritual development, they will be quite incapable during life on Earth of *feeling* or *understanding* the love of the Youngest for their dual part. Love for the dual part can thus in no way be regarded as an ideal model for neighbourly love.

Only love of their own selves can be held up before human beings as an ideal of love for their neighbours. If human beings could only learn **never to do otherwise unto others than they would have others do unto them,** then would much in truth be gained. If human beings could learn to show their fellow humans the same compassionate, sympathetic and charitable love that they would themselves wish to be shown when afflicted by sickness, sorrow, spiritual suffering or poverty, then neighbourly love would soon gain acceptance and understanding among all human beings.

But this will unfortunately take a long time to achieve. For most people *demand so much* of their fellow human beings while *giving so little* themselves. Not until *demands to receive* are in exact balance with *willingness to give will the proper relationship exist*.

Therefore, if a sublime neighbourly love is to thrive among mankind, all human beings must *reform themselves on the basis of the best, the noblest and the purest feelings of the self*.

41.

Is it true to say that God created the beautiful primal prototypes of earthly plant life out of love for his children – the human beings?

No! Not even God can take any action *out of love for non-existent beings!*

At the time God formed the primal prototypes of earthly plant life, the beings that according to His resolve should one day populate the Earth had not yet been created. *Out of concern* for His uncreated children God sought to make them a splendid dwelling place that would be suited in every way to the spiritual level they should occupy at their creation.

But with the fall of the Eldest these primal prototypes became distorted and made ugly through the fertilization by Darkness of the latent seeds. However beautiful it might become under the beautifying and harmonizing influence of the Light, and through human attempts at cultivation, earthly plant life can never develop as God had planned on the basis of the primal seed prototypes of the Light that He had laid down.

When God formed the spheres around the Earth His actions were similarly based upon *feelings of concern*. For the human spirits had not yet been created at that time. (See "Toward the Light" p. 17:6).

But when God made abodes for His first-created children – the Eldest and the Youngest – He did so out of *His Fatherly love.* For these children had been created before God made their abodes. (See "Toward the Light" p. 5:4).

And when all the human spirits are gathered in God's Kingdom in millions upon millions of years' time, *each one will then find his or her beauteous abode, created by God out of* **His deep, His infinite Fatherly love.**

42.

How should we correctly understand "the blasphemy against the Holy Ghost"? (Matthew 12:31).

Since the so-called "Holy Ghost" exists only as a thought-phantom created by human imagination, and therefore has no real existence, one cannot very well sin against such an *imaginary being.*

In "Toward the Light", p. 55:3, Jesus says in discourse[1] with some of the scribes: "But that which you sinned against the holy in you, that shall you not be forgiven until you have suffered for it and repented of the evil you have done". And in the footnote on the same page it is stated that the "holy" in human beings is the divine element that every human being receives from God.

With this pronouncement Jesus states that the scribes speak *against their better knowledge.* They sin thereby against the divine – against the spark of divinity – in the self. It is thus a perfectly *conscious* sin that these scribes commit. And such a conscious, deliberate sin will always bring about pangs of conscience in their worst form and thereby cause the transgressor deep spiritual suffering. For what took place will invariably reappear from time to time and beset the mind with an overwhelming power, no matter how much that person seeks to repress the memory of the unpleasant facts.

This spiritual suffering can be ascribed not only to the admonitions or reproaches of the guardian spirit, *but mostly to the person's own "spiritual self"* that because of its divine origin will react quite automatically and intuitively to each reappearing memory of sin committed. And the higher the level of the spiritual self, the more heavily will the memory and guilt of sin oppress the mind and thought until all has been fully acknowledged and repented of.

When God judges the actions of human beings, He distinguishes sharply between the actions that spring from *premeditated plans* and those that take place *spontaneously, without forethought.* For whenever an individual is fully aware of the consequences of the evil plans and intentions, the sin becomes far greater than if it occurs spontaneously. (See also "Toward the Light" p. 278:3).

Therefore, if a person for example deliberately kills one or several fellow human beings, and the act is not caused by insanity, that person has sinned against the *holy, against the divine within the self.*[2] But if the killing is committed in vehemence – without any deliberation – or in defence of oneself or others, it becomes a sin against *the divine laws,*[2] but not against the holy within that human being.

Or, if someone *deliberately plans* and causes one or several fellow human beings to lose, for example, their livelihood, their fortune or other property, then a sin is also committed against the holy within the self. For deep inside, that person knows this to be an act against law, justice and truth. But if an individual through ill-considered behaviour or through, for example, impulsive, thoughtless remarks

---

[1]) Identical to the discourse in the New Testament referred to in the Question.

[2]) The individual who sins against the holy within the self will of course also sin against the divine laws.

causes others to lose their life or livelihood, then that is also a transgression against the divine laws, but not against the holy within the self.

But *irresponsible* and *thoughtless words and actions would vanish from human life* if people would truly understand what it means *to think before they act*.

The Eldest incarnated by Ardor present a somewhat different picture concerning pangs of conscience in their human existence. For the Light-personalities of these Eldest were destroyed when they left God's Kingdom at the dawn of time in order to go their own way. And the infinitely faint spark of Light that remained in their personality – because that which stems *directly* from God's own Being can never be annihilated except by God Himself – *was so feeble that it was unable to react against all the evil, the sins and the transgressions that the Eldest plotted and carried out in their human existence*. Not until earthly death once more released them from their human body was this spark of divinity able to react against what had happened. Through their spiritual sufferings and their subsequent grief and remorse many of the Eldest have returned to God, that is to say, *have voluntarily submitted to the Law of Retribution*.

But there are still many people – the Eldest incarnated by Ardor – who can truthfully say: *"We feel no pangs of conscience for our wicked acts, we are not oppressed by the memory of our misdeeds, our killings and our transgressions"*. But when life on Earth has ended for these human beings and they awake from their "sleep of death" – **then will the reaction set in.**

43.

How can the thought and the urge to make offerings that is inherent in human beings be explained, and where does it originate?

The idea of sacrifice and the urge to make offerings can be traced back to the earliest, primitively thinking human races. It derives originally from the times when human beings began to unite under the elder of the tribe, or under a chief or leader. At gatherings around the camp fire, for instance, the chief and his nearest kin were entitled to the best places. But those who were in possession of material goods could by offering part of these to the chief obtain the better places by purchase or barter.

From the time when the worship of idols began various items of value have been offered up, such as weapons – clubs, spears, bows and arrows and the like – jewelry, harvest of the field and fruits. Later,[1] also captured enemies, lawbreakers, birds and domestic animals were sacrificed to the most important of the gods in order that they should provide the benefits desired by those making the sacrifice. Similar offerings were also made to appease the wrath of the gods against the individual or against the people as a whole.

This human urge through various offerings to purchase desired blessings, or to buy the forgiveness of the gods – and especially that of the highest god – thus occurred in all the most ancient primitive religious rituals that expressed the servile and uncritical worship of its gods by mankind. And from those early days the urge to make offerings has been "inherited" from generation to generation through the "astral brain".[2]

The belief in Jesus' death on the cross as an offering of atonement for all humanity sprang from such ancient "heathen" thoughts and ideas **implanted in the human race by Ardor and by his helpers.**

44.

Since it is a known fact that the Jewish people in ancient times practised human sacrifice, why does "The Doctrine of Atonement and the Shorter Road" state that prior to the crucifixion of Jesus Jehovah had not demanded human sacrifice?

Long before the so-called Mosaic Law was adopted and observed by the Hebrews, human sacrifice – especially child sacrifice – was common practice among these people, as it was with so many others. *But with the Hebrews these sacrifices had nothing to do with atonement for the transgressions of the people.* Child sacrifice was carried out mainly in order to make their souls guardians of the homes and secure the members of the household good fortune and happiness in life. But these offerings were also carried out to secure a good result in some great work of construction, for example the first wall around Jerusalem. Both children and adults were sacrificed as offerings of thanksgiving if the deity had granted victory to the king or the commanders in battles against the enemies of the land. These customs persisted for several centuries after the "Mosaic Law" had been adopted as the guiding principle for the sacrificial acts of the Hebrews. But as time passed they gradually died out.

---

[1]) At still later times children or elder relatives were sacrificed for many different purposes.
[2]) See "Toward the Light" p. 283:2 to p. 285:4.

45.

Did the Jewish people expect a Messianic Kingdom, a human or divine Messiah at about the time of the birth of Jesus?

During the time both before and after the birth of Jesus, Judaism embraced several religious sects, each with its own conception of the Messianic Hope. Thus, the Jewish people were expecting both a "God's Kingdom" on Earth in the form of a human king selected and anointed by God, and also a "divine being".

These expectations are quite similar to those held by people to this day. Some expect the Kingdom of God – the Millennium, others expect the Second Coming of Christ as a deity accompanied by a host of angels, and still others expect a new incarnation of Jesus as a man. But all such expectations are and will be in vain. *The Second Coming of Christ has already taken place* – although in a way entirely different from that expected or desired by human beings. *Invisible, with a human being as intermediary and interpreter, Jesus Christ has spoken to mankind in accordance with God's wish and God's Will.* (These speeches can be found in "Toward the Light" pp. 109-137, and in "The Doctrine of Atonement and the Shorter Road" pp. 23-33 respectively).

A Kingdom of God can never be established on Earth. The spiritual purity and maturity required for this to come about does not exist among human beings in the earthly world of Darkness. All humanity must make the long and toilsome pilgrimage *to* God's Kingdom, to the Fatherly Home, *from where each human spirit sprang and where some day all will meet in unity, love, beauty and happiness* **in an eternal life with their loving Father.**

46.

According to modern biblical scholars the father of Jesus was an architect or a mason, and not a carpenter, since the houses in Palestine were mud-built huts for which no timber was used. What in fact was Joseph's occupation?

Joseph was both a carpenter and a joiner.

Although the houses of the rural population and the houses of the poor in the towns were built from mud, many houses in the larger cities were constructed according to the Greek or Roman style of building. Both carpenters and joiners were therefore much in demand for the construction of these houses. In Joseph's time many a rich man's home was built in Tiberias, and Joseph often worked there. The Romans brought their own slaves, many of whom had been taught the various skills and crafts of the building trade. If the Romans were the builders they used mainly these slaves, but when for some reason it was necessary they also took the local people into service, and since they always gave ample wages they were never in want of labour. However, the Jews looked askance at their compatriots if they worked for the foreign rulers of the land.

47.

Has Jesus ever thought or said that he was in any human sense the Son of God, born of a virgin and conceived by the Holy Ghost?

No statement of this kind has ever been made by Jesus, no such *blasphemous thought* has ever gained access to his mind.

None of his contemporaries, not even his mother, had that perception of him – that Jesus was conceived by the "Holy Ghost"!

Jesus' teaching was that God was his and all mankind's Heavenly Father – *he taught thus of a spiritual child-relationship.* He taught that the Jewish people's perception of God was much too imbued with human attributes, he taught that the ancient traditions expressed an erroneous view of God's nature. (See "Toward the Light" p. 37). And he also taught that the proper understanding of God could be *fleetingly discerned in the ancient Scriptures.*

It emerges clearly from the genealogy given in the Gospels *that Jesus was the son of Joseph and Mary.* It is Joseph's lineage that is given in order to show that Jesus was of the house of David, as people believed had been prophesied of the awaited Messiah.

All talk of "virgin birth" and supernatural conception is no more than human fantasy and delusion, which have their roots in heathenism and Darkness. **Truth it is not!**

48.

It is stated in "Toward the Light" on page 207 that: "Since the 24th December has come to be honoured as the birthday of Jesus, the eldest of the Youngest does not wish this date to be changed." Is it correct to make this statement, since the day is also celebrated on the 25th December, as for example in England?

Yes, this statement can be made, even though the day is considered by others to be the 25th; for no statement is made in the relevant passage to the effect that the 24th December is honoured as Jesus' birthday *throughout all Christendom*. It states only that this date has become time-honoured, which no one can deny, since Jesus' birthday *is celebrated* in numerous places in the Christian world *on Christmas Eve the 24th December,* even though the birth of Jesus took place on the night before the 25th, according to the Church.

However, the account of the birth of Jesus in the Gospel of St. Luke is legend throughout – and nothing more. But even if this legendary account is maintained it makes no statement regarding the time of the year or the time of night at which the event took place. It merely states: "And there were in the same country shepherds abiding in the field, keeping watch over their flock by night. And, lo, the angel of the Lord came upon them, and the glory of the Lord shone round about them: and they were sore afraid. And the angel said unto them, fear not: for, behold, I bring you good tidings of great joy, which shall be to all people. For unto you is born[1] this day in the city of David a Saviour ...". It cannot be deduced from the wording of the legend whether the nocturnal vision of the shepherds occurred before or after midnight, which is the hour that divides the departing day from the day to come. The expression "this day" can thus apply just as well to the time before midnight as the time after. And since the eldest of the Youngest wished to establish a particular day on which all those who would in the future accept "Toward the Light" could join in commemorating his life on Earth as Jesus of Nazareth, he chose the 24th December. According to tradition the 25th could equally well have been chosen, but since the wording of the legend does not establish the time of the birth itself, it should in this case be quite irrelevant which date was chosen, the more so since the birth of Jesus did not take place in the winter half of the year at all.

It should moreover be borne in mind *that Christmas is no more*

---

[1] Luke 2:8–11. None of the other Gospels has this account of the birth of Jesus.

than the last vestige of the ancient heathen sacrificial feast to the sun. On the introduction of Christianity in Scandinavia this feast – the feast of the Winter Solstice – was quietly adopted by the Church as a model for the Christian "Christmas", which was held on the established birthday of Jesus.

Should mankind at some future time have outgrown the childish manner in which Christmas – the feast of the birth of Jesus – is now celebrated in most parts of the Christian world, then they may of course themselves decide whether to continue to celebrate this day – perhaps in a more dignified manner – or to omit it altogether. *No one will offend Christ's feelings if this festival disappears completely.* But one thing is certain, *the correct date of the birth of Jesus of Nazareth will never be revealed to mankind.*[1]

49.

Since Jesus according to the accounts of the Gospels was known as a humble man, his speech in the synagogue at Nazareth (see "Toward the Light", page 36) does not seem to stem from him, as it does not accord with this humility.

Nothing of that which is emphasized in the Gospels' distorted[2] accounts of Jesus' speech in the synagogue at Nazareth could rightfully have offended those present to the point where they desired to put him to death because of his pronouncements. But the speech which is presented in "Ardor's Account", p. 36, is the speech that was in fact given, and it is of such a nature that it unavoidably gave the deepest offence to those present. However, it was especially his statements concerning the equivocal nature of their "god" that aroused their anger.

A discussion between Jesus and the people is rendered in John 8:39-47. This dialogue is in fact a composite of several different conversations, but it clearly demonstrates the constant assertion by Jesus: *that the Jews had not one but two gods – the true God and the Father of Falsehood.*

After the incident in the synagogue at Nazareth Jesus became the personification of blasphemy to the entire clergy. His speeches stung

---

[1]) Many years ago this date was revealed at the wish of Christ to the two people who had assisted him in achieving the removal of the earthbound spirits from the astral plane of the Earth. But this information was given with the stipulation that no others should be informed of it.

[2]) Matthew 13:54-57; Mark 6:2-3; Luke 2:42-50 and John 7:14-20.

them, for he did not "show proper respect"[1] for the Mosaic Law, which can be seen by the fact that the priests and the Pharisees constantly rebuked Jesus for breaking the Law. (The Gospels clearly demonstrate that he neglected to observe the precepts for washing, and he violated the Sabbath as well as other religious rules). Similarly, it is always the letter of the law his adversaries confront him with so that with *his interpretations* he could provide them with material for accusations. But if according to the Gospels we are only to see Jesus as a humble man, how are we then to understand the so-called *"prayer of a high priest"* in John 17? For this "prayer" does not in any way portray a humble man. On the contrary, it is expressive of *a grandiloquent, complacent and proud man.* Therefore, let it at once be said that this "prayer of a high priest" *does not originate from Jesus;* indeed, it has nothing whatsoever to do with either his words or his thoughts. The author of this "prayer" will alone carry the responsibility for what has been presented, since it is at no point in accord *with the inner nature of Jesus.*

But also elsewhere in the Gospels can it be seen – according to the wording of these accounts – that Jesus was by no means always meek and humble, although he was never pompous, arrogant or complacent. For since Jesus had quite a violent temper, his answers would often to a great extent provoke his accusers. And since he hailed from the common people he very often used words that were quite strong, to say the least. Only a few of those utterances have been preserved, for example: "Ye serpents", "generation of vipers", "whited sepulchres", "children of the Father of lies", and so on.[2]

When Jesus thus inveighed against his persecutors it was only the *purely human aspect of his nature* that manifested itself, just as it would often be Ardor who, unseen by him, incited him to counter his adversaries with rash words in order to provide them with material for complaints against him. The reason why so many of these irascible words[2] and impetuous incidents have been forgotten can be explained by the fact that the Gospels were not written down until *long after the death of Jesus.* It is common knowledge that when relatives and friends have departed, the living try to remember only the best and to forget, or "cover with the cloak of charity", any rash and hurtful words or violent scenes.

---

[1] The originator of this question was of the opinion that Jesus showed deep respect for the Mosaic Law.

[2] Some of Jesus' utterances put forward in the less conventional idioms of the language that have not been included in the Gospels, because they had been forgotten, were for example the following aimed at the Pharisees: "You are like the camel's dung left in the dust of the road, yea, you are like running sores and stinking boils. – You are like swine that wallow in their own mire."

Therefore, although Jesus is known as a humble man through the Gospels, these also contain records that in their rendering of his words and actions show him to be impetuous and quick-tempered as well. *But all this was only the purely human aspect of his nature.*

50.

Why was Jesus crucified by the Romans when it was the Council in Jerusalem that had condemned him to death? Surely the Jews had a free hand in questions concerning their own religion.

Although many of the scribes had begun to resent Jesus after he had spoken in the synagogue at Nazareth, others among them observed at a distance his proclamations about God. They saw that the words of Jesus gained considerable power over the people, and they understood that his authority could possibly be employed to further their own interests.

In "Toward the Light", p. 56, it is written that a member of the Council in Jerusalem, Joseph of Arimathea, asked Jesus if he were the expected Messiah, and also suggested that he step forward under the leadership of the clergy as the awaited "King on Earth". Similar suggestions were later made by other members of the clergy and the Council. But Jesus firmly rejected these attempts to persuade him to promote an uprising of the people against the foreign rule. Despite his vacillation in accepting the thought that he was the Messiah,[1] Jesus knew with certainty that the matter in which the priests and the Council desired his help *was not his task*.

But when rumours that Jesus was a claimant to the crown reached Pilate he decided to imprison him before any rebellion began, for he was aware that the priests and the Council must be behind the plot. However, the Council in Jerusalem learnt of what was afoot, and its members considered the possibility that Jesus, under questioning before Pontius Pilate, would reveal the fact that it was they who had urged him to come forward as king. Such testimony would then place in Pilate's hands a potent weapon against the chief priests, who sought constantly to harass him. This had to be prevented but the Council could only do so by forestalling Pilate's plan. Jesus was therefore hastily imprisoned by Caiaphas and accused of having blasphemed God by calling himself the son of the "Most High".

During interrogation the further accusation was made that Jesus

---

[1] See "Toward the Light" p. 35 and p. 226.

had in mind to rouse the people to rebellion. Caiaphas had foreseen this, however, and since Jesus' own words had condemned him (see "Toward the Light" p. 62), Caiaphas was able to deliver him to Pilate on the pretext that he had learnt through the testimony of witnesses that Jesus had attempted to rouse the people to overthrow the Roman rule. By this action the Council – the Sanhedrin – disclaimed before Pilate *any part in the contemplated uprising against the overlordship of Rome.*

The members of the Council thus *sacrificed Jesus so as to escape any possible accusation themselves,* reasoning that should Jesus now testify during interrogation before Pilate that the chief priests had sought to induce him to start an insurrection against the Romans, his words could only be regarded as the *vengeance of a convicted man upon his judges.*

Pilate was well aware of the object of this proceeding, but since his own position at that time was far from secure and although he knew that Jesus was innocent of this accusation, he dared not dismiss Caiaphas' petition and release Jesus, or let the Council itself carry out the sentence of death according to Jewish law. The hope that Pilate had nurtured – to strike a blow at the members of the Council by *himself* imprisoning Jesus – had now been thwarted by the prompt intervention of Caiaphas. Pilate saw clearly that if he dismissed Caiaphas' petition the Council would gain the advantage of him, and as he did not wish this to happen, *he sacrificed Jesus* just as the Jews had done, *so that he himself might go free.*

But with the handing over of Jesus to Pilate – to the Romans – the manner of his death was inevitable: **death on the cross.**

51.

Why was the preceding Question not included in "Toward the Light" and answered there?

Because at the time that "Toward the Light" was given, no question was raised on this subject. Neither was any question asked regarding Jesus as a claimant to the crown, and for this reason it was not possible from the transcendental world to give a more detailed account of the interrogation and conviction of Jesus. And since it was known both from the Gospels and from other ancient documents that Jesus had also been convicted for posing as the King of the Jews, and thus as a *rebel,* there was strictly speaking no reason for further elaboration on this subject. For in order for the Council to be able to surrender Jesus to Pilate there had to be at least a suspicion that Jesus had *transgressed the Roman laws*. Otherwise the Council could have convicted him and carried out the sentence of death according to its own laws without the interference of the Romans.

But the main reason why no attempt was made from the transcendental world to elicit further questions on the interrogation and conviction of Jesus was that both Pilate and the members of the Council had *laid all the blame upon a quite innocent man* in order to escape from a difficult situation themselves. They had done this to *a much greater extent* than could ever be proved on Earth through normal scientific investigation, and since Christ did not wish the guilt either of the Council or of Pilate to appear greater than was already known to human beings, no details were given on any matter regarding which no questions were raised.

Information had, moreover, already been given under the Question of Joseph of Arimathea's relationship with Jesus (see "Toward the Light" pp. 55-57), which showed that at least one member of the Council had urged Jesus to come forward under the aegis of the chief priests as the Messiah on Earth, as the King of the House of David. A thoughtful reader could therefore easily have drawn the conclusion from that information that the Council's surrender of Jesus to Pilate was possibly, indeed probably due to their fear *that Jesus would hold them responsible for this attempt to raise a rebellion of the people against the Romans.*

52.

Who and what was Barabbas? Why was he released in preference to Jesus! (See "Toward the Light", page 228).

Barabbas originated from the tribe of Levi, and at the time Jesus was convicted he was known among the people as a shabby, old and mentally deranged beggar. The name "Barabbas" was his by-name. He was for ever acting in defiance of the Roman soldiers, he sought in various ways to annoy them, he swore at them in coarse language and cursed them as "the Roman potentates". As a rule the soldiers left him alone, mainly because they did not quite understand his abusive language.

One day when hostilities flared up between a number of beggars and some donkey and camel drivers in one of the back streets of the Jerusalem slums, the Roman guards arrived to disperse the contending parties and the onlookers that had gathered. As Barabbas happened to be in their way they pushed him aside so that he fell. Embittered by this ill-treatment Barabbas picked up some stones and hurled them at the soldiers. One of the stones struck a Roman scribe who happened to be passing, and as the blow was fatal, Barabbas was arrested. However, his imprisonment aroused great anger among the people assembled, since they had witnessed the incident and felt that the Roman soldiers were themselves to blame for the conduct of Barabbas. The crowd followed along to the prison, clamouring for his release. Pilate then conceived the idea that he could possibly resolve his own dilemma with respect to Jesus by offering the people to release one of the prisoners on the occasion of the Passover. He then requested them to choose between Barabbas and Jesus. He presumed the people would choose Jesus, who had bestowed so many benefits on the poor and the sick, whereas Barabbas had demonstrably killed a human being and was thus guilty unto death. Pilate's view of the matter was that Jesus was a man free from any guilt, even though he had been convicted by the Sanhedrin (the Council in Jerusalem), but he dared not oppose the judgment on account of his own insecure position and strained relationship with the Council, although he did see through the proceedings on their part to surrender Jesus to him accused as a rebel. (See the answers to the two preceding Questions). But despite Pilate's appeal to the gathering that they should choose Jesus, they demanded that Barabbas be released. *Thus the fate of Jesus was sealed.*

"The Council condemned him, the priests condemned him, the people condemned him! **Human beings themselves delivered him unto death!"**[1]

53.

Were the words "Eloi, Eloi, lama sabachthani?" (Mark 15:34) which have been attributed to Jesus in fact spoken by him?

No, these words were not spoken by Jesus.

In "Toward the Light", p. 64:5, it is stated that the mother of Jesus was present at the crucifixion. Deeply grieved over her son and frightened by the waning daylight, the thought occurred to her that God through this deep darkness demonstrated His wrath that her son had renounced the belief of his forefathers, and she cried out:

---

[1]) Quotation from "The Doctrine of Atonement and the Shorter Road", p. 20.

"Behold, the Most High has forsaken you!" – In the course of time these words, like so much from that period, became distorted until they were attributed in the above form to Jesus. But Jesus never thought, nor did he ever pronounce, **that God had forsaken[1] him in his hour of need.**

54.

Does the Bible provide any support at all for the assertion made in "Toward the Light" that Jesus' death on the cross was not a death of atonement?

Several passages in the Gospels indicate that Jesus knew nothing of being chosen by God to atone for the sins of human beings through his death on the cross.

For instance, in discourse with some of the Pharisees (Matthew 9:13) Jesus says among other things: "But go ye and learn what that meaneth, *I will have mercy and not sacrifice*[2]". If Jesus had known that he had been chosen by God as the "sacrificial offering" for mankind, he would never have quoted this text; for in that case he would also have known that *sacrifice* and not mercy was precisely what God *demanded*. But *Jesus knew nothing of such a provision*. And if his death on the cross were to be truly regarded as an "offering" for the sins of all humanity, such a sacrifice would not have served its purpose unless Jesus himself knew of its significance and *voluntarily gave his consent*. Besides, the interpretation of the "death of atonement" of Jesus violates the Jewish precepts for sacrifices for sin altogether and can never, despite all argumentation, be brought into accordance with these precepts. (See also "The Doctrine of Atonement and the Shorter Road", pp. 5–20).

In Matthew 12:36-37 it is also written: "But I say unto you, that every idle word that men shall speak, they shall give account thereof in the day of judgment: *for by thy words thou shalt be justified and by thy words thou shalt be condemned*[3]". Had Jesus known that by his death on the cross he would atone for the sins of humanity, he would never have spoken these words; for then he would have known that this provision would not apply to those human beings who believed in his sacrificial death. But Jesus knows nothing of any

---

[1]) That is to say, failed him.
[2]) Jesus quotes a text from the Old Testament. See 1 Samuel 15:22, Hosea 6:6; Micah 6:7-8, and several other places.
[3]) The passage quoted contains the incorrect word "condemned".

such dispensation, what he says here *holds true for all human beings*.

This should suffice to show that the Church on this question teaches one thing, **but that Jesus teaches quite another.**

55.

"If the robber on the cross could enter Paradise under the shelter of Christ, then surely everyone else should be able to do so?"

In "Toward the Light" on page 228, chapter 27, it is written that the two thieves who were crucified at the same time as Jesus were deeply stupefied by the drink they had been given, and hence that any talk between them and Jesus would have been impossible. It is thus out of the question that God should accept this *false human deduction* from a dialogue *that never took place*. And since the thief did *not* enter Paradise "under the shelter of Christ", clearly *no* human being can do so.

In order possibly to awaken understanding of how mistaken the teaching of the Church is also on this point, the following earthly illustration, although somewhat imperfect in its reflection of reality, is given for comparison:

Let us imagine an earthly prince and his son, both endowed with an abundance of love and compassion greatly exceeding the human measure. They live their lives in the greatest beauty, purity and splendour, and own all that earthly power and riches can provide. On one of his journeys the prince's son meets a wretched, exhausted and ragged man, soiled by every kind of filth, a man who has sinned greatly against the prince and his son. Out of love and compassion the prince's son takes this man into his care, covers his rags and his uncleanliness with his magnificent cape and leads him to his home, where the prince and his court receive him in their midst. How would this man feel in these surroundings? Even if we imagine that the cape of the prince's son had a magic power, and not only covered the man's rags and filth but also cleansed him and mended his attire, and possibly even cleansed his mind and thoughts, would he not still feel, and feel deeply, that despite all the love and forgiveness shown him, this was not his rightful place? Against the background of his earlier life, the environment in which he grew up, he would *never* be able to feel at home and at ease in these – to him – so strange surroundings.

Thus no one who is not *in mind and in thought* cleansed from within of sin, evil and folly could feel at ease in Paradise, God's Kingdom, let alone live in the nearness of God.

But slowly, through the many reincarnations, the human spirit must be cleansed and purified before it can enter the Kingdom of God, *before God* **from His heart can bid His child welcome.**

56.

"Should not those who attack the Church's Doctrine of Atonement take care to accord due recognition to all its merits?"[1]

In "The Doctrine of Atonement and the Shorter Road" it is written (p. 22:1, line 2): "Upon my return our Father bade me to remove the cornerstone from under the House that you, the human beings, have built upon my *presumptuous* interpretation of the death of Jesus of Nazareth".

Our God and Father has thus enjoined Paul to remove the cornerstone, the foundation that *he* laid, and upon which *the Church* has built further with *its* doctrine of Jesus' death of atonement. It was thus not Paul's task to expose the error in the doctrine of the Church, but rather to show the error *of his own teaching* – the cornerstone – and this he has done with all possible clarity and authority. The doctrine of the Church, all its embellishments, its possibly "higher ethics", *must be torn down by the clergy themselves.*

But everyone should be able to understand that if an error is made in the first step of a longer calculation, then the final result based upon this initial error cannot possibly be correct. Everyone should be able to understand that if the cornerstone is full of flaws and cracks it is unusable as the foundation for a building. *Sooner or later it will crumble – and the building will collapse into rubble.*

Let us, however, look more closely at pages 15–17 of "The Doctrine of Atonement and the Shorter Road". Paul has reached the point in his investigation of the Doctrine of Atonement where it must be determined whether Jehovah, the divinity of the Jewish people, sent Jesus unto humanity so that he could give himself once and for all as a pure and unblemished offering.

In order to do this, Paul had to draw a comparison between this action of Jehovah and the actions of human beings: the father who

---

[1] Refers to Paul's account of the manner in which the Doctrine of Atonement arose. See "The Doctrine of Atonement and the Shorter Road" pp. 15–17.

in his human anger demands corporal punishment for his wicked and disobedient children, which is indeed a befitting parallel to Jehovah. *The father of the parable* acts toward his children in the same way that *Jehovah,* according to the accounts of the Old Testament, acted toward the Jewish people time and again, that is: *he chastised them with his wrath.* Paul demonstrates through this parable that if Jehovah had *demanded* the sacrificial death of Jesus, he would have been guilty of an act that placed him *beneath* the level of human beings. Paul therefore concludes that Jehovah could not have sent Jesus with the intention that he should accept punishment for the sins of others. And since Jehovah could not have sent Jesus upon this mission, Paul concludes correctly that neither could *the God and Father of whom Jesus himself speaks* - and who is far above Jehovah - possibly be the originator of such a mission. *God* must have had other reasons for a mission requiring His beloved Son to live on Earth among human beings - and Paul then gives a brief outline of *God's intended plan* for the mission of Jesus. See "The Doctrine of Atonement and the Shorter Road", page 19.

Paul criticizes his own teaching, including the parable, from today's point of view in order to demonstrate how reprehensible it is for the Church to have continued to build upon *his* Doctrine of Atonement rather than dissociate itself from it - which the Church should have done a long time ago - as something **entirely unworthy of God.**

By refuting *his own* doctrine so clearly Paul has removed the cornerstone from under the Doctrine of Atonement *of the Church.* But no one has demanded that he also tear down the ornamentation and the embellishments with which the clergy have adorned it through the ages. For this is entirely the task of the clergy. (See "The Doctrine of Atonement and the Shorter Road", p. 21, line 11 and p. 22, line 5 from the bottom). But once the cornerstone is removed from under a "house", it has already become so undermined that the adornment is of no importance - the "house" will fall sooner or later; *for the result of the reckoning is false because the first calculation, Paul's calculation, was false!*

In the criticism of his Doctrine of Atonement Paul makes no mention of how the religious conceptions of the Jewish people, and thereby his own, had in various ways been influenced by the religions of the neighbouring "heathen" peoples. But since Paul, when the Doctrine of Atonement was formulated, was truly a child of his people and of his time, he did not perceive in which areas and in which manner his thoughts were influenced by his knowledge of the other peoples' religious perception of the divine, of the transcendental. Therefore, it does not rest with him to account for these relationships, especially since people themselves through critical studies of the Bible can point out, and have indeed pointed out, characteristics and similarities with other religions of his time.

57.

"It was, of course, human beings that gave him (Jesus) death. But it is quite without foundation to say that we would now put the blame on God. And that we should have invented the Doctrine of Atonement for that purpose is completely beside the point."
What comment can be made on the foregoing extract from a letter?

As stated in the reply to the preceding question. *Paul* was the originator of the Doctrine of Atonement. But through the ages *the clergy* have in various ways built further upon Paul's foundation, so as to make the doctrine more ethical and more worthy of God in the perception of human beings. It would therefore be quite incomprehensible to the laity if the Church should now maintain that mankind gave Jesus death *without this death being pre-ordained by God,* for in that case Jesus' death could not have been a *death of atonement*. Should the clergy recognize that the death of Jesus must be solely attributed to human beings, *all teaching* – ethical or otherwise – *of Jesus' death of atonement* would immediately collapse. *For in that case Jesus could not have torn down the dividing wall of sin* that was raised between God and mankind at the fall of the first human being – from the biblical point of view – *and no human being could then enter Paradise "under his shelter", cleansed or protected by his "innocent blood".*

It cannot be denied that "belief" in Jesus as Saviour and Redeemer has in the course of time brought forth many fine, true and genuine feelings in a not inconsiderable part of humanity, and neither can it be denied that the Doctrine of Atonement has been held as the full truth by many while they lived on Earth. But how does it benefit human beings that during earthly life they live by misconceptions and misunderstandings of the nature of God and of the beyond? Thousands upon thousands of Christians have had to acknowledge with grief and despair after earthly death that the road to "Paradise" is infinitely long and hard; and they have had to acknowledge that only they *themselves* can *atone for* what they have sinned, and *themselves* – in a new life on Earth – *rectify* the wrong they have done; and they have had to acknowledge that "belief" in

Jesus as Saviour and Redeemer *has neither sanctified nor justified them, nor has it brought them to their goal – Paradise*. But it is precisely all these sorrows and spiritual sufferings in the beyond that Paul and *the* Youngest who have contributed to the appearance in the human world of "Toward the Light" and "The Doctrine of Atonement and the Shorter Road" have sought to spare human beings in the future. And now that Ardor – Satan – has returned to God, it is in the hands of human beings themselves whether they will accept, understand and be guided by the truths presented to all humanity through these works; for those who will accept this guidance *will be spared much grief,* **will be spared much spiritual suffering.**

58.

Can one explain the fact that many religions of ancient times, like Christianity, are based on a "divine trinity"? Does anything occult lie at the root of this?

Yes, occult memories form the basis of the "divine trinity" that exists in various religions.

Those of the Youngest who had the mission in life on Earth to bring humanity knowledge of God, of His Being, of His relationship to human beings, and also had been given the task of teaching about life in the spiritual worlds, have from the oldest times found it exceedingly difficult to bring their messages in full accordance with the eternal truths. Ardor and the disincarnated Eldest continually sought to prevent the incarnated Youngest from fulfilling their mission in the proper way, partly by obscuring their memories of eternal life in God's Kingdom, partly by enshrouding them in accumulations of Darkness that prevented their free thoughts from developing in the direction indicated by God, and also by implanting false and misleading thoughts in them. Similarly, the incarnated Eldest have in various ways had a disturbing, destructive and misleading influence by distorting that which the Youngest brought human beings in the field of religion.

The occult basis for the "divine trinity" is the incarnated Youngest's dim memory of God as *the Creator and Father,* who within His Being embodied *both the male and the female primal principle,* and their memory of the eldest of the Youngest, who *was their leader in the beyond.*

Through the many thousands of years that have passed since the concept of a divine trinity first gained acceptance in the world of human "belief", it has formed a basis which has been built upon again and again, either in parallel or diverging series of steps. Time after time – incarnation after incarnation – have the incarnated Youngest tried to bring human beings a completely truthful teaching of God and the divine. But all their efforts remained more or less vain attempts until the time of Ardor's return to God. The Jewish people and the Mohammedans with their monotheistic concept of the godhead have on that point come the closest to the truth, although their understanding of the nature of God, of His relationship to humanity, their conception of the beyond, as well as other concepts, are marked by human fallibility.

Thus, behind the various religions which from the earliest times have built, and still build, upon a "divine trinity" lies the memory of God's Being and of life in the beyond. *These memories have by Ardor and his emissaries been drawn downward into Darkness, have been* **distorted and perverted.**

59.

How did the thought of a Messiah chosen by God arise?

Also through the occult memories of the Youngest, since many of the incarnated Youngest during their lives on Earth retained a memory of their loving, faithful and untiring leader – the eldest of the Youngest, Christ. They had a recollection of him who been chosen by God[1] to lead them in their work for humanity's journey toward the Light. They retained a memory of him, the radiant, shining figure who from time to time, at long intervals, became embodied as a man in order to teach his fellow human beings love for God and love for their neighbour. And during their earthly lives, when the yearning for the Heavenly Home, the yearning for their beloved brother and leader became too strong, they spoke to their fellow human beings of him *who should one day come,* spoke of him *whom God had chosen to be Lord and King*[2] *of the "Heavens"*[3] *and Ruler over all the Kingdom of the Earth.*

But Ardor also succeeded in distorting and perverting this beautiful memory, the truth, which lay behind the thoughts and words of

---

[1]) See "Toward the Light" p. 16:6.

[2]) The eldest of the Youngest had been chosen by God to become the leader of humanity, but not "Ruler of the Kingdom of the Earth". This distortion of the mission of Jesus was implanted in the thoughts of the incarnated Youngest by Ardor and has no connection with the

the incarnated Youngest – and thus *the doctrine of "Atonement" and the doctrine of the "Kingdom"*[2] *of Jesus became* **the visible manifestation of Darkness, originating from a truth of the Light.**

60.

In "Toward the Light" it is written on page 334 that no human spirit can come into the immediate presence of God without being absorbed into Him, for which reason Christ must act as the Father's representative to human beings. In view of this statement it must be assumed that God cannot visit the Earth. Is this the case?

As a consequence of His absolute capacity for *self-limitation* God can visit the plane of the Earth whenever He wishes and remain there as long as He desires. Through the power of His Thought and Will He then limits the Light-radiation of His personal Being so that it fully harmonizes with the Light-radiations present at the place where He wishes to be; for no human spirit and no human being can remain in the proximity of God when His Light-radiations are at their full intensity. If God is on the plane of the Earth and wishes to be near a human being, He creates a "dividing wall" between Himself and the human being by the power of His Thought and Will, having first reduced the intensity of His own Light-radiations. The substance of this dividing wall corresponds on the side toward the respective human being exactly to the degree of strength inherent in the radiations of Light or Darkness that are emitted from the personal being, whereas the side turned toward God has a Light-radiation that corresponds to the reduced strength of Light that is emitted from God's personal Being at that moment. By this arrangement an imperceptible transition is created – often from radiations of Darkness – to the reduced Light-radiation emanating from God.

If it could be imagined that God Himself had assumed the leadership of humanity instead of entrusting this to Christ, He would have had to create an abode in the outermost sphere around the Earth and reside there together with His twelve Servants. But in that case it would have been necessary for God not only to reduce His own Light-radiation but also that of His Servants, so that the Earth and the spheres should not be absorbed by the intense and radiant sea of

---

truth. It is the mission of Christ to lead all human spirits to God's Kingdom, but not to "rule" over them.
  [3]) The spheres.

Light that emanates from them all. The Youngest – as disincarnated spirits – would obviously have resided here with God in the same sphere. But if God had made such an arrangement His Kingdom would have stood empty, and even if the Youngest had sojourned there from time to time between incarnations, they would not have been able to receive the necessary help – through God's radiation of Light – for new incarnations. For God's full strength of Light would not have been available at the place where it was required. The zeal and capacity for work of the Youngest would therefore have gradually declined in the course of time rather than increased – *and their work on behalf of humanity would have become hopeless and impossible to complete.*

God is, however, the Supreme Leader, although Christ is responsible for the more direct leadership of the human beings on Earth and of the human spirits in the spheres. By this arrangement God can reside in His Kingdom together with His Servants and there they can all unleash the full strength of their radiance in the purest and most resplendent sea of Light. But even though God's permanent abode is in His Kingdom, *He is still able to visit the Earth* **whenever His presence there is necessary.**

61.

The idea that God has not existed through all eternity seems quite inconceivable!

God has of course existed through all eternity, but for untold eternities He was "Thought and Will" – an impersonal "something". God arose as a personal Being on the absolute union of the divine Thought and the divine Will. *But He has existed through all eternity.* (See "Toward the Light" pp. 3–4 and p. 159 to p. 160:2).

62.

Since God was for a time impersonal – and thus passing through a state of development – was He then subject to the natural laws?

All natural laws[1] have their origin in God's Thought and Will. But He had to have exact knowledge of all that lay hidden in the primal

---

[1]) At the dawn of time God established regular laws both for the spiritual and for the

power that is called "Darkness" before He could give laws that fully subjugated this Darkness, this primal force, and only through His own experience could this be achieved. While God was Thought and Will, while Thought and Will were not equal, not united in an inseparable whole – so that the Thought did not desire what the Will was not able to fulfil – He was not the absolute master over Darkness and could not arise as a personal Being, as the Almighty Power who by virtue of His Thought and Will had gained victory over *the evil that was in the Darkness*.

The existence of the personal Being God as Thought and Will is therefore the development that the divine male and female primal principle had to undergo in order for these principles to emerge as a unified, balanced and consummate "Divine Being". Thus, the natural laws – in this case the spiritual – are the issue of the Divinity's struggle out of Darkness, a struggle whose ultimate result became the personal God, a Being of universal knowledge and universal power.

Just as God had to struggle out of Darkness in order to become a personal Being, so must human beings struggle out of Darkness in order to become perfected personal beings: and in order to bring this struggle to its conclusion, they must time and again be incarnated into the Darkness of life on Earth until the final victory has been won.

Since the spiritual self of human beings has its origin in and from God, the human spirit carries within itself a reflection of the laws under which its development takes place. These laws that have been given by God, but were non-existent while He strove toward victory, ease the way for the human spirit in its struggle out of Darkness.

Human beings are highly different in nature, and the difference between them is among other things due to the longer or shorter development which their spiritual selves have undergone through the ages. Thus there are people rich in thoughts and emotions whose will is weak and ineffective. There are others where the reverse is true, so that the will has become the predominant characteristic of the personality, while the thoughts and emotions have been developed to only a limited extent. And between these two extremes there are a great many variations in degree of strength and differences of mani-

---

molecular Darkness. But when the Eldest began to experiment with the Darkness that had precipitated from the surrounding Light much of the molecular Darkness thereby evaded the direct control of God, and as a result many of its various manifestations no longer conformed to the regularity of God's laws. But in the course of millions of years the Light has had a regulating, harmonizing and stabilizing influence upon this Darkness, whereby several of these irregular and unpredictable manifestations have quite automatically been brought under the control of more regular or completely regular laws. The "natural laws" referred to here are the laws for the spiritual Darkness.

festation of the human thought and will. Only very rarely is it possible to find a person on Earth about whom it can truly be said that his or her intellectual and emotional life is in complete balance with the will. Such a human being will – in earthly terms – by the power of its will master the thought to perfection. And the thought of such a human being contains not only that which specifically concerns the sorrows and joys, the spiritual and bodily sufferings of the self, but also the sorrows and joys of other beings. And by virtue of the strength of the will that is balanced with the thought, such a human being will through its actions be able to bring help and joy to fellow humans, not only through the daily work of life within a narrow range of activities, but also outward to humanity at large. But in order to arrive at the ideal of so strong and perfected a personality, the spiritual self must have lived through numerous incarnations, *in other words, have undergone a very long development.* Only the individual who has experienced spiritual and bodily sufferings to the full is able to help others with love and compassion. Only the individual who has personally struggled through the grief, sin, evil, poverty, suffering and misery of many lives on Earth has the full loving understanding of the sufferings of fellow human beings. *For only through its own struggle, its own victory, has the human being become capable of understanding its fellow human beings and of bringing the help that is needed out of a loving heart.*

But once it has been understood that only through *self-recognition,* through *self-experience* can the individual attain understanding, attain perfection, it will also be understood that He, the Highest of all Beings – the Divinity whence the human spirit sprang – *must have personal knowledge of all that the human spirit has to endure in life on Earth.* It will be understood that He, who knows all, must also Himself have struggled through Darkness toward the Light, must also have striven toward the complete union of Thought and Will in order to emerge as the perfect Victor, as the All-knowing, the Almighty. Through His struggle out of Darkness God has gained full understanding of the grief and suffering that human beings may meet in life on Earth. He has gained knowledge of the sins and temptations to which human beings succumb, so that He, *from His absolute knowledge, can meet every human supplication for help* **with the most profound understanding, compassion and love.**

Therefore, through the struggle out of Darkness by divine Thought and Will, God had gained such knowledge of the many and various manifestations of spiritual Darkness when He arose as a personal Being that, apart from being the sovereign Ruler, He also was, and still is, fully able to be the loving, understanding and compassionate Father, who out of His loving Thought and through His strong Will is in every way able *to help all His children to gain victory in the long and bitter struggle* **out of the snares and temptations of Darkness.**

63.

If God is a personal Being and the loving Father of the human spirit, why is human life then so full of suffering, disasters, crime, wars and all forms of horror? Why does He not in each case intervene and prevent such things from happening? Is He not almighty?

It is explained in "Toward the Light" that humanity owes its existence on Earth to God's fallen children – the "Eldest". As the Earth is a world of Darkness and therefore subject to the natural laws[1] that are to be found within the primal power that is called Darkness, none of the suffering, dread and misfortune resulting from natural disasters can be prevented. They will therefore never cease so long as the Earth exists. But since Darkness will diminish significantly in the course of millions of years, natural catastrophes will occur more seldom and with less violence as Darkness is eliminated. It will take many, many ages, however, before this effect can be observed in the earthly world.

But if human beings were *less irresponsible than they are,* natural disasters would claim many fewer victims than they do at present. Why are cities and dwellings built on the slopes, or in the proximity, of active volcanoes? Why are cities and dwellings located on lowlying river banks and small islands without adequate defences against flooding by storm surge or sudden thaw? *On such matters mankind still has much to learn.*

For the suffering, sorrows and disasters that in so many ways cast a shadow over human life on Earth, human beings themselves bear most of the blame and responsibility. Many sufferings, griefs and misfortunes could be avoided if human beings would always be mindful that every individual has a great responsibility in life, a responsibility that no one can escape *when the account of the individual's life on Earth must – after death – be rendered unto God.*

---

[1]) The laws for the many and varied manifestations of molecular Darkness. These laws are not all as regular and firmly established as are the laws for "spiritual Darkness". See the footnote to the preceding Question.

Let us consider some examples from everyday life to illustrate the matter:

1) A mother leaves her small or infant children unsupervised at home. During her absence the children find a box of matches, and while playing with these the curtains, the children's clothes or other easily inflammable articles catch fire, and the children perish in the flames before help arrives. What grief, what horror will such an experience cause the irresponsible mother – or both parents! And how many curses have been hurled at God on such occurrences! But who is guilty, who bears the responsibility? *The guilt and the responsibility lie with the persons who left the children without supervision and without help.*

2) The children run about – without supervision – in the streets, on the roads and in parks, exposed to traffic or to the danger of drowning in marshes, ponds and lakes. Who is guilty, who bears the responsibility if accidents occur? The guilt and the responsibility lie with the persons who left the children to look after themselves.[1] *Such misfortunes would not occur if human beings were aware of their full responsibility.*

3) A third example from everyday life: Two trains collide, many lose their lives and many are maimed. Who is guilty, who bears the responsibility? The guilt and the responsibility lie with the persons who overlooked the stop signals, or with the person who forgot to set the signal. *But if they were aware of their full responsibility such accidents would not occur.*[2]

4) And the carelessness shown by many drivers of motor vehicles similarly brings accidents, suffering, maiming and death. Who is guilty? The drivers! *If they were all aware of their full responsibility, far greater care would be exercised.*[3]

5) And what sufferings and horrors follow in the wake of war! But who is guilty, and who bears the responsibility? Also in this case are

---

[1] Should anyone comment on the above examples that in many cases the parents are forced to leave small children and infants unattended because the mother, or both parents, are obliged to earn their livelihood outside the home, then there is only one response: no small or infant children must ever be left on their own. If accidents of any kind occur God will always lay the responsibility on the mother, or on both parents, where it rightfully belongs. But if people have small children whom they cannot support without being absent from home – and if they cannot afford supervision – then they must apply to the relevant public authority for help, however humiliating this may be for them. There is no other way. (See further "Toward the Light" p. 126:3-8).

[2] Railway accidents can of course arise in many other ways, but where they are not due to natural catastrophes it is usually human beings who bear the responsibility.

[3] Many other examples could be given, for there is indeed enough to choose from in the matter of human transgressions: recklessness, foolhardiness, competitive sport, irresponsibility – and human malevolence.

human beings themselves to blame for what occurs, also in this case do they bear the full responsibility. "Toward the Light" states clearly and concisely that **all warfare contravenes the laws of God.** And not until all have learnt the true meaning of the ancient commandment *"Thou shalt not kill"* will earthly conditions – in respect of war – improve.

But the Question asks why God lets all this occur instead of intervening and preventing it. To this there is but one answer: God is the *Father and Mentor* of the human spirit, but He brings up His children so that they will gradually learn fully to understand their responsibility, both toward Him and toward their fellow human beings. God does not *hold* His children *by the hand* for ever, for then they would never become spiritually mature beings. If God intervened and prevented all untoward occurrences, then human beings would never change, then they would never learn the deep-rooted significance of responsibility. It is therefore the task of human beings themselves to ensure that the importance of responsibility is learnt and understood. And this should be achieved through the education given to children and the younger generation by parents, in schools and in institutions.

But even though God does not prevent disasters from affecting human life, He helps in many ways by letting the guardian spirits give warning both to those about to cause disasters and to those who through no fault of their own may be exposed to them. Many people can testify that due to a sudden impulse they had decided not to travel on a given train, ship or other means of transportation, and that by following this impulse they have escaped possible injury or impending death. However, the majority of people fail to follow such impulses or pay heed to the warnings of their guardian spirit; but in that case *these people must share in the responsibility* for their own death, maiming or suffering, although it does not *lessen* the guilt of the person chiefly responsible for the disaster.

In those cases where the disasters are caused by the ether-recordings of Ardor (see "Toward the Light" p. 253:5 and p. 254:1) a warning will always be given through the guardian spirit to people who might be exposed to danger. But if disasters are caused exclusively by thoughtless, foolhardy, careless, forgetful or irresponsible people, not even God can anticipate when, where or how possible accidents may take place, because of the human free will. But also in these cases will it be attempted through the guardian spirit, if a disaster is about to happen, to issue a "call" of warning to the person responsible, that is to say, evoke a sudden impulse to exert caution. Many people can testify to such an experience, if they wish to do so. (For further reference see "Toward the Light" p. 306:1,2 and p. 252:3-4).

God *is* a personal Being, God *is* the loving Father of the human spirit, and God *is* Almighty. He seeks in every possible way to bring up His children *with full justice to all, with fervent and profound love for them all. But he does not act against His own laws, He does not act against human free will for good or evil - the free will with which God has endowed every human being, and which for a time and in many ways* **limits His omniscience and therefore His omnipotence.**

64.

In "Toward the Light", page 160, the possibility is mentioned that primal Thought and primal Will might have attracted each other under the influence of Darkness, and that the being who would have arisen at the moment of uniting would in every way have become the absolute antithesis of God. Can it be explained how a cosmos of Darkness would have evolved under the leadership of such a being?

Only God can answer this question in full, but probably it will not be answered in every detail until all human spirits are gathered in God's Kingdom and wish to know the answer.

However, anyone is entitled to attempt to elucidate the question on the basis of what "Toward the Light" teaches about the powers and properties of Darkness and of the Light.

Therefore, if we imagine that primal Thought and primal Will met and became united under the influence of Darkness, thus resulting in a Divinity of Darkness, an absolute antithesis of the God of Light that we[1] know, love and revere, the following facts must first be taken into account: 1) that the Deity of Darkness despite his power would be incapable of destroying the primal Light, since this *embodied and still embodies eternal life;* 2) that the primal Light would therefore remain in its place, as a core in the primal Darkness; 3) that the Deity of Darkness would be able to create from Darkness, but not from the Light, since he could have no knowledge of the properties of the Light, since primal Thought and primal Will before becoming united[2] had existed only in Darkness and not in the Light;

---

[1]) The Youngest - the spiritual leaders of humanity.

[2]) One must imagine that Thought and Will reacted to the influence of Darkness while they existed on the border between Light and Darkness. See "Toward the Light" p. 159:3.

4) that the beings, objects, globes and worlds which the Deity of Darkness might create would be transitory *since death or extinction, was and is in the Darkness;* and 5) that he, even though his ability to survive could be extended through countless aeons, would ultimately disintegrate and be extinct, because the life of Darkness *is not everlasting.* One could imagine two possibilities for the development of life in a cosmos of Darkness:

1) The Deity would to a certain extent be able to control the Darkness, but since Darkness is chaos, nothing but chaos would result from his work, his actions and his reign. He would probably have created children in his own likeness, dreadful creatures, endowed with all the ferocity, malevolence and hideousness of Darkness, worse than the worst of the fallen Eldest. The Deity would incessantly be at war with his creatures, for evil and hatred would dominate the dealings between them. Love, compassion and mercy would be concepts quite incomprehensible, indeed quite unknown to all of them. "Thought" would stand against "thoughts", "Will" against "wills"; for the Deity would never have attained complete control over his children's insatiable greed for power, since having created beings of thought and will, he had thereby weakened *his own thought and will.* And as the eternal, *inexhaustible* radiations of Light would lie beyond his reach, there could be no prospect for him of renewing the energy of his own thought and will in order to assert himself before his children.

Thus it is conceivable that the many evil wills would ultimately emerge victorious over the Deity whose will had been weakened through his acts of creation. And when he had been conquered by his children, *then his dissolution and destruction would be inevitable.* The many who had defeated the one would necessarily continue the constant struggle for power, for they would obviously all desire to be the first, the uppermost, and no one would yield, none would submit. And this struggle would continue until all had ceased to exist as personal beings, for the last, the lone survivor on the field of battle, would not enjoy any sense of victory for long, for he would surely be torn apart by the boundless evil and ferocity of his thought and will of Darkness, *because his "thought" and "will" would have absorbed and assimilated the "thought" and "will" of all the annihilated beings of Darkness* – fragments of primal Thought and primal Will. But when the disintegration of the last remaining living being of Darkness had taken place, then it could be conjectured that one of the following two possibilities would occur:

a) With the disintegration and dissolution of the personal being, his thought and will would also *be split apart, dissolved and absorb-*

ed by Darkness. But the explosion that had taken place would at the same time depolarize the Darkness, after which it would revert to its *original state of dormancy,* and together with the Light – also in a state of dormancy – *exist in all eternity with no prospect of once more being polarized, since primal Thought and primal Will had been annihilated.*

b) Or the following could happen: At the moment that Thought and Will were split apart the explosion would be so powerful that Darkness would not be able to dissolve and absorb the primal Thought and the primal Will. These would therefore revert together with the depolarized Darkness to the same dormant state as that in which the Light still existed, and after countless aeons of rest would be ready for renewed activity in connection with Darkness or with the Light – *according to the way in which primal Thought and primal Will were influenced by the radiations of the two mutually opposing forces.*

2) The other possibility for a cosmos of Darkness could be presented as follows:

It could be envisaged that some of the creatures of the Deity of Darkness, would out of curiosity experiment with the Light – *the core of Darkness.* But once they had come under the purifying, regulating and harmonizing influence of the Light the result would necessarily be that the Light slowly and gradually transformed their personalities of Darkness, so that these in the course of aeons of time were changed completely into *personalities of Light.* And when these beings had lost all contact with Darkness *the Light would become their true eternal home and Kingdom.*

The possibility could furthermore be contemplated that one among these beings of Light would more extensively than the others explore the properties and characteristics of the Light, and that as a result of his greater knowledge, his greater authority and power, he would necessarily become the uppermost, the leader whom all others by the power of the regulating and harmonizing influence of the Light would love, follow and obey of their own free will. But when this Divinity of Light felt and understood his power, *and was conscious to the full that he was master of the Light,* then he would most likely turn to Darkness and explore its powers and properties. And then he would find the beings of Darkness, the beings who together with their Deity had remained in the Kingdom of Darkness. But since in their strife with one another, nourished by hatred and lust for power, they had all probably quite forgotten the fellow beings who had apparently been absorbed into the Light, these beings of Darkness would be completely mystified by that Being of Light who now searched them out in their Kingdom. However, since the Divinity of Light would quickly come to understand that the inhabitants of Darkness could not be *assimilated* by him and by the other beings of Light, he would presumably initiate a struggle against the Deity of Darkness and his creatures. *And the Divinity of Light would then necessarily emerge as the victor.*

But whether he would gain victory by virtue of the understanding he by that time would have achieved *of the all-vanquishing power of love,* or whether by virtue of the strength of the Light, it is not possible to determine. In the first event the inhabitants of Darkness would under his influence and control be purified and transformed in the course of countless aeons *into beings of Light,* and so be received *into his Kingdom of Light.* In the other event he would, by virtue of the mighty strength of his thought and will, *dissolve and obliterate them all.*

65.

Has there really existed a "Hell", and if so is this Hell now annihilated?

Hell – the "ravaged Kingdom" around the Earth – *has existed as a reality in the transcendental world, but by the power of God's Will it has now been removed for ever.*[1]

But it has never been God's intention to punish His disobedient and recalcitrant children by banishing them to a "Hell". It was the disincarnated Eldest who dwelt in the "ravaged Kingdom", where by the power of their evil thought and will they bound sinful human spirits to be their slaves and servants in this realm of Darkness. And these sin-bound human spirits were often held there for centuries – or longer – before the Youngest succeeded in bringing them help and deliverance.

However, now that the ravaged Kingdom has been annihilated, neither the human spirits nor any of the Eldest live in *a real Hell.* But if during their earthly lives they have sinned gravely against God or against their fellow human beings, and have not tried to obtain forgiveness for their sins while they lived on Earth, they will suffer "the torments of Hell" in their consciousness of sin, until grief and remorse set in and temper their minds. During this hard time of self-searching the sinful spirit is to all appearances alone in its dwelling in

---

[1]) See "Toward the Light" p. 101:9.

the spheres, for none of those who went before, neither relatives nor friends, are permitted to be present. But even in this *apparent solitude* God provides for the human spirit; for the spirits of Light will often be near, speaking to the lonely spirit. But since the spirits of Light are invisible to sin-bound human spirits, the sinner can only hear the voice in the same manner in which human beings on Earth hear their "conscience". The sinners are therefore not aware of having received help in their hour of need until grief and remorse set in – *then they see the helper who faithfully and lovingly has been watching over them.*

66.

Why does "Toward the Light" denounce the Book of Revelation? It is claimed to be inspired by Ardor – Satan – but are there no truths of the Light in the letters to the various congregations?

The Apocalypse has absolutely nothing to do with the truths of the Light. It was produced through Ardor's inspiration and through his ether-recordings, which were read intuitively by the human author of the book, who is not identical with John, the apostle. Besides, the Apocalypse contains numerous reminiscences of the "visions" of the Old Prophets. Nor do the letters to the various congregations originate from God or from the spirits of Light. They are a mixture of Ardor's inspiration and figments of the author's imagination.

The entire book is *a grotesque, misleading document of Darkness, a collection of fabrications, many of which are rooted in the darkest depths of paganism.* And no matter how much human beings contemplate interpretations of its many prophecies, this will certainly not make them *into eternal truths of the Light.*

"Revelation" is the *big, fanciful, mysterious fairy-tale book* of the Christians, and not until the people who are spellbound by this book have progressed beyond their spiritual infancy will it loosen its hold on the human mind. Children "love" fairy-tales, no matter how gory, how gruesome or how senseless they may be: to children – at least to most of them – the fairy-tale adventures are truths to which they return again and again. But when the stage of childhood is over these once admired and "beloved" stories are seen for what they are – **just fairy-tales and nothing more.**

The Apocalypse is thus a test of the maturity of the human spirit. Those who shun this work with revulsion in mind and thought have progressed beyond the stage of spiritual childhood; but those who really believe it to be a work of beauty and exalted truth – they are in spiritual respects like young children who are equally pleased with a glittering bracelet whether it is made of *base alloy* or of *the purest gold*. Unfortunately there are also Christians who feel deeply repelled by the Apocalypse, but who nevertheless outwardly embrace this work as if it truly were a divine relevation. These people bear an infinitely heavy responsibility, as does Luther for his action in including the Apocalypse in the New Testament; for in his mind and in his thought he has no appreciation for this work.

While reading the so-called "Revelation of St. John the Divine" Christians should think of the fairy story of "The Emperor's New Clothes"; **for this work is but an insubstantial fabric of the mind, whose warp is the hideous, false and perverted imaginings of Darkness and whose weft is the fantasies of human thought.**

67.

Why does God not delete all the ether-recordings of Ardor, that is, in each single case prevent their realization on the plane of the Earth? Many disasters and much suffering could surely be prevented in this way.

In order to explain the continuing capacity for action of the ether-recordings, even though their author – in this case Ardor – would have them obliterated, we must draw an analogy with a somewhat similar phenomenon in the earthly world:

Once a so-called wireless message is transmitted, the sender can neither stop it nor delete it in its passage through space. Not until it arrives at the receiving station can a subsequent request possibly cause the recipient to destroy it. But in reality it is then too late, for by that time the recipient will already know the contents of the message. But these wireless messages can sometimes be intercepted by other stations than the one for which they were intended; and in a similar manner can mediums, for example, under favourable conditions intercept psychic ether-recordings that were not addressed to them. And in the same way that wireless messages on Earth are not prevented from reaching the main receiving station because of interception by other stations, neither are psychic ether-recordings deleted because of interception by mediums. Such messages and ether-recordings are transmitted *according to established laws,* both in the earthly and in the psychic worlds. Therefore, no one in the earthly or psychic world can delete anything already sent, broadcast or recorded.

It must all follow its determined course until – under the established laws – it fades away, dissolves and vanishes. God never goes against the laws once they are given, but He and the Youngest can lessen the impact of Ardor's ether-recordings by directing them to power-centres in distant space, so-called "receiving stations", or they can under favourable conditions even halt them completely, as these recordings can "adhere" to the power-centres. But if the "main psychic receiving station" – in this case Earth itself – exerts sufficient attraction through, for example, large accumulations of Darkness, or through the collective thought of many people revolving around the "known" recordings[1], thereby attracting them, they usually enter the plane of the Earth as real events despite the efforts of the Youngest to divert them. It is therefore important to the greatest possible extent to dissuade people from paying heed to, and "believing in", such things as the prophecies of the Apocalypse, or the predictions of mediums who have intuitively intercepted Ardor's ether-recordings.

But whenever Ardor's schemes – ether-images – for the life of human beings are about to enter the plane of the Earth as real events, despite the efforts of the Youngest to prevent them, a warning can be given by God through the guardian spirits to those who are endangered by, or in some way exposed to, involvement in the impending events. In this way the ether-images can occasionally *at the very last moment* be prevented from becoming reality in life on Earth. If, for example, one of Ardor's plans for future wars is about to enter the plane of the Earth, God will issue warnings to those within whose earthly power it lies to determine whether the imminent threat of war is to result in hostilities – *or be resolved through peaceful diplomatic means.* However, if these people do not listen to the questioning and warning voice of their conscience but issue the necessary orders to start a war, then nothing can prevent the ether-image from becoming a reality in the earthly world. For God never goes against the human free will for good or evil. But anyone who truly has the will for the good does not have to become enslaved by the Darkness that streams toward humanity from Ardor's ether-images.

Therefore, people should not "believe in" the prophecies of the Apocalypse, should not "believe in" the predictions for the future given by astrologers, by spiritualistic mediums or other fortune-tellers. *These predictions may be true enough in their origin –* **but they do not necessarily have to come true in the earthly world.** (See also "Toward the Light" page 253:5 to page 255:1, and page 202:1 to page 202:4).

---

[1]) Through predictions, prophecies, visions and the like.

68.

Why did Satan's return to God take place precisely in our time? And why has he chosen to bring humanity the Message of the eternal truths?

Many people will of course find it difficult to believe that the return of Satan – Ardor – to God has taken place in our time. However, since God and the Youngest have striven toward this goal for millions of years their work would certainly meet with success sooner or later, and so it happened that the goal was reached in the year 1912.

But how many people while still alive on Earth understand that they live in *an historical age?* Most people forget that each individual becomes a part in the formation of the destiny of humanity. The earthly events therefore do not become "History" until the moment arises when the various events can be combined and observed from a distance. Only very few are capable of recognizing and understanding the history of the "future" in the events that take place in their own lifetime. For instance, how many of the contemporaries of Jesus understood the future significance of his mission?

When Ardor had returned to God *he must necessarily have been the one chosen to inform mankind of what he had sinned against God and against human beings.* Thus "Ardor's Acount" is a confession, a penance, which God has requested of him, in order for him in this way **to obtain the forgiveness of human beings.**

Whether people who come into possession of "Toward the Light" will trust in its message *is a matter between them, their conscience and God.*

69.

Since Ardor has returned to God, why does God continue to create human spirits? Does He not thereby become the slave of the promise He gave millions of years ago?

If God gives a promise He is necessarily bound by it until it is fulfilled. But God gives no promise until its every aspect has been carefully considered, so that He knows full well that it can be carried out as He promised. And even though God binds Himself for long periods of time through His words, He never becomes a "slave" to His promises, precisely because He knows their future implications in every detail.

Human beings, on the other hand, often make themselves the slaves of their promises, partly because they usually do not seriously consider – and indeed cannot always consider – all the implications, partly because they very often make promises against their conscience, and partly because these may be given in a moment of deep emotion without thought for the possible consequences. Human beings therefore *fail* time and again to keep their promises, which inevitably gives many of them pangs of conscience, if not in this life then after death when the time of reckoning approaches.

But God never fails to keep His given word – *nor will He do so in this case.* And so long as mankind is bound to the "Eldest" still incarnated here on Earth, God will do that which He promised[1] His fallen children at the dawn of time, namely, prevent the astral counterpart of the human body from becoming a "shadow" without thought and will. For not until the last of the Eldest incarnated by Ardor is dead will human beings be released from their creators – **and at the same time God will be released from His promise.**

70.

Is there any substantiation in the Bible for the forgiveness of Satan – Ardor – by God and by human beings?

Not directly, but such evidence is given indirectly in the New Testament.

In Matthew 5:44 and Luke 6:27-28 it is written: *". . . love your enemies, bless them that curse you, do good to them that hate you, and pray for them which despitefully use you, and persecute you."*

Having spoken these words Jesus does not continue by saying that *Satan shall be excepted from this injunction*. And since the archenemy of mankind is – or rather was – Satan, or Ardor, human beings must therefore also learn 1) to *"love"* Satan, the creator and enemy of mankind; 2) to *"do good"* to him, who most of all has sinned against and hated them; 3) to "bless" him, who has hurled the most and the worst of all curses upon them; and 4) to "pray" for him, who most of all has abused and persecuted them. For human beings cannot wholly and fully comply with these words of Jesus *unless Satan is included.*

Next, there is the parable of *"The Prodigal Son"* – Luke 15:11-32.

However, this parable was among those current at the time of

---

[1]) See "Toward the Light" p. 14:19 and p. 322:1.

Jesus, and did not originate from him. But he used it frequently, because it *expressed for him God's true, all-pervading and all-forgiving Fatherly love*. During his life as a human being it gave him certainty that the fallen but beloved brother, despite all straying from the path, *would nevertheless one day find the road and return to their Father's home*.

Expounded according to Jesus' thoughts, mankind is the son in the parable who remained at the father's home – the father being God. The son who journeyed to a far country and there led a riotous life is Satan. When the father in the parable sees his degenerate son, grief-laden, wretched and in rags, coming along the road to the father's home, *he runs to meet him,* embraces him and forgives him from the fulness of his loving heart and mind; and he forgives all the sorrows, all the sufferings that this son has caused him through his sinful life, and *the father rejoices in his home-coming*. But when the son who had remained at home – mankind – hears of the welcome that their mutual father has given the returned son, he does not rejoice in this event but becomes *envious and angry*. He does not understand the father's gladness, does not understand that genuine fatherly love excuses and forgives everything when deep-felt grief, the true remorse completely fills the sinner's heart and subjugates his defiance.

(Jesus only retold this parable, he did not interpret it for his listeners. He usually let them draw their own conclusions from the parables he employed).

In his human existence Jesus saw clearly that as in the parable, so it would happen at some future time when Satan – one of God's children – would return in remorse to the Fatherly Home, and mankind in one way or another learnt of this event. He foresaw that many, in their *narrow-mindedness,* in their *self-assertiveness* and in their *lack of neighbourly love* would not understand that God could in His heart forgive a being *who had fallen so deep as Satan fell*. He foresaw that many would not be able to comprehend that God must rejoice a thousandfold more in the return of a son *who was thought to be lost for all eternity* than He would rejoice in the children *who live under His immediate care and in His keeping*.

But if the parable were applied to purely human relationships – between father and sons – God would then, if He had not been able to forgive Ardor, His beloved, lost and new-found son, *be far inferior to the human father of the parable*. But would this not be inconceivable? Must not God in His Fatherly love *greatly transcend* even the most loving of human fathers? Indeed, if human fathers in life on Earth are able to forgive their wicked children, how much more must not God – the Father of all – be able to forgive each and every one of His children *without preference,* even though human beings may feel that the transgressions of Satan cannot in all eternity be forgiven.

But the reason why people do not understand God's forgiveness of Ardor is rooted in their lack of neighbourly love, their great selfishness. For as long as they themselves can be saved, Satan is no concern of theirs; *he fully deserves his sufferings, so why take pity on him or have compassion for his sufferings?* However, everyone should lay to heart Paul's beautiful words about love: **"Though I speak with the tongues of men and of angels, and have not charity, I am become as sounding brass, or a tinkling cymbal".**

71.

If it is true, as stated in "Toward the Light", that Satan – Ardor – has returned to God, why can this event not be felt in life on Earth? To all appearances, we have as much sin and misery, as many crimes and misdeeds as before.

That Satan – Ardor – has returned to God and has received His forgiveness *is a fact;* otherwise this information would not have been given in "Toward the Light". But it is quite inconceivable that this fact should immediately be felt in life on Earth. Only unthinking people can in all seriousness present the point of view that Ardor's removal from the Earth would necessarily at once be reflected in the thinking, conduct and actions of human beings. For any thoughtful human being should be able to understand that many generations must pass before there will be any indication that a revolution has taken place in "spiritual life" on Earth. Not until millions of people have not only come to know the message of "Toward the Light", but also as a result of this have fully forgiven Ardor, have fully understood their responsibility both toward God and toward their fellow human beings and have learned to live in accordance with their conscience, *not until then will there be any improvement in humanity's religious, ethical or moral understanding and perception of life.* For it should be remembered that Ardor for millions of years has sown the evil seed of Darkness in the minds and in the thoughts of human beings, and this seed has flourished and spread widely wherever humans exist. The hideous, evil-smelling fungus and weeds of sin still grow and flourish and spread the fertile seeds of Darkness through all mankind; and this spreading and flourishing will continue until all human beings with all their strength seek to uproot the fungus and weeds from their minds and thoughts, until each individual has learned to purge the self of all impurity and ugliness of sin. *For no "miracle" can with one stroke change the impure, sinful human race into perfected beings of the Light.*

Humanity can be compared to *a flower garden overgrown with weeds.* Even though the mother plant of the weeds is removed to the very root, this will not suffice to clean the garden. Each single shoot of weed sprouting forth must be uprooted before the flowers can grow freely, can develop new shoots and new leaves, can bud and blossom forth. Each individual must therefore carefully weed the flower garden of the mind and thought, for if this is not done, the weeds of sin and Darkness will smother all the goodness and beauty *God has implanted in the inner being of every human spirit.* But such purification of the human self requires an exceedingly long time to bring to its conclusion, and the human spirit must live through numerous incarnations before it can fully succeed in cleansing the self of the earthly Darkness. For it is of no avail that the Christian peoples with all their might cling to the belief of Jesus' death of atonement; these people must be told again and again: **The blood of Jesus does not cleanse the impurities of sin, Jesus did not atone for the sins of human beings through his death.** Indeed, belief in the reality of the Doctrine of Atonement does in no way benefit the Christians, it only prolongs and makes harder their journey toward the so very distant homeland – God's Kingdom, *the true Paradise.* But if Christians will persist in clinging to faith in Jesus' death of atonement, and if they continue, whenever mention is made of "Toward the Light" – God's message, to refer to the words of Jesus about "false prophets" – words that were never spoken by him – then it could well be *that the Christians will be the last religious community fully to accept the Message that God has sent to all humanity.* It may possibly happen thus – no one knows – but one thing is certain: they – all the Christian communities – ought to be the first to break with the clerical, man-made dogmas **that strive against God's innermost Being and conflict with all common sense.** But all who listen to God's message will always be able to invoke His direct help in the struggle against Darkness, in the cleansing and purification of the self. For all who in their love of God, in their trust in His Fatherly help, submit to His leadership *will soon feel encompassed by the strengthening, life-giving rays of the Light, will soon feel themselves protected by His strong hand.*

The era in which humanity now lives can best be regarded as **a great interregnum.** The prince of Darkness and of mankind, Satan –

Ardor – has renounced his rule and laid down his crown and sceptre. The Kingdom of Darkness – the Earth – has no "sovereign" more – *his throne stands empty!* For Ardor was the Prince of the Earth and of humanity from the moment when the first human beings were created for earthly life. And even though God at the dawn of time when certain of the Eldest sought His help for their wretched creatures, promised to help them, He did not for that reason become the King and Prince of humanity. But God knew that at some future time through the leadership He had given in order to bring spiritual life and Light to human beings – so that they might overcome the sin and temptation of Darkness – He would win back His eldest fallen children, and some day **be fully recognized as the God, spiritual Father and Supreme Leader of all humanity.**

The first goal has now been reached by God: Ardor has returned to God, to his Father, and mankind is no longer subject to Ardor's rule, to his direct influence and direct inspiration. But mankind has still far from attained *in full unity, in mutual love and trust in God acknowledgement of Him as the Father of their spirit, as the Supreme Leader of life on Earth, and as Lord and Prince of the Earthly Realm.*

Not until the greater part of the Earth's many millions of human beings have learnt to know the *true God,* as He really is, have learnt to love Him and submit to Him alone, have fully learnt to forgive Ardor, the creator of the human body, not until then will it truly be felt **that Satan's throne stands empty!**

In "Toward the Light" God has called upon all His beloved children; *for He longs for the fullness of their love; He yearns for their perfect trust!*

Yea, God hath called upon His beloved children!
But – when will they heed His calling voice?
When will they answer Him?
When will they, from deep in their hearts, meet His profound and infinite Fatherly love with the fullness of their love, with their perfect trust?
God hath called!
And God yearneth!

ADDENDUM

The great problems of *marriage, birth control and abortion,* which are the subject of much debate at this time in many civilized countries the world over, are of such fundamental importance to humanity that certain indications from the transcendental world will be given here, so as to assist in finding the proper solutions to these problems. Human beings must then themselves decide whether to accept this advice or whether to ignore it.

Since none of those who have joined in receiving the message of "Toward the Light" has posed any direct question relating to these problems to our interpreter, our medium, with the desire of obtaining an answer from the transcendental world, these matters will be treated separately in an Appendix to this Supplement to "Toward the Light". This is done so as to keep these comments separate from the answers given in response to direct questions from the human world.

Marriage, Birth Control and Abortion.

By their creators – Ardor and the Eldest – humans were created as *polygamous beings,* because Ardor's purpose was to ensure the survival of the species, so that he should not in the future be faced with any need to attempt further creation. His objective was therefore to render human beings capable of becoming fruitful, so that they could multiply, replenish the Earth and subdue it.

While human beings were still exclusively the creatures of the Eldest they lived a life similar to that of polygamous animals. The primal human beings thus roved in great herds under the leadership of a single male, or with three or four males as leaders. But there were continual and violent fights between these leaders and the younger males of the herd, especially because the sexual drive was not confined to certain seasons of the year. For this reason periods of greater peacefulness between them were precluded. On account of these polygamous relationships, and because of the primal human beings' total lack of spiritual intelligence, these creatures had no sense whatsoever of kinship with one another. Only the maternal instinct prevailed, as it does in the female of numerous animal species.

When God at the dawn of time granted the prayer[1] of some of the Eldest to take upon Himself the care of their ill-conceived creations – the human beings – He gave these creatures of Darkness, as explained in "Toward the Light"[2], a spark of the Light from His own Being, so as to endow them with spiritual life – that is, with thought and will. At the same time God's children – the Youngest – pledged themselves to assist their Father in drawing the human beings away from the influence of their creators and under the influence of God and the Light. The Youngest who were bound to human bodies had so much of their mighty intelligence withheld through the interaction between the "life-giving cord"[3] and the physical, astral and psychic brain[4] that – spiritually speaking – they were brought to a level only slightly above that of the other human beings whose bodies God had endowed with a spark of His own Self.

It now became the task of these incarnated Youngest in their life as human beings to be the guides, leaders and pioneers of mankind in all aspects of life on Earth. From the very first incarnations, improvements could be observed in many different areas; and one of these was the area of sexual life.

Exceedingly slowly, under the regulating and harmonizing influence of the Light *through millions of years,* the all-important, primordial sexual urge became sufficiently subdued for the *then existing* civilized human beings to lead a monogamous life, although polygamous relationships still existed in some places. This restraint of the sexual drive was due to the influence of the Light as well as to a large number of the Youngest, who continually let themselves be incarnated among human beings. And these "personalities of Light" had by the power of their will tempered and regulated the sexual instinct of the families in which they had been incarnated; this subdued instinct was then passed on as inheritance to the offspring.

However, when the Eldest conceived the idea of incarnating themselves among human beings, these incarnations represented a strong countermove against the work of the Youngest. Until that time, despite the spiritual influence of the disincarnated Eldest in the direction of Darkness, the Youngest had step by step brought much of humanity forward toward the Light and toward a communal life protected by good and well established laws. Very positive results had

---

[1]) See "Toward the Light" p. 14.
[2]) See "Toward the Light" p. 18:3.
[3]) See "Toward the Light", p. 278:4.
[4]) See "Toward the Light", p. 278:4 to p. 279:2.

thus been attained through millions of years under this steady, slowly progressing development. However, because of the influence of Ardor and the Eldest, most of the communities were still highly belligerent in their internal relationships and affairs, as well as in their dealings with other communities.

About 12,000 B.C. a multitude of the Eldest were incarnated among mankind as human beings (human beings have lived on Earth for about five million years). But these incarnations brought about a profound change in the prevailing conditions, for with respect to intelligence those of the Eldest who had been incarnated by Ardor were infinitely superior to the Youngest who were incarnated at that time. Consequently, the Eldest gained absolute leadership in life on Earth over the incarnated Youngest, and over ordinary human beings as well. In an appallingly short time a drastic decline – a complete regression into Darkness – took place everywhere and in all areas of human life.

One of the first things these incarnated Eldest undertook was to institute a formal "religious" cult of the sexual relationship between man and woman. Gods and goddesses of male and female fertility were each given their separate magnificent temple and their own priesthood and rituals. And large numbers of maidens, and in some places also young males, were consecrated to these gods and goddesses. At prescribed times of the year great, shameless orgies were staged in which all the people, both high and low, took part under the leadership of the priesthood. The ill-famed orgies of these days were far worse in sexual excesses and savagery than were the Festivals of Dionysos of later times,[1] known today through scholarly research into the history of antiquity.

Thus, through the continued incarnations of the Eldest the suppressed sexual drive flared up anew with a violent, almost explosive force, a force the Youngest have been unable to subdue during the almost 14,000 years that have elapsed between the first incarnations of the Eldest and the present. Today, however, there are numerous families throughout the world whose members, with a few exceptions, are no longer dominated by this drive but have brought it under the control of their will. This does not mean that all the Youngest who during this 14,000-year period continued to be incarnated among the human beings as leaders and pioneers never succumbed to sexual temptations and aberrations. It should be obvious that

---

[1]) The earliest "pictorial" representations of the myth regarding the life of Osiris that were demonstrated, or re-enacted, before the people by the priests and priestesses of Ancient Egypt were likewise sexual orgies, just as the cult of Astarte had its own orgies. Also the festivals of the ancient Scandinavians for their god Tyr (the Bull) were highly immoral.

Ardor tried in every way to lead God's emissaries astray, especially in sexual matters. But God in His wisdom had arranged that numerous of the Youngest should be incarnated during this era with the sole purpose of subduing the sexual instinct in those peoples where it was most predominant. And these Youngest had by God been endowed in such a way that through their will they were able to withstand the onslaughts and temptations of Darkness in this respect. But those of the Youngest who pioneered in the various arts needed all their power of will in order to bring their particular mission to a favourable conclusion, for which reason the will was not always quite prepared to withstand the onslaughts of Darkness in sexual matters. And it was especially these who at times gave way to the temptations of Darkness and to the influence of Ardor in "erotic" matters. But these lapses did not spring from deep in their inner being.[1]

The continued arbitrary incarnations of the Eldest have also in the course of time distorted the attitude of human beings to culture. For it was God's intention – through the unquestioned leadership of the Youngest in all matters – to bring mankind forward toward the Light and spiritual life in such a way that the sexual problem would be solved simultaneously with the advance of culture. But the incarnations of the Eldest brought to a halt this slow but steady progressive development in all aspects of life. In order to combat the incarnated Eldest in a reasonably effective manner God was time and again obliged, when the Youngest should be incarnated, to raise their spiritual intelligence many degrees, so that it came to equal – and in some cases to exceed – the intelligence, the knowledge, that the Eldest brought with them into life on Earth. But for this reason "culture" has been raised to a much, much higher level than can be assimilated

---

[1]) The following allegory can serve to illustrate the relationship of the Youngest to mankind in this, as in all other areas:

There is a coal mine in the neighbourhood of a nobleman's family estate. Several members of the family, who have heard of the wretched conditions in which the miners toil in the dark galleries of the mine, are seized with compassion. They decide to share for a time the miners' lot, to become their equals, or in other words to work alongside them, taking upon themselves the same strenuous, exhausting labour and exposing themselves to the same hazards. They do this in the hope that through talking with the miners they might awaken their spiritual interests, and by their own example teach them greater patience in their daily toil. While the noblemen work in the dark tunnels of the pit they become, like the other workers, coal-blackened and marked by cuts and bruises, so that it becomes difficult to tell the noblemen and the labourers apart. But when work is done and they emerge together with the other miners into the light of day, then – when all have washed and changed their clothes – it can easily be distinguished which of them are the true labourers and which are the noblemen, for their features are quite different.

In this allegory the coal mine represents the Earth, the labourers the human beings, the noblemen the Youngest, and the state of being washed, clad in clean clothes and being in daylight represents life in the spheres after rendering the account of the completed life on Earth to God.

by the average human being. As a result of this, human sexual life remains at a much lower level than it should by now have attained in relation to the existing culture.

———

With the spread of Christianity within the countries of Europe the polygamous relationship, which thrived side by side with monogamous marriage, became more and more to be regarded as sinful. This attitude did not, however, eliminate polygamous relationships, but only caused them to flourish more strongly in secret, while monogamous marriages were clearly by no means always *"monogamous"*. Under Christianity the Church authorities assumed more and more power in the various domains of human life – though not always with equally good results. And the certification of marriage was drawn under the "protection" of the Church, as were so many other matters.

The ancient biblical myth[1] of Adam and Eve in the Garden of Eden is apparently symbolic of the human monogamous relationship. But this myth stems originally from one of the Youngest, who attempted during life on Earth to give an allegorical exposition of the concept of "Dualism", of Darkness and of the Light, of the life in God's Kingdom of His first-created children – and of the fall of the Eldest. And the ancient maxim of the Church: "What therefore God hath joined together let not man put asunder" – or, more correctly, "no one" – applies in reality to the dual relationship to each other of God's first created children, but in no way does it apply *to human marital relationships*. There is therefore no justification whatsoever for its application to human beings, except in connection with the duality[2] of the human spirit. For in the great majority of cases God has nothing to do with contracted marriages. God does not demand of human beings that they should enter into matrimony with any particular fellow human. In this respect everyone has a perfectly free choice, God makes absolutely no particular selection in this matter.

When a human spirit shall be incarnated – born to a life on Earth – God gives a plan in broad outline for the coming life, a plan[3] which the human spirit is made aware of, and which is imparted to the guardian spirit as the basis for guidance. These draft plans for human lives often indicate the desirability that a particular person should be

———

[1] See "Toward the Light" p. 325, Note 2 regarding this myth.
[2] See "Toward the Light" p. 187:1-3.
[3] See "Toward the Light" p. 184:3.

chosen as companion in a marriage relationship during incarnation. This is normally done so that these future human beings can in this way offset the transgressions committed against each other in previous incarnations, or so that they can be of help to each other in some cultural undertaking. The latter applies especially to the incarnated Youngest. But it *is not demanded* that these suggested unions *must take place* according to plan. God is thus not the institutor of earthly marriages. But once human beings have made their choice, whatever that may be, God seeks through the guardian spirit to make the best of the union, although all too often marriages sadly fail to succeed. And the supervision of marital relationships by the Church has contributed to the fact that they often fail as completely as they do in so many cases. For many couples continue living together out of religious considerations despite the unwillingness of one or of both parties. The Catholic Church in particular has caused almost irreparable damage by its sanctification of marriage, since it has thereby prevented any possibility for the two spouses to create better conditions, a better life for themselves through a dissolution of their marriage.

However, many years ago an increasing number of Lutherans already showed more and more of a tendency to circumvent the Church in marital questions, just as the desire to consider marriage an entirely social and not a religious matter has at times been strongly expressed. However, until this day it has not been possible to make the so-called "civil marriages" obligatory for all, and thus leave it to the individuals to seek the "blessing" of the Church *after* the civil marriage has taken place.

Since the transcendental world has now shown that it imposes no rules on marital matters, does this not imply a denunciation of the Church's jurisdiction to act as guardian in the contracting of marriages? Yes, it does! Church authorities should never have intruded in an area which definitely does not belong within their domain. Furthermore, bringing marriage under the guardianship of the Church has violated ethical aspects of religious life, for example the metaphorical representation of the congregation as the "Bride of Christ", or the nun, who is also referred to as the "Bride of Christ" at her consecration. If Christ were truly God, such descriptions would be **entirely blasphemous.** But since Christ is not God, they must be regarded as being *both highly unethical and inaesthetic.*

Rather than engage in seemingly endless debates on the problem of marriage, the members of the various societies should first of all exclude the Church from all connection with the entering into and the dissolution of marriages and make marriage a social institution.

Next, an obligatory civil wedding should take the place of the church wedding, but with permission temporarily granted – if it is so desired – to obtain the blessings of the Church after the civil ceremony. But, as it has already been stated, this permission to obtain the blessing of the Church should only be temporary, *since as human beings mature spiritually* they will undoubtedly request fewer and fewer of such blessings until they finally desire them no more. For it must be remembered that God takes no greater interest in marriages blessed by the Church than in marriages entered into on the basis of a "civil wedding ceremony". But when matrimony wholly and completely becomes a social institution, provisions should be made at the same time that in no way impede the dissolution of a marriage, if it transpires that the partners are unable to live together without making life a "hell" for each other and for any children they may have. Not only should ordinary breaches and transgressions of the marriage pact be regarded as grounds for divorce, but also spiritual differences between the partners should especially be taken into consideration. And the provisions made should also ensure that one partner cannot refuse to consent to divorce, and thereby hinder or delay the dissolution of the marriage. Once the necessary formalities have been concluded – and financial provision made for any dependent children and for the wife – the divorce should not be preceded by a lengthy separation, since such a period of separation is in many cases of no benefit whatsoever, but only serves to aggravate the situation. For if the marriage is dissolved with a new marriage in view – either for the one partner or for both partners – the separated parties will often live together in secret with their future marriage partner, despite the provisions of the separation period. This so-called separation period should therefore be abolished; although after the dissolution of the marriage there should be an obligatory waiting period of about four months, which is more than sufficient to determine whether or not the wife is pregnant. If it can be proved that she had conceived with her husband, and not with the man chosen with a view to future marriage, then the child should be named after the husband, who should then also assume the financial responsibility for the birth and upbringing of the child until the age of majority.

These are therefore the first principles that should be observed in providing a basis for more orderly and secure relations within marriage. Many will undoubtedly object, however, that the situation would deteriorate rather than improve if divorce were made possible without difficulties of any kind. There is only one answer to this: that sound, pure and happy marriages would not be affected in any way by easier access to divorce, while bad, unhappy marriages where either or both parties have relations with some other partner would only gain by such an arrangement. For if the partners know that their marriage can be dissolved at any time they wish there is a better prospect that they will be more tolerant toward each other and thus overcome their disagreements and difficulties. But if they feel tied and hampered by rigid rules and regulations, or if they feel bound by religious considerations, such obligations will often be the only reason they continue living together and will thereby create a still worse domestic situation, both for themselves and the children, *for whom the parents should provide a good and peaceful home.* Also, such a continued marital relationship lived with ill will toward the other, lived in mutual anger and hatred, will only give impetus to illicit relationships outside marriage.

The ideal for human marriage is of course to be able to go through life with the one and first chosen partner. Indeed, the ideal[1] which people should strive for is this: under all circumstances and difficulties of life, in sorrow and in gladness to stay together, kindly and calmly without quarrels and strife to yield to each other, to be like good friends throughout life and to be fully agreed on the upbringing of the children, to correct and guide them with loving patience and understanding without foolishly spoiling or idolizing them. However, human beings on the average are still quarrelsome in mind and in thought, are self-assertive by nature and in their conduct. Therefore, God also knows how difficult it is for them to be mutually tolerant, which is the reason why He believes that the best road to improvement in the area of marriage is to make marriage not a compulsory but an entirely voluntary relationship, legalized through a civil office with easy access to dissolution, even if it is *desired or demanded by only one of the parties.*

The proposals for trial marriages and companionate marriages should also be discussed in this context. These suggestions were brought forward primarily to allow early co-habitation for the young, a relationship that might otherwise prove difficult, for financial reasons among others. People are of course free to choose also in this matter, but once easy access to divorce has been instituted, these suggestions for "marriages" should no longer be discussed. It could be arranged for the young partners, *after a civil* marriage, to remain in their respective homes.[2] For companionate marriages that

---

[1]) See Speech of Christ in "Toward the Light" p. 127:6 to p. 128:1.

[2]) The above suggestion was presented by human beings during the various discussions and is included as it has some merit.

are not legalized in the ordinary manner could easily cause the very young to be drawn further and further downward, because their sense of responsibility would be lessened and the will to curb the demands of the sexual drive might grow weaker rather than stronger. A chaste young woman would also in most cases suffer under such insecure circumstances. Yet another factor should be taken into consideration: if companionate marriages were tolerated, it is likely that quite casual relationships would soon be regarded as "companionate marriages" to people in general. And despite all provisions the young would easily be tempted to live not in one, but in several "companionate marriages" at the same time; but under such circumstances society would again experience polygamy, although under a new name and under a new form.

Therefore, the basic condition for improving the circumstances for marriage should be to exclude the guardianship of the Church from the domain of matrimony, to provide obligatory civil marriage for all, easy access to divorce, and secure provision for the wife and dependent children in the case of divorce. But this is far from sufficient. For the problem that in most cases will cause the largest amount of friction and the deepest discord between marriage partners – who often began living together in love for each other with a sincere desire to create a good life together – is *the problem of the children.*

In the myth of the Creation of Man, Genesis 1:28, the narrator makes God say to the newly-created man and woman: "Be fruitful, and multiply, and replenish the Earth, and subdue it . . . ." This "command" has been faithfully followed by human beings; they have indeed multiplied, and – almost – replenished the Earth. To this day, millions of people are following the command of fruitfulness. But never was this command given to the first human beings, nor did God give it to mankind. For God did not create "Adam and Eve", nor did He request them to multiply beyond all limits. The sexual drive was implanted in mankind by Ardor when he and his fellow beings created the first human bodies. And later he instilled the idea of fruitfulness in the minds of human beings after God had endowed them with a spark of His own Self. None of this therefore originates from God, it is rooted in Darkness and not in the Light. Never has it been the wish of God that the Earth should be overpopulated, and never has He requested human beings to produce so many children that they would be unable to provide their offspring with proper living conditions. And never has He reproached the human spirits upon their return after death for not producing offspring. But God has time and again reproached them for their thoughtlessness and irresponsibility in leaving behind far too abundant offspring. Therefore, let it clearly be stated once and for all: **God has neither part nor lot in the number of children that human beings bring into the world.** All who say *"God has denied us children"* or *"God has blessed our marriage with many children"* should know that these pronouncements **have nothing to do with the truth.** But God requires that every father and every mother account for the upbringing of their children and for the living conditions they have provided. He places the responsibility for their children's conduct in life *upon their shoulders;* for no one has the right to throw his offspring to the four winds. And as human beings take care of their children, so does God take care of human beings. Therefore, if human beings wish to ensure favourable circumstances for themselves in future incarnations, then they must provide a good, secure environment for their children – otherwise retribution will come upon them in one form or another. God thus demands that every parent should account *for every single child,* whether or not the child is born in legal wedlock. All human children are equal before God; *He recognizes absolutely no difference between "legitimate" and "illegitimate" children.* God gives human beings free choice in respect of how many children[1] they will bring into the world, but He demands that these children be provided for in every way – none shall suffer neglect because their parents cannot or will not provide for their needs. *Such is the law of God:* **this is God's message to mankind.**

Since the question of whether or not birth control should be permitted is under such heated debate at this time it is emphasized from the transcendental world *that birth control is permitted to the extent desired by each individual,* and by the means or method best suited to this purpose, provided that the means or method employed is not injurious to health. It is not demanded, for instance, that one, two, three or four children must first be born within a marriage before any limitation of the total number can be allowed. Even those who do not wish to have any children from their marriage will after death receive no reproach from God for this decision.

Birth control is thus allowed by God to the extent desired by each person. And one thing is certain: this limitation will produce more, better and happier marriages. For in many cases the woman's continual pregnancies and the many mouths to feed lead to a constant struggle for existence. These difficult circumstances thus very often impose disproportionately hard work upon the man, the provider –

---

[1] There are, of course, cases in which people are unable to have children, even though they may wish to do so. But since this pertains to diseased or abnormal conditions of the body, it is not discussed here.

and in many workers' homes also upon the wife – in earning the daily bread and maintaining the home. Frugality is a good thing, but a life of toil and drudgery, in constant struggle for daily necessities, a life of annual childbirth and constant care of the offspring, is not the best background for a happy marriage. And many a man and woman have been defeated in this struggle for existence, in this joyless life that they have created for themselves by bringing so many children into the world. Many a marriage that began in mutual love has thus ended in daily quarrels, in impossible demands, in anger – and in hatred. Neither must it be forgotten that a woman who is pregnant year after year and is tied to "the cradle and the nursery" for years on end cannot continue to be a good companion[1] to her husband, neither sexually nor in the area of spiritual matters. Furthermore, if on account of the long succession of pregnancies the woman withdraws from sexual relations with her husband, this often provides the first occasion for him to seek extra-marital relations – which thus leads to polygamy and to so-called "illegitimate" children. Rather **limit the number of children – and enjoy a happier marriage!**

In order to assist in creating the best possible circumstances in the future, both for marital relations and for any resulting children, the following guidance is given for the most appropriate course of action.

Let us begin at the beginning, *which is the attitude of parents toward their children on the subject of sexuality.*

Every father and mother must as a necessary duty take it upon themselves to explain to their children how they originated, and the reasons for the differences between the male and the female body. But this can only be done by fully and wholly considering the matter from a natural point of view. Bring the whole question into the full light of day, so that the sexual relationship does not become shrouded in any kind of mystery. When the child begins to ask questions on these matters they must be answered clearly, calmly and decently, and in a manner appropriate to the child's age. No child must be dismissed with evasive words such as "this is something you are not old enough to understand"; nor fobbed off with the old tales of "the angel" or "the stork", and so on. All such should long ago have become a thing of the past, although this is far from the case in very many homes. If the child does not ask spontaneously, the parents themselves should lead the child's thoughts toward these problems,

---

[1] There are, of course, some women who despite much childbearing can also be good helpmates to their husbands in everyday life, but this is the rare exception to the rule.

so that he or she is prepared for what lies ahead before reaching the normal age of puberty. No parents should keep a child in ignorance of the phenomena of this difficult age, since this can easily cause damage to a young mind, a kind of damage that can affect the child's whole life. For not only can the child be led into potentially damaging sexual practices, but its mentality can also deteriorate, or be partly or even wholly destroyed. Not only the sexual differences between men and women should therefore be discussed and explained, the parents must also teach the child that there is nothing secretive about bodily union, that it is neither nasty nor degrading, but that it is – within limits – essential for the physical well-being of the body, and that the propagation of mankind is similarly dependent on it. The young should be taught to be pure of mind and thought and not to yield to obscene imaginings and desires. This will be much easier for the young to avoid if they are fully informed about sexual matters. For once all this is clear to them, there will be no reason for their thoughts secretly and incessantly to circle about the subject, which can otherwise produce a situation that is almost unbearable for an impressionable young mind. Teach them also the responsibility they take upon themselves by bringing more children into the world than they are able to support. Teach them to curb their sexual drive – to a certain degree – so that it does not dominate their body, and teach them that they can control this drive by virtue of their spiritual development and by exerting their will. Teach them that through this exercised self-restraint they can pass on a refined sexual instinct and thereby help future generations overcome the difficulty that stems from the fact that the sexuality of the human body is modelled upon that of the animals. And teach them *that through a prayer to God – if it is sincere and deeply felt – they can always receive help in subduing the sexual drive.*

But not only in their homes should the young be made aware of these problems, also schools and institutions should have a part in this aspect of the education and development of the young. "Sex hygiene" should therefore in the future be an obligatory subject in all schools of all the civilized countries the world over, not only in schools of higher learning but also in every hamlet and village school. Young male and female doctors could undertake the teaching of this subject.

As a transition from the existing situation until these suggestions can possibly be implemented, the authorities in the various civilized countries should accept the task of arranging free public lectures for both the married and the unmarried, so that all can be enlightened on the origin of and the problems relating to sexual life. All who so desire should also receive clear and thorough instruction on the best ways and means of limiting the number of children without endangering their health. Young medical specialists might undertake this educational work, for a suitable remuneration, of course. Furthermore, contraceptives should be dispensed free of charge to those of limited means; they might, for example, be distributed through Red Cross centres at central locations in all cities, and through suitably located regional centres in the rural districts. Such services should not be rendered as "relief" or "charity", *but as a right to which these people are entitled;* for they should be given the same opportunity to limit the number of their children as have their fellow human beings in better economic circumstances. It is of course possible that a number of people who can well afford the cost will be tempted to have contraceptives dispensed free of charge on the pretext that they are unable to afford them. However, it would be far better for this to happen than to deny free dispensation to one single individual who is entitled to it. As all the other administrative details fall into place, also this aspect of the matter will surely be solved to everyone's satisfaction.

These suggestions may well serve as the best basis for the transition from the existing state to that of the future – which is prepared and shaped through this work – and which will provide the young people and the coming generations with knowledge of sexual matters. As already stated, this education should be given in a direct, seemly, clear, adequate and natural manner to every child before the normal age of puberty.

Finally there is the problem of *abortion.*

From the earliest times of human history God's emissaries – the Youngest – have time and again taught mankind that **no one must take the life of another human being!** This ancient commandment applies also to abortion, even though the foetus is no more than an incipient human being. Only in one specific case is it permissible to destroy the foetus, namely if the life of the mother is endangered either by physical ailment during pregnancy or by various complications arising during the process of birth. In such cases the doctor must decide what action is to be taken. The decision can if necessary be made by one doctor, but it would be desirable that a consultation with one or several colleagues take place, since it is always a very difficult decision for a single individual to make, no matter how competent he or she may be. Once they feel convinced that the best decision has been made, neither the doctor, or doctors, nor the mother will be held *responsible for the interrupted life of a future human being.* These people will therefore in future incarnations not be confronted with the task of saving a fellow human being from sudden death[1] as an atonement for the life they have terminated.

But many will undoubtedly ask whether this applies if motherhood has been forced upon a woman, either by the brutish demands of her husband or because of rape by an assailant? Does she not in these cases have the right to interrupt the pregnancy that was forced upon her? **No! She has no such right whatsoever!** In the first case she can – according to the aforementioned arrangements for easy access to divorce – have her marriage dissolved if the husband's demands develop in a brutal manner. Neither in the second case – enforced pregnancy as a result of rape – does the woman have any right to rid herself of the foetus, for such action is considered by God **as an act of premeditated murder;** *and this applies both to the woman and to any who assist her.* However, the same rule applies as previously discussed: if the mother's life is threatened the foetus may be sacrificed, but not otherwise.

The only comfort that can be given to the distressed and unfortunate woman whose pregnancy results from rape – *with no part of the blame upon her* – is this: that on account of the wrong that has been done her and the suffering that has been brought upon her, God will seek in one way or another to offset her misfortune against her own earlier and as yet unexpiated sins and transgressions. God will also often bind one of the Youngest or a highly advanced human spirit to the foetus whose existence is due to rape, so as to counterbalance the injustice that has been done. The enforced motherhood, despite its cruel and deplorable origin, has often for this reason brought joy to the mother in the consciousness of having given life to a diligent, honourable and gifted citizen.

If a child owes its conception to assault and rape[2] everything possible must be done to assure its existence in life. In consideration for its future the child should thus bear neither the father's name – even if this is known – nor the mother's family name. It should be given a neutral name that has no connection with the existing family names. Only if the mother truly wishes should the child be named after her. And since in many cases the father cannot be traced, because he will generally stem from the shadier section of the populace, and for this reason the child cannot claim financial inheritance from him, as would otherwise *be its right,* and if the mother will not assume the burden of its upbringing, then the State must act as representative

---

[1]) See "Toward the Light", p. 114:6.

[2]) Since a beginning has been made in recent times in the special treatment of sexual problems relating to the mentally defective, the question of sterilization is not discussed here.

for the father. "Children of rape" should thus be brought up at the expense of the State, not as cases of "poor relief" or "charity" *but as their right.* This can take place in institutions intended partly for this purpose, but it must be carried out under such circumstances that the child's feelings will not be exposed to hurt, for example by veiled hints as to its origin; for so much can be destroyed in the mind of a child by that kind of thoughtless or malicious remark from classmates or others. The management of such institutions should therefore be entrusted to highly cultured, understanding, considerate and trustworthy persons.

And when the child has reached the age of majority the state must also provide suitable employment and in due course adequate funds to enable the individual to acquire the means of a secure livelihood. If the father can be traced, and if he belongs to the more prosperous section of society, this child has the same rights of inheritance from him as have any of his other children. If he is well placed financially the State should recover all the costs of the child's upbringing from him. The relevant authorities must themselves decide on the penalty to be imposed on the rapist, although this should not be such as to exceed humane limits.

The legislative authorities of all civilized countries should therefore give urgent consideration to the problems of *marriage, birth control and abortion.* And while new and improved regulations for these matters are being prepared it must not be forgotten that all children[1], whether born in legal wedlock or otherwise, *have equal rights of inheritance from their father.* For so-called "illegitimate" children have the same rights in respect of inheritance – *according to God's law* – as are enjoyed by "legitimate children". If this *law of God* should become *a law of mankind* it would rapidly result *in a significant reduction in the number of illegitimate births.*

We hereby impart to humanity this solution to these difficult problems, a solution which human beings may use as they wish: accept these recommendations – or reject them because they do not welcome intervention from the transcendental world in these earthly matters.

But never forget: **As the law is, so are the people!**

---

[1] Since it goes without saying that so-called "illegitimate" children have the right of inheritance from the mother, this is not referred to above.

QUESTIONS AND ANSWERS

SECOND SUPPLEMENT
TO
"TOWARD THE LIGHT"

PREFACE

In the first Supplement to "Toward the Light", published in September 1929, the following footnote is given on page 28: "There is a possibility that a further Supplement will be forthcoming if a sufficient number of questions is asked while our female helper still lives on Earth".

When the first Supplement had been published, only a few answers remained as the basis for a second Supplement. But the aforementioned footnote prompted one student of "Toward the Light" to submit a list of no fewer than twenty-eight questions, to which further questions were soon added, both by him and by many others. On 20th October, my wife therefore turned to her spiritual guide, who promised to answer these questions. Some were put aside as being of minor importance, but even so, sixty-six answers were given between 20th October, 1929 and the middle of February, 1930 – excluding the three weeks at Christmas. This was indeed a remarkably short time in view of the difficult and complex nature of many of the questions.

My wife receives the thought-inspiration of her spiritual communicator through intuition, in the manner that has been explained many times (for example, in the Preface and Postscript to "Toward the Light", and in the Preface and in the Answer to Question No. 1 in Supplement I). It is therefore not a question of trance, automatic writing or similar spiritualistic forms of communication. My wife remains fully conscious; she need only exclude her own thoughts, so that her brain is available for the use of her spiritual informant.

As in Supplement I, the sequence of answers has been determined from the transcendental world; neither my wife nor I have had the slightest influence on this aspect of the matter.

We have been advised that with the publication of "Toward the Light", and "The Doctrine of Atonement and The Shorter Road" together with the two Supplements, the subjects on which God wished to inform humanity have been dealt with, and the guidance that human beings should follow has been given. No further questions will therefore be answered from the transcendental world during the remainder of my wife's lifetime. However, my wife will always be able to obtain any necessary help in dealing with letters, public debate in newspapers, or the like, that may ensue from the publication of this work.

As I wrote in the Preface to Supplement I, we know that many of these answers will arouse opposition. I must therefore repeat: they are all approved and authorized by God, our Father. It will then be for human beings to decide whether to accept or reject them, in accordance with the dictates of their *conscience*.

19th February, 1930
The Publisher

CONTENTS

Question	Subject	Page
1.	Mark 12:29, on the subject of a divine trinity	9
2.	The question of an Original Gospel	10
3.	The demand of Jesus on Joseph of Arimathea	11
4.	Jesus' search for Joseph of Arimathea on the astral plane of the Earth	12
5.	The attitude of Jesus to Caiaphas' question as to whether he was the Son of God	14
6.	Jesus regarded as the groom and the congregation as the bride	15
7.	The significance of baptism as practised by John the Baptist	17
8.	Speech of Christ on the development of the human spirit through earthly rebirths	18
9.	Increased total time of incarnations	22
10.	The "divine language"	23
11.	The origin of languages	24
12.	The style of language in Ardor's Account	26
13.	Production of "Toward the Light" in the Danish language	27
14.	"Toward the Light" based on questions asked by human beings	28
15.	The style of language in the Commentary to "Toward the Light" and in the two Supplements	31
16.	Birth control and the Law of Reincarnation	32
17.	Ultimate effect of birth control on world population	33
18.	Divorce	34
19.	The demand for sexual abstinence	35
20.	The meaning of adultery	36
21.	Ratio of God's first-created children to the human spirits	38
22.	Spiritualistic mediums and manifestations of spirits	39
23.	The voluntary incarnation of the human spirit	40
24.	Mediums calling on the "dead"	42
25.	Christian Wilster's poem "Memento"	43
26.	The role of "coincidence" in human life	44

27. Predetermination of the human life span in
    relation to accidents 46
28. The Law of Retribution and the sufferings of humanity 46
29. Compassion for those suffering under
    the Law of Retribution 49
30. The Law of Retribution and the prevention
    of accidents 50
31. Form and appearance of the spirit-body in
    the spheres 51
32. Why a deformed spirit-body retains its
    characteristics 56
33. Imprints of the physical organs on the spirit-body 57
34. Euthanasia 58
35. Harmful stimulants 59
36. "Prohibition" and the "Temperance Movement" 60
37. Liberalism versus Socialism 61
38. The thickness of the insulation layer 61
39. The Earth's location in the universe 62
40. The diverse development of God's children 62
41. The first sinful thought of the fallen Eldest 63
42. The desire of the Eldest for the leadership of the
    contemplated beings of the Light 64
43. The delight of the Eldest in the newly-created
    world around the Earth 66
44. The prayer of human beings for Ardor 67
45. Christ and the Youngest in relation to the
    prayer for Ardor 68
46. God's Servants 69
47. Christ and Ardor as leaders of the Youngest
    and the Eldest 70
48. A correction to the first edition of Supplement I 71
49. The relationship between the Eldest and the Youngest
    in God's Kingdom 71
50. The concept of time, the time-rhythm in the two primal
    forces of Darkness and the Light 73
51. The problem of the nebulae 75
52. a) The removal of the Eldest from the Earth 76
    b) The barring of the Eldest from the outer world 78
53. Creation of new human spirits in relation to
    the most primitive human races 78
54. The number of human spirits 79
55. The height of transcendental beings 79
56. The mystery of the uncreated 80

57. Primal Thought and primal Will 81
58. The relation of primal Thought and primal Will
    to Darkness 83
59. The purpose and value of existence 84
60. Evil by contrast accentuates world harmony
    (light and shadow in a painting) 86
61. God and His knowledge of the future 88
62. The element of spiritual Light from the Eldest 90
63. The spark of "God's flaming Being" that was bestowed
    upon the "shadows" 90
64. The influence of Darkness on the spark of divine Thought
    and Will bestowed upon each of God's children 91
65. The spiritual enhancement of the divine element in human
    thought and will 100
66. a) The longer time of incarnations for human spirits in
    the future 101
    b) The burdensome lot of the Youngest 101
    c) The fallen Eldest who never took part in the unlawful
    incarnations, and those who did 102
67. Material causality and the laws of conservation of
    energy and matter 104
68. Free will and the theory of energy 105
69. The exalted remoteness of God 106
70. "Toward the Light" as a religious system 109
71. The subconscious and the supraconscious 112
72. The future of humanity 118
73. The form and appearance of God 120

CONCLUDING REMARKS

1.

When one of the scribes asked which commandment was the greatest, Jesus answered – according to Mark 12:29 – "Hear, O Israel; The Lord our God is one Lord". Since Jesus quoted this ancient Hebrew tenet with deep conviction, should we therefore not assume that Jesus himself taught that God is One?
How then can the Church teach that God is three equal beings – the Father, the Son and the Holy Ghost – who together are One?

This question should in fact be directed to the clergy, as they should have all the qualifications to answer it in accordance with the truth, even if it would seem difficult enough to make these words of Jesus conform to the "Dogma of the Trinity". But so as not to inconvenience the clergy, we shall answer the question according to the knowledge we possess.

Jesus did not, of course, "believe" in a *divine trinity;* indeed, such a concept in relation to the personal Being of the true God was completely unknown to him. God was to him *the Father* – **the One, the only One!**

The teaching of the trinity is the work of human beings. But behind the original thought of this dogma was Ardor. The unity of the Son with the Father was agreed upon *at the Church Council of Nicaea* in the year 325 A.D., according to the current calendar, in other words long after the lifetime of Jesus. The "Holy Ghost" was included in parenthesis as the third link in this entity. But *at the Church Council of Constantinople* in the year 381 A.D. – likewise according to the current calendar – the parenthesis was deleted, and the "Holy Ghost" was given equal status with the Father and the Son.

As many people know, and as *everyone* should know, numerous alterations have been made both in the so-called Synoptic Gospels and in the Gospel of St. John, as a result of which none of these Gospels appears in its original form. In order to make all the four Gospels conform to the teachings of the then existing Church during the first centuries much in the various manuscripts was deleted or amended – or rather fabricated – according to the best judgment of the learned Fathers of the Church. But through this arbitrary action of deleting from or adding to the text, the inherent contradictions of the Gospels became even more conspicuous than they had been from the outset. The place referred to in Mark 12:29 *was simply overlooked during these revisions.*[1] In the corresponding passages in Matthew 22:37 and Luke 10:27 *the first part* of Jesus' *answer is missing,* namely the sentence: **"Hear, O Israel; The Lord our God is one Lord"**. (Anyone can easily verify that these words are missing by looking up the passages in question). The learned Church Fathers had "overlooked" Mark 12:29, and when it was discovered it was already too late to correct the error. The "camel" *was there to stay!* And generation after generation of prelates have "swallowed the camel" without feeling any obligation to reinstate the words of Jesus and expunge[2] the Doctrine of the Trinity, the work of human beings, from the teachings of the Church. However, many a sensitive mind has felt deeply disturbed by this pronouncement of Jesus, and because of this overlooked quotation many people have dissociated themselves from the Church Doctrine of the Trinity.

We await that man of the Church who in view of these words of Jesus, overlooked[3] **at the Church councils of Nicaea and Constantinople, will have sufficient courage to undertake this necessary purging of the Christian teaching.**

2.

Some biblical scholars are of the opinion that an ancient Original Gospel is the source of the now known Gospels. Did such an Original Gospel exist?

The existing Gospels, both the Synoptic and the Gospel of St. John as we know them, are *only copies of copies.* As a basis for these Scriptures there was not one – *there were several "Original Gospels".*

As it is not our task to restore the Gospels[4] to their original form

---

[1]) The scribe's reply to Jesus, Mark 12:32, was also overlooked. In this answer he confirms that God is One. This confirmation has been deleted in the two other Synoptic Gospels.

[2]) In this connection it is of no consequence that different sects and societies have been established in various places to proclaim that God is One. Nothing will help until the Church itself undertakes a complete purging of its own teachings.

[3]) In several other places in the Gospels and the Epistles there are words by Jesus that have been overlooked and that are not in accordance with the teaching of the Church. The original evangelists, the actual authors of the "synoptic books" and of the Gospel of St. John cannot, of course, be held responsible for the numerous distortions, deletions and additions. It was these original authors who received help from the transcendental world. (See "Toward the Light" p. 233:2,3). But despite this help, the first scriptures were still deficient and often misleading.

[4]) See "Toward the Light", p. 233:2.

and wording – which would in fact be an impossible task – we shall not elaborate upon this, but shall refer to that which is stated about Jesus, about his life, his words and acts in "Toward the Light", both in Ardor's Account and in the Commentary, as well as in the two Supplements, *for what is stated in these works is the truth!*

We must also point out that Jesus himself had some knowledge of the older mystic religions,[1] and that his beliefs and pronouncements were therefore influenced in certain respects by his knowledge of the ancient cults. It would thus be a hopeless task for any biblical scholar to attempt to prove the authenticity or otherwise of the many doubtful passages, for despite the many distortions, arbitrary insertions and deletions **all the Gospels contain glimpses of the truth and words genuinely spoken by Jesus.**

3.

Why did Jesus demand of Joseph of Arimathea that he should give all his great riches to the poor and renounce all power, honour and esteem? ("Toward the Light" page 57:2). If he had declared himself as a follower of Jesus, could he not have exercised great influence upon his fellow citizens, precisely because he was a rich and respected man?

Although Jesus did not belong to the Essene community, he nevertheless felt that many of their ideas were fine and exalted and therefore practised many of them himself. He was thus in complete agreement with the Essenes that the material things of life should be shared by all, and that none should amass unnecessary wealth for themselves. He therefore reasoned from his strictly human point of view that those who possessed an abundance of worldly goods should share them with those who had none – that *they should be poor among the poor.* He was for the same reason contemptuous of all earthly power and esteem.

Had Jesus suggested to Joseph that he should contribute a part of his great wealth for the benefit of the poor he would then have been in accordance with God's Thought. *For God at no time demands of the rich that they should give away* **all their possessions** *and retain nothing for themselves.* God greatly respects the individual's rights of ownership. And Joseph's situation in earthly life was indeed such that in accordance with God's intention and desire, he could have

---

[1] See "Toward the Light", p. 208:6.

supported Jesus by virtue of his wealth, esteem, authority and power.

Jesus was thus in this case all too stringent and too much influenced by the human aspects of the self in his demands upon Joseph.

4.

It is stated in "Toward the Light" on page 145 that Jesus had to search the plane of the Earth for centuries before finding Joseph of Arimathea. Must this be understood to mean that Christ was completely absent from his task in the sixth sphere during this long period of time, or did he only search intermittently? In the former case it seems to human eyes to be an unreasonably severe penance that was imposed on Jesus for his apparently insignificant guilt in this matter. Why could he not with God's help find his missing brother much more quickly?

During the time that the eldest of the Youngest – Christ – sought after Joseph he could return to his home in the sixth sphere as often as he wished. He also discharged in full the task[1] that God had entrusted to him – *to be the leader of the Youngest and of mankind.* But all the time that he could spare each day he used to search for him.

But in the centuries that passed before he found Joseph he was *never once in the Fatherly Home with God.* This should be compared with the parable of the "Two Brothers". The son in the parable says to the father: "Father, I shall go forth and seek my brother – I will not return, except that I bring him with me". This is thus a penance **that the son – Christ – lays upon himself,** and is not a penance *that is imposed upon him by the father – by God.* For in the parable the father says: *"Take up your staff and turn back; seek until you find the brother who fell behind you on the way!"* He does not say that the son may not return until he is able to bring his brother with him.

The inquirer feels that this was a severe penance for the apparently *insignificant* guilt that can be ascribed to Jesus in this matter.

But God did not look in this way upon *that* which passed between Jesus and Joseph in Palestine at that time. The guilt that Jesus in his earthly life incurred toward his "brother" was – in God's view – *by no means an entirely trivial guilt.* For on account of his uncompro-

---

[1] In the parable it is stated that "he bore no burden upon his shoulders", which only means that he was not incarnated.

mising attitude he rejected Joseph instead of drawing him closer, *as had been God's intention.*

Among the Youngest God had chosen these two, who are known to human beings under the names of *Jesus of Nazareth and Joseph of Arimathea,* to work together during life on Earth. He had chosen them to support each other in the difficult task that He had laid upon them; *together they should counter the anger, hatred, misunderstanding, opposition and condemnation of their contemporaries.* But by his attitude, which he maintained despite the urgent promptings of his conscience to draw Joseph toward him, Jesus thus became partly guilty in the failure of their joint mission. Similarly, he cannot be held entirely without responsibility for the fact that Joseph followed the ways of Darkness, that he committed murder so that his old servant should not reveal that he had removed the body of Jesus from the tomb. This guilt might possibly appear less significant in the eyes of human beings, but to God it was important. And the penance *which God* imposed upon the eldest of the Youngest was therefore no more than just: **that he was to search for the missing brother and help him find the road back to their Father, because he had failed during life on Earth to concern himself with the fate of his fellow-worker, because he never once on the road of his journey had turned to call his brother back.**

God knew of course where Joseph was to be found. After many years of wandering aimlessly about on the astral plane of the Earth, he had sought to hide in the Darkness of "Hell", drawn there by his guilt of sin. And God could of course have conveyed this to Christ; but would that have been of any use? Joseph could still not return, he could still not be released from the bonds of Darkness until he was overcome by grief and remorse. But there was a possibility that Christ in searching for him could evoke this grief and remorse, when he suddenly stood before him as the good Samaritan who sought for the one he could help and sustain. And thus it came to pass: when Christ suddenly stood before Joseph in the deep darkness of Hell, *when the radiant figure of Christ cast a clear light on the dismal surroundings, then a yearning for the Father's forgiveness awoke in the darkened mind of Joseph.* **And he followed his brother.**

But behind this search of Christ was God's Thought, and the moment God saw the first feeling of unease emerge in Joseph's mind, when He saw him seized by the first shudder of horror at the memory of his act of murder, God led Christ to his brother's refuge. For He knew that there was now a possibility that the son who was lost in the depth of Darkness might be overcome by grief and remorse over the failure of his earthly life. For He knew *that there was now a possibility that the son might return home to ask his Father's forgiveness.*

5.

According to "Toward the Light"[1] Jesus confirmed before Caiaphas that he was the Son of the Most High. Did Jesus mean to say that he was in fact[2] the Son of God and thus of a different nature from God's other children?

Through his spiritual struggles, Jesus had come to a full understanding *that he was the Messiah, God's emissary.* He had a faint recollection *that in the Heavenly World he held a special position as the chosen one among his equals.* He faintly recalled *that God had entrusted him with the power and authority over beings who lived and existed in the "Heavens".*[3]

"My Kingdom is not of this world" is one of the statements often repeated by Jesus, and it clearly indicates his perception of the special position that was his in the world invisible to human beings. *However, he felt that not only he, but all human beings were children of God, and that as such they were all equal.* When Jesus spoke of God he would as often say *"my Father"* as *"your Father"* or *"our Father".* And in his teaching he pointed out time and again **that God was the loving Father of all.**

At the time when Caiaphas questioned him, Jesus was a tired man. He knew that he had been chosen to be sacrificed, that he was to pay with his life *for the attempted revolt by the priests and the Sanhedrin*[4] *against the Roman overlordship.* He knew that his an-

---

[1]) Page 62:16.

[2]) See Supplement I, Question No. 47, regarding Jesus as the Son of God in the earthly sense.

[3]) These faint recollections of the beyond brought Jesus through his spiritual struggles to an understanding of the fact that he was the one chosen by God, the "Anointed One", God's emissary.

His conscience (God's voice) constantly reminded him that he was the Messiah, that he must teach the Jewish people of God's love and compassion, that he must lead the people away from and out of the constraining Mosaic Law. But Jesus was not able to bring these thoughts into accordance with the expectations of the people concerning the mission of the coming Messiah. For neither did he feel that he was the "King of the House of David", nor that he was the "Saviour" of all the people, sent by God. His conduct with respect to those matters therefore became uncertain. However, if according to God's intention he had openly acknowledged that *he* and no one else was the "promised" Messiah, he would have stood forth with much greater authority, and the Jewish people would perhaps have understood that *their conception* of the mission of the Messiah did not conform *with God's* intention.

[4]) See Supplement I, Questions Nos. 50 and 51.

swers would be of no consequence, for Caiaphas would be certain to turn and twist his answers so that they would express exactly that which he desired to hear in order that he might surrender him to Pilate. *The Sanhedrin was determined to be rid of him* – **and Jesus knew this.** When Caiaphas asked if he were the Son of the Most High, Jesus could have answered according to his teachings: *the Most High is my Father as He is your Father and the Father of all human beings!* But, as stated before, Jesus was a tired man when he stood before Caiaphas, and his answer was not well considered. His words were such **that the Sanhedrin saw blasphemy in them** – *and the fate of Jesus was thereby sealed.*

6.

In the Appendix to Supplement I, page 114:6, the clergy are rebuked for the use of the expression "The Bride of Christ" for the congregation in the terminology of the Church. But can they be reproached for this, since for example John 3:29[1] and Revelation 19:7, 21:9 and 22:17 can be said to set a precedent for this expression?

The wording of the various passages referred to in the Question has its origin in *the older mystic religions.* These words *stem from ancient rituals* – quoted incorrectly[2], in fact – and were spoken at the feasts consecrated to the nuptials of the God of Fertility and the Earth. At this feast the God of Fertility was represented by a handsome youth chosen by the priests of the temple from among the young disciples, while the Earth was represented by a fair maiden chosen by the priestesses from among the young temple maidens. The chosen youth had to submit for a long period of time to various ceremonies in order to render his body a worthy abode for the "god" during his stay on Earth. These ceremonies closed with a "baptism" during which body and soul were cleansed of all sin and earthly impurity. After the baptism the youth was led to the altar, where – kneeling in a prescribed posture – he inhaled narcotic vapours rising from the glowing embers in a metal bowl before him. And at the moment he swooned in a stupor, *the god took possession of his body!* After subjection to a number of stimulants he awoke to consciousness once

---

[1] The words ascribed in this passage to John the Baptist were, of course, never spoken by him. There have been numerous alterations to the original form of this Gospel.

[2] For example, Rev. 19:7 originally read: "the nuptials of the God are come". Later, "Lamb" was substituted for "God". Rev. 21:9 read "the wife of the bridegroom", and Rev. 22:17 included "bridegroom" where it now says "spirit".

more and was *hailed by the priests as the god descended from heaven* – **the bridegroom.** Outside the temple as the mid-point of a semicircle formed by white-robed, flower-bedecked priestesses and temple maidens stood the chosen bride – herself white-robed and flower-bedecked – awaiting the bridegroom's arrival. The priests, chanting softly, led the "god" to his waiting bride. The many priests stood before her, the high priest stepped forward, raised his staff and called out: "Behold the bridegroom is come! Who is the bride?" The priestesses answered in chorus: "The Earth stands adorned as the bride, longingly she awaits the coming of the bridegroom!" Again the priest called out: "Behold, the bridegroom is come! Where is the bride?" Then the young maiden stepped forward and bowed deeply before the god. Under alternating chants by the priests, priestesses and temple maidens the chosen bride was delivered unto the "god" – the bridegroom ...

The mystic cult from which this account is taken belongs to the more ancient cults, but we are not permitted to reveal from which people or from which time it originated. In ancient times this feast, or rather this drama, was enacted with a certain chaste beauty and solemnity. Only those who had been chosen to take part in the invocation were present. And a tragic drama it was! For the moment the youth had enacted his role as the God of Fertility, he was slain by the chief priest so that the god who had descended into the body of the youth could again be released. This was also done so that the earthly body that had briefly served as an abode for the god would never be tainted by sin or earthly impurity.

Also this once so exalted and solemn feast later developed into an orgy in which all the people participated.

The comparison of Christ with the heavenly bridegroom therefore springs from an ancient mystic cult. And bearing the above in mind the congregation, the bride, thus becomes **an expression of earthly fertility.**

With the knowledge that the quotations from the New Testament given in the heading are offshoots of an ancient pagan cult, a symbol of the union of the God of Fertility with the flourishing Earth, one can rightfully say *that it is unethical, inaesthetic and unseemly to compare Christ to the bridegroom who awaits his bride, the congregation.* And if the Church had not brought human marriage contracts under its domain, this metaphor of Christ's relationship with the congregation would probably *long since have been removed from the terminology of the Church* **as a most offensive expression.**

7.

Why did many of the followers of Jesus and the Apostles believe that baptism[1] – as practised by John – cleansed them not only of sins already committed but of future sins as well, even though Jesus repeatedly explained that baptism was no more than a symbol?

Both in his day and at earlier times the general populace of Jesus' native land knew as much about the older mystic cults as the general public of, for example, Denmark today knows about the ancient pagan feasts of the Winter Solstice (now "Christmas"), the New Year and Shrovetide.

"Baptism" was thus widely known in Palestine as an initiation, as a cleansing that purified and consecrated the individuals who dedicated their lives to the service of the mystic god. But then came John the Baptist and made baptism available to all – with his ceremony of baptism he consecrated all who would accept his teaching. But when he took water from the River Jordan and poured it over his disciples he said: "As with water I cleanse your bodies of earthly dust and soil, so shall the Lord cleanse your hearts with heavenly fire, cleanse you from the soil[2] of sin and evil." This was therefore *a twofold cleansing*, for the heart – the soul – should be purified by the "heavenly fire" of the Lord. Many therefore understood this to mean that the Lord let His fire cleanse their soul while John poured water from the river over their body. And when the fire had purified their "heart" of the uncleanliness of sin and evil, being thus doubly cleansed they could no longer be soiled by sin – *even though they sinned*. A remarkable logic, but thus they reasoned! And it was this misconception that Jesus sought to root out by countering the question of baptism with the analogy of the daily cleansing of the body, as told in chapter 19 of Ardor's Account.

---

[1]) See "Toward the Light", p. 51, footnote 2, and p. 52, ch. 20.
[2]) See "Toward the Light", p. 38:6.

8.

Christ says in his Speech (see "Toward the Light" page 113, line 19): "For there shall be no progress for you, nor shall you be able to begin a new life on Earth, before you have acknowledged your errors, before you have repented of your sins." But on page 112 he says: "...for what you sin, each one of you must atone in full. But if you refuse to restore what you have destroyed – for no one compels you to do what is right – then you cease your progress toward the Light and the Kingdom, then through many lives on Earth you remain at the same place". Do not these two pronouncements contradict each other?

No! These two statements are in perfect harmony with each other, and they supplement each other completely.

In the first quotation Christ says that the human spirit must acknowledge and repent of its guilt of sin before a new life on Earth can be commenced, for otherwise there will be no progress for the spirit, in other words, *it cannot progress in spiritual development.* According to God's Law of Incarnation each new earthly life *normally advances the human spirit in development, knowledge and experience.* It is this that Christ emphasizes by saying: *"For there shall be no progress for you."* But – and it is this that Christ emphasizes in the second quotation – neither is any progress possible for the spirit that refuses to submit to the Law of Retribution,[1] that is to say, *refuses to atone for its guilt of sin.* Provided that it has repented of its guilt, a spirit that refuses to atone for this guilt can well be incarnated for a new life on Earth, but that earthly life *will never advance it in spiritual respects, in spiritual development.* The spirit will therefore remain at the same level that it had reached when it refused to atone for the errors and transgressions committed in its last normal incarnation.

In the second passage quoted in the Question, which is taken from the section dealing with the Law of Retribution, Christ does not speak of prior repentance, he speaks only of spirits who *refuse* to restore what they have destroyed, *refuse* to atone for what they have sinned. But in the other quotation Christ speaks of repentance, the

---

[1]) If the human spirit cannot obtain the forgiveness of the victim of its transgression, it becomes subject to the Law of Retribution, and must atone for its sin through the sufferings for which it is itself to blame. For example, in cases involving murder or killing, including also infanticide and abortion, the forgiveness of the victims can seldom be obtained, since the "deceased" reside in a higher sphere, or because they have entered upon a new incarnation. Transgressors cannot in these cases be confronted with their victims in the spheres in order possibly to obtain their forgiveness.

remorse that all must sooner or later fully experience *before a new earthly life of progressive spiritual development can begin.*

Numerous human spirits are willing enough to acknowledge their errors and repent of their sin, but however deep and true their remorse may be, many a spirit will still attempt to evade *the Law of Retribution,* evade *the atonement,* and many refuse outright to submit to the provisions of this law. Since no one, however, is incarnated under the regular Law[1] of Incarnation without their consent, the spirits who refuse to atone for their sins must remain in their home in the spheres with no possibility of further progress. (See "Toward the Light", p. 184:4). Thus they do not take part in any preparatory instruction that could be of use to them in their coming incarnation. However, this idle and lonely existence will in most cases soon bring the spirits to their senses, so that they willingly submit to the provisions of the Law of Retribution. But if it transpires after a given time that the spirits are still unwilling to submit to the Law, permission will be given for them to be incarnated rather than stay in their home in the spheres. This permission *has always been accepted,* since everyone prefers to live on Earth as a human being among other beings, rather than remain completely alone in their home in the spheres. *But such an extraordinary incarnation does not bring the individual any spiritual progress.* In such cases many incarnations are often required before the recalcitrant spirit yields. But when the human spirit finally understands *that almost all contemporaries have progressed further, have moved on to higher spheres,* the full weight of solitude will make itself felt and the spirit will submit to that which cannot be avoided – **the incarnation of atonement.**

These extraordinary incarnations *do not count in the development of the human spirit,* and it is this circumstance that Christ refers to with the words: "... then through many lives on Earth you remain at the same place."

In his Speech – see "Toward the Light", p. 111:1 – Christ says: **"I speak unto you of some of our Father's laws!"** Thus it is only the most important laws that are mentioned in the Speech of Christ, namely the laws all human beings should know of. But it goes without saying that under the principal laws there are *numerous sections and subsections,* each of which is highly important for the pro-

---

[1] See "Toward the Light", p. 249:3, concerning the law for spirits who visit the Earth without permission, drawn by the demands of relatives, friends and mediums. See also the Answer to Question No. 23 in this Supplement.

gressive development of the human spirit, although it is not essential that they become known to mankind. If information on all these sections and subsections were to be given, that subject alone would fill numerous volumes, and this would therefore be an impossible task. However, there is one exemption clause, referred to in Question No. 18 of Supplement I, that we shall describe in greater detail. This clause, which is found under the normal rules of the principal law for the incarnations of human spirits, *pertains to the position of "Christian" spirits under the Law of Retribution.*

The great majority of human spirits who have lived and worked in Christian societies during their last incarnation will during the contemplation of the errors and sins of their earthly lives sooner or later come to understand the erroneous implication in the principal dogma of Christian teaching, namely: **the teaching of the Death of Atonement of Jesus.** They realize that it must be absurd that someone else should atone or suffer for the sins *which they have committed during their lives on Earth.* And even though numerous human spirits have sighed and grieved because they had to renounce this – to them so convenient – mode of atonement, they fully concede *that a loving and just divinity would never allow a "Christ" to suffer or atone for the sins of mankind.* And having made this concession they understand *that only they themselves can make amends for their errors and atone for their sins.* These spirits will enter their incarnation of atonement in the normal manner. But among the "Christian" human spirits there are unfortunately a great many with whom it is impossible to reason. All arguments founder on that one single, at times differently formulated, but invariably repeated tenet: *"Jesus Christ has atoned for my sins, and I am saved and absolved of my guilt of sin through my belief in his death of atonement".* Remorse is out of the question for these beings, they will not repent because, as they say, they have *already repented* when they partook of the Sacrament of the Communion on Earth *and received the "forgiveness of sin".*

But when God has seen that their repentance on Earth is superficial, is anything but deep, then they must indeed carefully consider the errors and transgressions of the life they have just ended, *until they become truly and deeply remorseful* – and this cannot be avoided. **For the forgiveness of sin through Communion is of no significance whatsoever to God.** But these obstinate "Christian" human spirits refuse to submit, and in most cases they are even highly dissatisfied with their stay in their home in the spheres: 1) *Because the spiritual self does not "sleep" until the "Day of Judgment",* as many imagine that it does after the death of the body. 2) *Because they are not in*

Paradise, although, to be sure, neither are they in the dreaded Hell. 3) They see no host of angels with great white wings, musical instruments or palm fronds. 4) There are no songs of jubilation, no hosannas, no hallelujahs! 5) **There is nothing of all that they had expected, hoped for or believed in.** There is only a grey and dismal existence,[1] a complete loneliness and absolute silence, when the conscience does not speak. But because of their trust in Christian teaching they cannot accept such loneliness and silence. Neither can they understand that this loneliness and this silence *are necessary for the voice of conscience to be heard in their innermost selves, so that everything from the completed life on Earth can be recalled and carefully considered.* They ponder therefore first and foremost upon how they may escape from this unendurable existence, which they find quite incomprehensible. Again and again they cry out **that they wish to return to life on Earth!** For they would much rather live in the human world among other beings than ponder in solitary silence upon the errors and transgressions that in their view had long since been forgiven through participation in the Sacrament of Communion, and wiped out by their belief in the Death of Atonement of Jesus Christ. When God sees after a time that nothing can be done with these human spirits He concedes *their demand* to return to life on Earth through a new incarnation. But although they are told that in the new incarnation they must themselves atone for the sins that they would neither consider nor repent, they all seize eagerly upon the prospect of living once more among their fellow beings. For they all hope *that in one way or another they will manage to avoid atonement when they become human beings again in a new life on Earth.* And not until they have endured one or more earthly lives in which – under the Law of Retribution – they have had to atone for previous sins and errors, do they concede and admit that they were wrong in their "Christian" views. But when this is conceded their defiant obstinacy is broken, **and then acknowledgement of sin and feelings of remorse awaken.**

It is undeniably a longer road that these "Christian" human spirits must travel; **but it is a necessary detour,** *and it must continue to be followed until human beings have understood that the dogmas, doctrines and postulates of the Christian religion are mistaken. Not until then can there be any expectation that all human spirits, when confronted in the beyond with their completed earthly life, will be more amenable in the matter of penance and atonement for the transgressions of their human life.* (See also Question No. 18 of Supplement I to "Toward the Light").

---

[1]) This state of existence lasts until feelings of grief and remorse awaken.

9.

In the Answer to Question No. 36 on page 54 of Supplement I, it is stated that the total time of incarnations will be longer in the future than it has been in the past. It must of course be assumed that the activities of the Eldest among human beings have greatly hindered and delayed their progress, and now that these activities have ceased it would seem that mankind should consequently make faster progress, which should then lead to the more rapid completion of the total time of incarnations. But the aforementioned Answer states that the converse will be the case – that the total time of incarnations will be lengthened. How can this be understood and explained?

This Question should need no further explanation beyond that given in reply to Question No. 36 in the first Supplement, where it is clearly stated *that the wilful incarnations of the Eldest have brought disorder to the calm and steady progress of the human spirits through earthly rebirth.* And since the nature of this disorder is explained with equal clarity in "Toward the Light", everyone should be able to grasp the reason why both the total number and the total duration of incarnations will be increased in the future rather than decreased. However, since it appears that the logic of this situation is difficult for human beings to comprehend we must provide a further explanation, even though this would seem to be unnecessary:

It must first and foremost be remembered that millions upon millions of human spirits remained on the astral plane of the Earth for thousands of years, and thus evaded the normal succession of rebirths. These millions must therefore atone in times to come not only for what they sinned in long since completed lives on Earth, but also for the guilt they brought upon themselves during their earthbound existence by participation – through the influence of their thought – in the crimes, misdeeds and transgressions of human beings. One must also consider the transgressions committed by human beings who have lived through several incarnations on Earth during the time of the wilful incarnations of the Eldest. *All these transgressions, misdeeds and crimes must be atoned for in full, which will inevitably demand a longer series of incarnations than was previously necessary for the earthly development of the human spirit – before the self-incarnations of the Eldest began.* But the questioner must not at this juncture exclaim that "this is surely an injustice that cries to Heaven!" *For this is in no way unjust,* **because this provision is founded upon perfect justice.** It must be remembered that the individual is perfectly free in deciding whether or not to give way to the influence of sin and Darkness. It should be remembered, *as it has often been stated, that all human beings are guided by their conscience.* And if the human beings during that period had followed their conscience and not let themselves be tempted or guided by the self-incarnated Eldest, there would of course have been no reason to increase the number of incarnations; *for then mankind would not have transgressed to the overwhelming extent that it has.* By studying world history from known ancient times to the present, anyone can learn of the misdeeds and crimes of the successive generations. But as human beings are easily tempted, as they easily submit to the guidance of the emissaries of Darkness, they must also fully atone for what they have sinned. *For they were not compelled to follow the ways of Darkness;* **if they had so willed,** *they could have chosen the ways of the Light.* But at some time in the future, millions of years from now when the atonement has been completed – **for there must be balance according to God's laws** – it is possible that the number of incarnations can once more be reduced. And since the Eldest who were incarnated by Ardor will at some time be removed from the Earth for ever, it is likely that as time passes the lot in life of human beings and the circumstances for atonement on Earth will be more favourable than would have been the case if the Eldest had continued their incarnations.

In the Answer to Question No. 36 of Supplement I it is stated: "...and since the sequence of incarnations of human spirits will be longer in the future than hitherto, the period of development in the worlds of Light *will be of shorter duration for these spirits* than for those who have been released from earthly life and now live in the worlds of Light". The reason for this is of course that these first mentioned spirits, through the numerous rebirths, will learn much *that was unknown when the previously released spirits lived through their periods of learning and development on Earth.*

10.

Words in the form we know them are of earthly origin. ("Toward the Light", page 3:3). Do transcendental beings also make use of an audible language for song and speech? And if so, do all spiritual beings speak one and the same language?

All spiritual beings can use audible language in speech and song; but all of them can also communicate by means of thought over short as well as extremely long distances.

The language by which God, His Servants and His first-created children – the Eldest and the Youngest – communicated, and still communicate, among themselves is very different from earthly language. *No more detailed information regarding this language will be given.*

The human spirits in the spheres speak the earthly languages with which they are familiar, but if they so desire they can also communicate by thought. They have no knowledge of the language spoken by God, by His Servants and by His first-created children. When they "speak" to human spirits, it is normally by thought or in the language the human spirits know from their last completed life on Earth. (Regarding God's speech to the human spirits in the spheres, see "Toward the Light", p. 186:2,3).

When the human spirits have been released from their earthly incarnations to continue their development in the distant transcendental worlds, they will also be taught the "divine language". **And thus all God's children will speak the same language once they are gathered in their Father's Kingdom.** *But they will also be able to communicate by thought and, if they so desire, by the earthly languages they once spoke.*

11.

The Youngest taught human beings the use of speech. (See "Toward the Light", page 19:10). Why then are languages so different and so grammatically complex?
Can we be advised from the transcendental world whether humanity should adopt an artificial language or one of the existing languages as a common tongue?

When some of the Youngest lived through their first lives on Earth, bound to the human bodies Ardor had created, their intelligence was at an infinitely low level. To enable the Youngest to live and associate with the animal-like human beings of pre-historic times, their mighty intelligence had to be reduced and limited to the lowest possible level. The spiritually life-giving cord that forms the connection between the psychic and the physical brain was therefore brought into contact with only a few sharply defined centres in the psychic brain of these Youngest. Consequently, the first attempts to establish any form of language necessarily had to be very hesitant, feeble and deficient. And since these Youngest – the first leaders of mankind – were incarnated at places scattered widely across the Earth, it was impossible for them to communicate with one another. Each one, guided by their guardian spirit, therefore had to think and act independently and according to the intelligence allotted to that individual. Thus it was quite impossible to create and develop a common form of speech for all people. However, as with each rebirth on Earth the life-giving cord of the Youngest was interwoven with more centres in the psychic brain, their human intelligence increased by some few degrees each time. They were thereby enabled to broaden the spiritual horizon of their fellow human beings, they achieved greater fluency of speech and were able to create new words, devise a better sentence structure and invent better designations. But progress was infinitely slow, fumbling and faltering, building always upon the existing but diverse forms of spoken language. Later, when the intelligence of human beings began to awake in earnest they themselves – within each nation – contributed new words to their language, new names for implements, animals, plants and natural phenomena, and so on. Later still the disincarnated Eldest began to interfere through the influence of their thought in what the Youngest were teaching mankind, so that the thoughts of the Eldest also left their mark upon the various language groups. During their many and long migrations from place to place in the earliest times, in the pre-historic era and in the age of ancient history, human beings again and again borrowed words and expressions from one another's form of speech, adopted them into their own language and in many cases built further upon them.

And when the Eldest incarnated themselves on Earth, beginning about 12,000 B.C., they improved and expanded the vocabulary and grammar of several of the existing languages through the mighty intelligence of their personalities. And further development took place in the course of thousands of years upon the basis laid down by the Eldest or upon their linguistic innovations. The forms of speech of the many nations and peoples were thus not created in a single event. They were all developed gradually in the course of time from the primitive, hesitant and unsure attempts to build a bridge between human individuals – *a bridge over which thought could be communicated in words that could be gathered into sentences and resound in audible speech, and thus convey to others the thoughts and feelings of the individual and express joy, sorrow, passion, pain and suffering.*

Human beings must themselves decide whether it is expedient and desirable to adopt some artificial language as a common means of communication between all nations, or whether one of the existing, living languages should be employed.

12.

Some readers have expressed surprise that Ardor should have used an archaic style of language in his Account. Is this because Ardor was most familiar with this style, or because the language would thereby acquire a more solemn and biblical tone?

Ardor did not employ an archaic form of speech in order to give his Account any Bible-like effect, but to give it a more solemn tone, since these older forms of expression have a much more serious and dignified sound than modern idioms and style, especially when read aloud.

He could, of course, have presented his Account in accordance with modern usage, but since he wished to give it a more personal stamp, and to show how beautiful and resonant the Danish language could be when shaped by a highly developed spiritual intelligence, he composed his Account in the form in which it now exists.

To compare the language of Ardor's Account with that of the Bible would be to the detriment of the latter.[1] The whole of Ardor's Account, from the first word to the last, is couched in an eloquent and graphically descriptive style. (Such cannot be said of the Bible, which is a work pieced together from manuscripts of widely varying quality). Especially the first chapters of Ardor's Account are phrased in such terms that any person of even moderate poetic appreciation will not only rejoice in the exceptional beauty of the language[2] but will also be able to picture the events of the narrative quite clearly with his inner vision. As Ardor moves into the age of history his language becomes less restrained and more graphic, though without losing his characteristic choice of words or his typical sentence structure.

Not until scholars of Danish language and literature undertake a close study of "Toward the Light" at some future time, will the full beauty of its poetic form be widely understood, for it is not given to everyone to recognize the linguistic beauty of this work without some guidance.

In order possibly to be recognized as the person he once was – Jesus of Nazareth – Christ gave his Speech in a language similar to that

---

[1]) The implied comparison is, of course, between the original Danish text of "Ardor's Account" and the Danish language Bible. – Translators' note.

[2]) Because of the overriding need for accuracy, the style of "Ardor's Account" has inevitably suffered in the translation process. However, the translators have endeavoured to the best of their abilities to reproduce the corresponding stylistic effects in the English language. – Translators' note.

used in the New Testament.¹ But it will soon become apparent to the observant reader that the Speech of Christ is in its form and choice of words much more poetic than the New Testament. His Speech is masterful, dignified and eloquent, and in every way transcends the quite ordinary usage of language in the New Testament.

But it cannot be expected that the general public will be able to judge the linguistic quality of "Toward the Light"; *though at some future time also that aspect of this work will be fully recognized, and this will happen when the spirit of the time has matured sufficiently to understand and acknowledge* **the unique significance of "Toward the Light" for all mankind.**

13.

Why was "Toward the Light" not given in a more widely used language, such as English, which would have made it accessible to far more people without translation? Was the reason for its appearance in Denmark similar to the reason for sending Jesus to Palestine?

At the time God incarnated a multitude of the Youngest, both male and female, so as to make them human helpers for Christ in his special task of winning Ardor back, they were incarnated in all civilized countries throughout the world. Among many other considerations, attention also had to be given to Ardor's ether-recordings, of which some *loomed ominously on the horizon of human life* at the exact point in time when these incarnated Youngest were to extend their help to Christ in his difficult mission. We refer to the so-called *World War* which had been planned and predetermined by Ardor, *but which was brought to reality through human action.* And when God saw that there was a possibility – although it was faint – that Denmark would remain neutral, He sent to that country some of the Youngest who in previous incarnations had proved to be especially suited to letting themselves be guided by the voice of their "conscience". Among these Christ succeeded in finding the necessary assistance.² *"Toward the Light" and the supplementary books were for this reason presented in the Danish language.* But with the

---

¹) The "Speech of Christ" in "Toward the Light", as well as his speech in "The Doctrine of Atonement and the Shorter Road", have both been translated into language that attempts to emulate the vocabulary and style of the Synoptic Gospels. – Translators' note.

²) Since these Youngest were merely to serve as Christ's earthly helpers in his special task, they were incarnated in such a way that their human personalities were only slightly above the level of the advanced human spirits.

knowledge people today possess of the languages of the various nations, it should not prove too difficult to find qualified people for the translation of the works, so that in time they may become *universally known,* may become *the common property of all mankind.*

14.

Why is the structure of "Toward the Light" based on questions asked by human beings? Would it not have been easier for the spiritual intelligences to create this work from their own knowledge of the truths that would be of importance to humanity?

This question can be answered both in the affirmative and in the negative.

It would have been a great relief for the spiritual intelligences if they had been allowed to proceed in this manner. But if the work had originated exclusively in the transcendental world, an exceedingly great difficulty that probably could not have been overcome would have presented itself when it came to "transferring" it to the earthly world. The only possible method would then have been for our helper on Earth to memorize the complete manuscript page by page during numerous nocturnal sleep releases[1] from her human body; and page by page the spiritual intelligences would during the following days have had to transfer the memorized subject matter from the helper's psychic brain to her physical brain. In other words, the same method that was employed by some "deceased" Danish poets when they produced a collection of poems, "Greetings to Denmark", *as a proof* **that the "dead" were alive and that they were able to send a greeting to their former native country and its people.** But even though the first part of the work, the production, the composition, of "Toward the Light" would have been an easy task for *the disincarnated spiritual intelligences,* the many nocturnal sleep releases[1] could have caused considerable harm *to their earthly helper,* just as the transfer from the psychic to the physical brain would have been a very difficult, perhaps quite impossible task. And since it involved so many significant truths and important explanations, which would have had to be reproduced exactly according to the manuscripts of the spheres, it was too risky a procedure to embark upon when in all likelihood it could not have been brought to a successful conclusion. But we cannot give an account of all these

---

[1]) See Postscript to "Toward the Light", p. 343:1.

many and severe difficulties, because human beings lack any basis for understanding them. We can only ask you to bear in mind that the human brain tissue will always lose some of its original elasticity over the years, a condition which in this specific case probably would have left "voids" in the manuscript while transferring it from the psychic to the physical brain of the earthly helper. And since it is highly unlikely that sufficient resilience could be restored to the slackened physical brain cells and brain-centres in order to fill possible "voids" by repeated transpositions of the missing sentences and paragraphs, it would still have been necessary to resort to a different procedure with respect to these sections. But the only recourse would then be to thought-dictation, the inspirational and intuitive procedure, or in other words the method that was in fact used for the production of the greater part of this work in the Danish language. (See also the Postscript to "Toward the Light").

But one other aspect of the matter must also be considered. If the work had been successfully conveyed to the human world from a manuscript prepared by spiritual intelligences, then human beings could with some justification ask: *"What should we in fact do with this work? We have surely had enough 'revelations'. Spare us from yet another of this kind",* and so forth. God pointed this out to the Youngest who had been chosen by Him to create "Toward the Light". He therefore said to them: *"Lead the thoughts of your earthly helper and her closest friends toward questions of religion, ethics, science and philosophy. Say to them that within those limits they may ask about anything that they believe could be of interest to them and to their fellow human beings. For then you can give them answers to their questions, for then they can receive answers to the questions which they believe it is necessary for them to ask, then they can receive solutions to some of the riddles over which human beings have puzzled for thousands of years and more without being able to solve them correctly".* In accordance with God's wish it was thus left to certain individual human beings to pose questions upon which "Toward the Light" could be based and drafted by the spiritual intelligences chosen for that task. But great freedom was also left to these intelligences to lead the chosen human beings to ask at least the most essential questions. Thus no one has any right to say: *This work has no significance for us, it does not tell us what we need to know, it gives little of the information that is of interest to us, the whole work is quite meaningless, our own interpretations are much superior,* and so on. For that which is *now* given to mankind through Ardor and several of the disincarnated Youngest **is the very answer to that which has been asked by human beings.** And those who have posed the questions show – through their questions – that they represent that part of humanity – though doubtless only a smaller part – *whose spiritual level is higher than that of the average human being.* This therefore means that only a few people – *few in relation to the total population of the Earth* – will be fully able to understand the answers given. But the others, the greater part of humanity, will at some future time *through numerous incarnations achieve the same spiritual level,* **if all will pay heed to the "Message" that is now given.**

At the time when our earthly helper announced that neither she nor her circle had any further questions to ask, the work was temporarily concluded. But as God had seen that there were still a great many matters of importance to mankind which had not been explained, because questions pertaining to these subjects had not been asked, He decided to augment the work that had been given with one or possibly two Supplements. God therefore entrusted some of the Youngest with the task – within a given number of years – of leading those people who had accepted or shown interest in the "Message" to submit written or oral questions to our earthly assistant, in order to have these questions answered *through her intuition and through the inspiration of the Youngest.* These Youngest thus became the helpers of the spiritual guide who had been assigned to our earthly interpreter and translator.

The structure of Supplements I and II is therefore also based on questions from human beings. Only the Appendix to Supplement I was, according to God's wish and His directions, given solely from the transcendental world[1], since it had not been possible to elicit any questions relating to sexual matters before Supplement I had been concluded.

Disincarnated spiritual intelligences and human beings have thus worked hand in hand. And the work will continue in this way until the point has been reached that was established by God as the ultimate limit in time for obtaining answers to questions *on spiritual, spheric, and earthly matters.* But if we succeed in eliciting the still missing questions and answering them before the time established by God has been reached, the work will be definitively concluded and no further additions allowed.

---

[1]) In the same way as, for instance, the Speech of God's Servant in "Toward the Light" and the speeches of Christ and Ignatius in "The Doctrine of Atonement and the Shorter Road". No questions from human beings form the basis of these speeches.

15.

Some readers are of the opinion that the style of language used in the Commentary to "Toward the Light" differs from the one employed in "Questions and Answers". Did the same intelligence originate both texts, or do their origins lie with several different intelligences?

To answer this question we must go back to the time when "The Doctrine of Atonement and the Shorter Road" was concluded. With the completion of that work, the promise given to our earthly helper that she should receive a gift consisting of *"three golden fruits"*[1] was fulfilled. However, as stated in the Answer to the preceding Question, there still remained a number of material problems to be elucidated in order to give human beings a more complete picture and a fuller understanding of the transcendental world, and of the circumstances that form the basis of the individual personality of the human spirit. There similarly remained a number of answers in "Toward the Light" that could well be further clarified and expanded through the posing of new questions, and thus contribute to a clearer understanding of the subjects already treated. Our Father then chose – as previously stated – some of the disincarnated Youngest to assist our earthly helper's spiritual guide, and He instructed them to elicit with the means at their disposal the missing questions from the people who had accepted "Toward the Light" and understood the significance of this work. With our earthly helper's permission the time-limit for the answering of such questions was set at the expiring of her life on Earth – which was of course the latest possible date. However, should it prove possible to elicit and answer the missing questions within a shorter period of time, *the work would then be brought to a final conclusion, so that all response to any further questions would cease, even though our helper's life on Earth had not yet ended.*

While "Toward the Light" and "The Doctrine of Atonement and the Shorter Road" were being given, *the spiritual intelligences were present in our intermediary's earthly home.* Invisible to her we each stood at her side and communicated what we had to convey with the help of our thought – *but these words and sentences of thought* **were expressed in the Danish language.**[2] The style of language thus *directly expressed the individual personality of each of the spiritual intelli-*

---

[1]) See "Some Psychic Experiences", p. 22.
[2]) Certain passages of these works had nevertheless to be memorized by our intermediary during nocturnal sleep release. See Postscript to "Toward the Light".

gences that was present. But this intensive and concentrated procedure could clearly not be employed in the case of the subsequent Questions, because the chosen Youngest – the helpers of the spiritual guide – first had to elicit these questions in the thoughts of several different human beings before the spiritual guide could answer them. Our Father then established **a direct spiritual "radio" link between our intermediary and her guide.** Wherever he happened to be in the spiritual[1] world or in the spheres, he would thus at any time be able to answer the questions posed through the intermediary. *These answers were given as usual by thought* – **but in the "divine language".**[2] When her spiritual leader's thought-messages reached our earthly helper's psychic brain, her thought[3] would automatically convert the given words and sentences to the Danish language. *And because of this* **"translation"** *minor departures have occurred from the literary style of the Commentary, which was conveyed in her mother tongue.*

16.

If the entire human race should follow the course suggested in the Appendix to Supplement I and thus refrain from begetting children – and there is no logical reason why this possibility could not be considered – how would the Law of Reincarnation then operate? Would it then not cease to function, and thereby bring to a halt that form of development of the human race?

A suggestion to limit the number of children is not the same as a command *not to bring children into the world under any circumstances whatsoever.* The questioner puts forward the view that there is no logical hindrance to envisaging the possibility that the whole human race might cease to beget children on account of the suggestion in Supplement I that human beings should limit the number of children. Can this truly be called a logical thought? *We do not think so!* 1) Because no consideration is given to the individual's need to

---

[1]) The globes of the Light, where human spirits abide after release from life on Earth.
[2]) See Question No. 10 in this Supplement regarding this language.
[3]) Even when the thought-messages are given in the Danish language there are instances – such as in the case of synonyms – where the intermediary's thought might take the nearest available word in her psychic brain and use it in rendering the "thought-dictation", although another word was used by the sender and would therefore have been more appropriate than the word chosen by the intermediary. This can thus occur whether the thought-dictation is given in Danish or in the divine language.

have children, the need to give love to beings of one's own flesh and blood. For this instinct cannot be eliminated from the human race by decree, much less by a mere appeal to limit the number of children. *This is quite out of the question.* 2) Because no account is taken of the primitive peoples, nor of the millions of human beings unfavoured by the benefits of civilization in, for example, China.[1] 3) Because no account is taken of the survival instinct[1] of the various races. It is hardly likely that any single race would willingly eliminate itself in favour[1] of any other.

Thus: *God does not demand that human beings should refrain from bringing children into the world under any circumstances whatsoever, since such a demand would be in deep conflict with His love for His children and with His sense of justice. But He does demand that no human beings should beget more children than they are fully able to support.* **And this demand is perfectly justified.**[2]

17.

Birth control could theoretically be practised to the extent that the human race eventually died out. How would God and the Youngest view such a possibility – or the prospect of a drastic reduction in the number of people on Earth?

A drastic reduction in the number of people on Earth *would only be welcomed by God and the pioneers of humanity – the Youngest –* for such a reduction would in every respect create better circumstances and conditions for mankind. However, *there is not the least danger far into the future* that the human race will become extinct through birth control. But if the possibility of extinction should arise at some time in the future, humanity would have no cause for anxiety, *for God would certainly know of other ways in which to continue the development and education of the human spirits according to His plans and wishes.* And this possible continuation would then take such a form *that it would create no injustice whatsoever for those human spirits who, if that hour should arrive, would have concluded their earthly development.*

---

[1]) Literally translated, the original Danish text included the expressions: "millions of uncivilized human beings of the Chinese race", "the instinct of self-preservation of the white race" and "in favour, for example, of the yellow race". In view of historical and semantic developments during the past half-century, it was felt that the words now chosen would less invidiously express the intended meaning. – Translators' note.

[2]) See also the answer to the following Question.

18.

Some people see a discrepancy between "Toward the Light", page 328, where it is stated that divorce should be "a means of last resort", and the first Supplement which recommends easy access to divorce. Should it be understood that the first statement applies as a moral obligation, and that easy access to divorce is demanded only because freedom strengthens the individual's sense of responsibility and facilitates divorce in those cases where it is definitely justified?

The statement – in "Toward the Light" – referred to in this Question, on divorce as a means of last resort, should not be understood as *a question of morality,* but *as a norm for marriage, a goal for which all people who are married should strive.* What is stated in "Toward the Light" is thus **the ideal** of human marriage, *an ideal which is pointed out also in Supplement I, p. 108:1.* Human beings can give substance to this ideal, and it has been fulfilled in numerous marriages both at the present time and in the past. But so long as people are bound by rigorous laws for the dissolution of marriage, and as long as marriage is regarded as a Sacrament and divorce in general as a disgrace, the average human being cannot attain this ideal. Also in this case should people be given the freedom of choice with respect to the dissolution or continuation of their marriage. The more difficult it is to obtain divorce, the heavier will be the "yoke of matrimony" for either one or for both parties. For it should not be forgotten *that average human beings are still at such a low level in a great many respects that it would be quite absurd to attempt to tie them down through rigorous laws for the dissolution of marriage.* Only anger, hatred and bitterness result from such regulations. Many married people who could have led a happy and peaceful life together with someone other than the partner they had first chosen have stagnated in life or broken down completely, *both morally and spiritually,* because their marriage was regarded as *a Sacrament* and its dissolution *a disgrace,* or because one of the parties had tenaciously clung to his or her *"right".* Human beings – especially men – must try to reject the archaic point of view **that marriage partners are each other's property. For according to the law of God, the man has no right of ownership over the woman, any more than the woman has over the man.** Both partners must be equally free in their relationship, but if this cannot be, divorce is much to be preferred, especially if there are children in the marriage. For the mental health of the children can be impaired considerably if they must constantly witness parental disputes and quarrels.

The questioner is right in stating *that complete freedom in questions of marriage strengthens the individual's* **sense of responsibility,** *and that easy access to divorce should be granted* **in all justified cases.**

19.

Many people will also see a contradiction between the insistence on purity and the easy access to means of contraception recommended in Supplement I. Should this be understood to mean that abstinence – also within marriage – is preferable when this is consistent with bodily and spiritual health?

Easy access to means of contraception should be seen from the point of view of *birth control.* For according to God's laws human beings have the right to give life only to that number of children that they can fully support and educate.
The demand for purity has nothing to do with birth control and nothing to do with sexual abstinence. And nowhere in "Toward the Light" *is there any condemnation of bodily union*. This union has once and for all time been given to humanity by the creator of the human body **as the basis for its propagation.** The sexual instinct and its satisfaction must be regarded as a part of human life in the same way as all other functions of the body. Human beings cannot refrain from taking nourishment, even though this may be an inaesthetic process, unless they wish to expose themselves to death from starvation. Nor can they retain in the body the waste products that must normally be expelled. For if humans act in defiance of nature they will simply destroy their bodies, even though their action is based on apparently aesthetic considerations. It is necessary for all to respect the various demands and processes of the body; no good can come of seeking to ignore the natural functions with which the human body was endowed by its creator at the dawn of earthly time. But everyone can – by the strength of the will that God has given to all – *subdue and refine* **the crude sexual instinct** *that dwells in the body*. Through the strength of the will human beings can thus govern and regulate their sexual life, so that the individual does not give way to the sexual instinct both at proper and improper times. For if human beings do not seek to govern this instinct, it may manifest itself in atavistic and abnormal behaviour and result in abusive or criminal sexual conduct.
Thus, God does not demand that bodily abstinence should be re-

garded as an ideal expression of "purity". For such a demand would be quite absurd in view of the once established natural functions of the human body. But what God does demand of human beings is **purity of mind and thought!** The will can also be employed for this purpose, for everyone can by the power of their will cleanse the mind and thought from that which gives impure, amoral and obscene ideas and fantasies. But those who are subjected to compulsory abstinence, for example through the Catholic vow of celibacy, are very seldom pure of mind and thought. For they often practice in secret – not only in thought, but often also in reality – what the vow of celibacy denies them.

If people practise abstinence within marriage, without damaging their spiritual and bodily health – and with the full agreement of both partners – then God makes no objection. **But He never upholds sexual abstinence as an ideal of "purity" either for the married or for the unmarried.**

Thus: the purity demanded by the laws of God is **purity of mind and thought!** But this does not mean that the individual must force the body to refrain from satisfaction of the sexual instinct. It means that *all, through the power of their will, should seek to hold the urges of the body within the normal and proper limits and not become slaves to their instincts, so that they are led to commit lewd, unchaste, atavistic, abnormal or criminal acts.*

Everyone should thus respond to the demands of the body within the limits that the self and the conscience believe to be proper for the satisfaction or denial of the sexual instinct.

20.

How should the ancient commandment[1] "Thou shalt not commit adultery" be properly understood, and how far-reaching is its significance?

Adultery, in the sense of the Old Testament, covers many different forms of transgression. Various sinful and wrongful acts against morality, both within and outside marriage, are listed in Leviticus 20:10–21. The transgressions within marriage that are discussed there, and whose penalties are cited, must first and foremost

---

[1] Obviously God did not engrave the ten commandments on the two stone tablets of the law, as related in the ancient myth. The commandments originate from human beings, although some of them were inspired by God's Thought, for example the commandment "Thou shalt not kill".

be judged in the light of the very stringent view held in those ancient times of the man's absolute ownership of his wife or wives, and of the inadmissibility and immorality of sexual relationships between close relatives.[1]

The sexually immoral, abnormal, lewd, atavistic and criminal conduct of human beings was far worse and more widespread in those times than it is today. Thus, from a human point of view there had to be severe penalties for these various forms of sexual offence and crime.

The New Testament not only supports the views of the Old Testament on such matters but adds a new element, namely the words of Jesus[2]: "Ye have heard that it was said by them of old time, Thou shalt not commit adultery: But I say unto you, *that whosoever looketh on a woman to lust after her hath committed adultery with her already in his heart".*

As stated earlier, Jesus agreed in a great many ways with the dogmas and ideas of the Essenes. He was deeply disturbed by the immorality of his time, and being chaste himself, he felt that the Essene demand for sexual abstinence was justified. But he saw deeper than his contemporaries, he understood that not only the act itself but also what preceded the act, the background for it, was highly important, namely *the feelings of the heart and the thought's desire.* Jesus thus touches upon what God demands of human beings: **purity of thought, purity of mind, purity of feeling!** *For if the mind and thought are clean, the individual is no longer drawn toward the unclean, toward immorality, toward sexual transgressions and sexual crimes.* But Jesus did not understand that even though a man's desire can be aroused at the sight of a desirable woman, *his desire can still be clean, his thoughts and his feelings can still be clean.*

Therefore, although Jesus went one step further by including the mind, the thought and the heart in the concept of adultery, *he was still unable* **to distinguish between clean and unclean desires, between clean and unclean thoughts.**

Every age has its laws for immorality and sexual crime. Each period in time has its views on such offences, but God alone can determine how deeply these sexual transgressions and crimes are rooted in the mind and thought of the individual. Consequently, no definition of adultery can be given from the transcendental world which will be fully valid for all peoples and for all times. Only this can be said: each individual must first of all strive to cleanse the

---

[1] Related both by birth and by marriage.
[2] See Matthew 5: 27-28.

mind, the thought and the feelings, for if this is done **that person's[1] attitude toward all sexual excesses, toward all abnormal or immoral sexual offences will remain clean.**

21.

In "Toward the Light", page 5:3, it is stated that God created thousands upon thousands of glorious, graceful figures – spiritual beings – the angels. Later on in the work the guardian spirits of human beings are mentioned and from this information it appears that the "angels" should be counted at least by the millions, rather than by the vague number "thousands upon thousands". Is it not possible to give the correct number of God's first-created children?

No! The actual number will not be given.

When Ardor rendered this part of his Account, he knew from a conversation with God that this number should not be revealed. But God also pointed out to him the fact that since the number of human spirits far exceeded the number of God's first-created children, Ardor should employ a numerical quantity *that would indicate this difference.* And this he did when he used the expression *"thousands upon thousands"* for the number of the angels, and *"legions of legions"* for the number of the "shadows". (See "Toward the Light", p. 18:2).

However, this refers only to the number of "shadows" as compared to God's first children – the Eldest and the Youngest.

In "Toward the Light", p. 18:3, Ardor explains how the shadows were transformed into human spirits, namely by God endowing them with a spark of His own flaming Being, that is to say with *Thought and Will.* But through millions of years this first contingent of human spirits was increased many times over through numerous new creations, whereas the number of God's first-created children *was established once and for all time.*

According to God's wish, no further information will be given concerning this matter. Human beings must therefore content themselves with each individual's own conception of the collective number of all God's children. Not until the pilgrimage of mankind to God's Kingdom has ended will the exact number be revealed, for human thought is too feeble, too limited in its scope to be able to comprehend this number in terms of living beings.

---

[1] This applies only to the normal individual and not to sickly, abnormal persons who are not in full possession of their faculties.

22.

Although there are no more earthbound spirits – according to "Toward the Light" – spiritualistic mediums can nevertheless communicate with all manner of spirits at any time of the day or night. But is it conceivable that the incarnated Eldest – during nocturnal sleep release – can be responsible for all these manifestations?

As so often stated, spiritualistic mediums have no further contact with "earthbound spirits", since that kind of being no longer frequents the astral plane of the Earth. *Genuine manifestations* are therefore due to the incarnated Eldest during their nocturnal sleep release, and to a number of human spirits from the fifth sphere and to some extent from the sixth sphere. But these human spirits have no permission to visit the plane of the Earth, and must therefore expiate their disobedience through an incarnation commencing at a much earlier time than would normally[1] be the case.

A further explanation is that the spiritual self of many mediums is one of the Eldest. The numerous "releases" through the unlawful[2] excursions during sleep of these Eldest have in many cases caused the connection between body and spirit to slacken in the course of time. And since several of these Eldest during life on Earth act as mediums – in the spiritualistic sense – *they are able to act simultaneously as both medium and manifesting "spirit", or "spirits".* It is not even necessary for these mediums to be in semi-trance or in complete trance. They may well be completely awake, apparently normal, because interaction – although weak – still occurs between the spirit and the respective human body. This type of medium can thus seem to be in contact with "several different spirits", but in reality it is the medium's *own spirit* that is released from the body and imitates, or poses as, different spirits. Even though the medium might appear trustworthy in everyday life, this is no guarantee that his or her claims regarding the origins of the many spiritual manifestations are true. For many human beings have a certain ability to hide their true nature from their fellow beings, and thus appear to be different in character from what they really are. In some cases the mediums themselves act in good faith, but in others they are knowingly fraudulent. It is self-evident, however, that such unlawful releases of the spirit, which must normally be firmly bound to the visible body, must in due course slacken the interaction between the psychic brain

---

[1]) See "Toward the Light", p. 249:3.
[2]) See "Toward the Light", p. 293:2.

of the spirit and the physical brain of the body. If these unlawful releases are continued over a longer period of years, they can result in insanity for a longer or a shorter time – *possibly for the remainder of the earthly life of the person concerned.*

All mediums who perform under the cloak of spiritualism act in contravention of God's law, for which reason it cannot be repeated too often **that no human being should attempt in a spiritualistic manner to act as a link between the "living" and the "dead".**

23.

In "Toward the Light" it is written on page 184:4 that the incarnation of the human spirit must take place voluntarily. But near the foot of page 249 it is stated that those spirits, who against their better judgment and without permission return to the Earth, will on each such occasion have deducted a period of time corresponding to one earthly year from the time otherwise allotted them for rest and development in the spheres.
How can these two statements be reconciled with each other?

Until the Spring of 1918 the new incarnations of the human spirit took place in the manner described in "Toward the Light" page 184:3 to page 185:1. But since a danger arose during the World War that a new lower class of spirits might develop on account of the prohibited, but in fact frequent, excursions of the spirits to the plane of the Earth, the provisions described on page 249 were adopted.

These provisions can be attributed in the first instance to a request from a multitude of spirits who frequented the plane of the Earth without the necessary permission. These spirits were greatly exhausted and distressed by the continually repeated visits to the Earth that were practically forced upon them by the demanding thoughts and wishes of friends, relatives and mediums. Many spirits saw quite clearly that they lacked the ability to harden their will sufficiently to resist the strong "earthly attraction" to which they were exposed. And they therefore appealed to God that they might receive some effective help. In order to increase the capacity of their will, God made a temporary law for these beings who had such difficulty in refraining from visiting the Earth. And this law was approved by all the spirits, even though it provided *that each unlawful visit to the Earth deducted a year* from their time of rest and learning in the spheres. God chose this procedure because He knew that the prospect of a curtailed sojourn in their homes in the spheres would cause the respective spirits *to strive to the utmost of their ability against the powerful attraction from the Earth.* And by thus exerting their will, they would in most cases remain in the spheres despite the compelling thoughts of relatives, friends and mediums.

This statute therefore applies only to those human spirits who visit the plane of the Earth even though they know such visits are not permitted. They know beforehand that they are violating the law, and they know that the consequence will be incarnation earlier than normal, that they must enter that incarnation without any preparation for the coming life on Earth, and that *the incarnation will not bring them any spiritual progress.* Possessing this knowledge, they themselves must decide whether to act against the law or not; **for it is only a question of will.** The will may freely choose between two alternatives: to visit the Earth without permission, which brings about an early incarnation, or to remain calmly in the home in the spheres, with a following incarnation after the period of time normally allotted.

In the various earthly communities human beings live under many kinds of laws with many sections and subsections, but they are still free individuals until the moment they in some way transgress against the laws of society, and these transgressions cause them to lose their freedom for a longer or shorter period of time. In a civilized society everyone knows that one must not kill, rob, steal, and so on. But if people nevertheless violate these laws of their own free will, they must suffer the allotted penalty. *The punishment is a natural consequence of the individual's misuse of the free will.* And the incarnations that the human spirits bring upon themselves, through their unlawful visits to the Earth, can only be regarded as a **"sentence of temporary confinement",** that is, an atonement invoked by violation of the section of the law in question.

The human spirits who are in fact immature, because of a poorly developed will, receive God's help in a different way; they are restrained by a Barrier across the Passage of Light that leads to the Earth. (See "Toward the Light", p. 249:2). This Barrier was established according to *the wish* of these beings at the time that they besought God to provide them with protection against the human, the earthly attraction.

Thus, the Barrier and the stated section of the law are **only temporary measures,** which at some time in the future will be abolished when people have learnt that **no one must call upon the "dead"** – *but several centuries may pass before this can be fully accomplished.*

24.

In the Answer to Question No. 6 in the first Supplement it is stated: "Daily thousands of human spirits are drawn to the Earth, and daily the spirits of Light lead these insubordinate spirits back to their homes in the spheres". How can the calling thoughts of mediums bring these comparatively advanced spirits from the fifth and sixth spheres to transgress so readily against the law, and to surmount the restraining Light-Barrier? Compared to earthly conditions, it can hardly be imagined that people would travel hundreds of miles in order to violate the law because of an external thought-influence.

The comparison between the situation in the spheres and on Earth made in the Question does not apply in this particular case, inasmuch as the thought-influence of one human being upon another *follows other laws than those which form the background for thought-influence of a human being upon a disincarnated spirit, or vice versa.* However, in the earthly world a *coded telegram* or a *coded message delivered over the telephone* would often have a similar effect. *A considerable number of people could by such a message be persuaded to travel hundreds or thousands of miles in order to commit an unlawful act.*

If a spiritualistic medium exerts thought-influence on disincarnated spirits, it should be taken into consideration that such mediums are normally the "Eldest", whose capacity for thought-concentration is enormous compared with that of ordinary human beings.[1] Many human spirits also have a strong yearning for their relatives and friends on Earth. These spirits are therefore readily attracted to the Earth, to their earthly homes or to spiritualistic séances, but usually only to say that *they are alive!* But others return again and again because their yearning for life on Earth grows stronger with each visit and because the Darkness on Earth gains ever greater power over them on account of the unlawful nature of their visits. The Light-Barrier offers no appreciable hindrance to spirits who are determined to visit the Earth. However, it does present an obstacle for those spirits who are drawn to the Earth *against their will.* Often they venture only so far as the Barrier, then they hesitate and return to their home in the spheres. But others fail to resist the calling from the Earth if the medium is one of the Eldest, and when they arrive at the Barrier of Light

---

[1] Concerning the mutual thought-influence among human beings see "Toward the Light", p. 310:1-2 and Supplement I, Question No. 1.

they penetrate it by the power of their will.¹ These distressing conditions for many of the human spirits cannot improve until the time comes when people have learnt to be less selfish in their grief over the beloved, departed ones; they cannot improve until all spiritualistic séances have ceased for ever. *Not until then will it be possible also in this respect to improve the general conditions of existence, both for the "dead" and for the "living".*

25.

Christian Wilster's poem "Memento" – reproduced on page 30 of "Greetings to Denmark" – contains the following passage: "I followed my life from birth until death, a hand unseen held me fast". Since the human being and the human spirit have a free will, how can "a hand unseen" hold him fast when he himself does not wish to review the course of his past life?

Recollections of the many stages of the earthly life just ended arise quite spontaneously in the thoughts of the spirit; no one – neither God nor the guardian spirit – forces the spirit to *"listen" to* the emerging thoughts or to *"look" at* the scenes of the past life as they pass before the eye. If the spirit does not wish to consider its past actions and *does not wish* to contemplate the visions of its past life then it can – by the strength of its will – suppress these things. But time after time they will reappear and invite reflection. It is this state of self-searching that Wilster poetically likens to *the grip of an unseen hand.*

The automatic appearance of these visions and memories of life is due to the **divine origin** of the human spirit. For the divine element will always react to any wicked, evil or unlawful thought or action that the respective spirit bears in its memory from life on Earth. What happens is thus the attempt of the spiritual self *to cleanse itself of earthly Darkness and cast off the oppressive yoke of the guilt of sin.*

During incarnation the guardian spirit is essential to the human being, since the divine spark in the self is often so faint that its "protests" are unable to penetrate the Darkness surrounding the spirit that is bound to the human body. The guardian spirit is thus the *"reinforced conscience"* of the human being. But when the spirit is released from its human body and finds itself in its home in the

---

¹) Concerning the Light-Barrier see "Toward the Light", p. 249:1-3.

spheres, far away from the earthly Darkness, then the spark of divinity – the divine element – is strong enough to react to the periods of Darkness in the completed life.

The task of the guardian spirit in the home in the spheres is thus to help and sustain its charge during the time of self-searching. It seeks with love and patience to reason with its charge and convince him or her that every aspect of the life on Earth must be considered, acknowledged and repented of **before rest and peace of mind can enter the spirit.**

26.

Since human beings by their own deeds pave the way for their life on Earth, what part does coincidence play through sickness, misdeeds and accidents of various kinds? Or does nothing happen by coincidence?

Since the Earth is first and foremost a world of Darkness, life there must by the very nature of Darkness be full of coincidences, and numerous of these are unavoidable.

The saying attributed to Jesus – **"Are not two sparrows sold for a farthing? and one of them shall not fall on the ground without your Father"** – does not reflect the situation on Earth. *For sparrows fall to the ground day in and day out without the Will of God being involved in the slightest.* **And thousands upon thousands of human beings die every day, long before the day and the hour appointed by God is reached – and thus without God's Will!**

In the parable of the "Two Brothers"[1] the father says to his returned children: *"Many of you came before I called*[2]*..."* This statement refers precisely to the return home of numerous human spirits before the time determined for the death of the earthly body is reached. Never does God predetermine the death of human beings through criminal acts, warfare or the raging forces of nature, or by accidents, whether these occur on land, at sea or in the air. But if human beings through no fault of their own are exposed to death through natural catastrophes, sickness, random accidents or criminal acts, God will always utilize the occurrence to counterbalance their previous guilt of sin. (See "Toward the Light", p. 306:2).

---

[1] See "Toward the Light", p. 141.
[2] The continuation of this passage refers to the many "earthbound" spirits who returned belatedly to the spheres.

The blindly acting powers of Darkness are not *directly* employed by God in framing His outline for the earthly lives of human spirits. If a human spirit for one reason or another shall live an earthly life *under the Law of Retribution,* then the spirit will normally be bound to a human foetus conceived in a family in which disposition for disease or deficiency is latent or active in the body or in the brain. *They are thus born to life in homes or surroundings that can produce exactly what is demanded by the Law of Retribution – a deformed and sickly body, mental deficiency or imbecility – or a life of poverty, want and misery.*

If a human being has been rendered liable under the Law of Retribution to suffer some accident or disaster, then God does not determine that the respective human being shall be afflicted by any particular catastrophe. He rather leaves it to "chance" to decide when and in what manner this will happen. Such a human being will therefore not be warned[1] by the guardian spirit if suddenly threatened by some imminent catastrophe during life on Earth. Should the respective human being thus die before the appointed time, the number of years of which the individual has been deprived will be *added to the time of rest in the spheres.*

And neither does God, in the case of a human being that under the Law of Retribution must save the life of a fellow human, determine that an accident will occur at any particular time, so that the human being in question can carry out a penance. But God informs the spirit – before its incarnation begins – that life on Earth is so full of various kinds of accident that it must seek its own opportunity to save the life of a fellow being. The guardian spirit will, however, assist in finding an occasion upon which this may be possible. If the spirit in the coming life on Earth carries out its penance and loses its life while saving a fellow human being from death, and therefore returns to the spheres sooner than it should, then it will not be reproached for this premature return. The missing years will also in this case be added to the spirit's time of rest in its home in the spheres.

But if the human being dies at the appointed time without having performed its penance, then the spiritual self – when it has rendered its account – will be incarnated to a new life on Earth in circumstances *parallel to those of the life just ended.* For no time of learning is needed for such parallel incarnations.

---

[1]) See "Toward the Light", p. 252:4.

27.

Since God determines the duration of the life on Earth of human beings and the manner of their death ("Toward the Light", page 185), how can the many deaths through apparently random accidents be explained?

The many deaths due to unpredictable accidents – such as bolts of lightning or other natural catastrophes, accidents at sea, on land or in the air, and fire disasters – are applied by God to the counterbalancing of the guilt of sin of the present or previous lives on Earth, provided that the particular human being is not to blame for what happened. **For in such cases there is no counterbalancing.**

If human beings themselves have in some way caused the premature interruption of their lives, *they must assume the full responsibility for that which has taken place.* And on the very day that had been determined by God to be their last on Earth, the spirit that was bound to the prematurely deceased body will be incarnated to a new earthly life, parallel to the one that was not completed. The time of the spirit's stay in its home in the spheres between such parallel incarnations *is regarded as a period of rest, but not of learning.* (Regarding the stay in the spheres of those who commit suicide see "Toward the Light", p. 114:3 and p. 185:1,2).

Even though God has pre-ordained the life span of every human being, the hour of death determined by God will in numerous cases not be reached. (See the Answer to the preceding Question). This is first and foremost due to the *blindly acting powers of Darkness, secondly to Ardor's predeterminations for the lives of human beings as individuals as well as for entire nations, and finally to human recklessness, foolhardiness, competitiveness, irresponsibility, and so on,* **but also because human beings fail to heed the warnings of their guardian spirit.**

28.

According to the Answer given to Question No. 16 in the first Supplement, it would seem that the Law of Retribution is rarely enforced in its full severity, since it is only applied to those who fail to repent in time. How then can the immensity of suffering on Earth be explained in terms of retribution for transgressions of the past?

Not all suffering in this world can be explained in terms of retribution for past transgressions. It has often been stated that human beings themselves to a great extent cause much and quite needless suffering: 1) *Such suffering is needless because it could have been avoided if people had exercised greater care and less irresponsibility.* (See Supplement I, Question No. 63). 2) One should also bear in mind *Ardor's "future-images" which human beings themselves cause to become reality on the plane of the Earth,* and, 3) we must also consider *the unpredictable suffering called forth, for example, through natural disasters.* None of this is in any way due to *retribution.* **It is, however, an entirely different matter that God employs this apparently "undeserved" suffering to counterbalance human transgressions of the past.** (See Answer to Questions Nos. 26 and 27 in this Supplement).

Perhaps the inquirer does not understand the true meaning of the expression *"in time".* For the meaning according to God's laws is this: *that human beings during life on Earth must fully repent of their guilt of sin, both toward God and toward their fellow human beings.* This means: *that everyone, during the same life in which the transgression is committed, must ask the forgiveness of both God and human beings;* **for there will be no retribution if the transgressor is forgiven by God and by human beings.** Yet, how many ask forgiveness? Some may during life on Earth attain a feeling of guilt of sin and remorse toward God. But if there is guilt among human beings, the anger and hatred between them is increased rather than diminished during their common life on Earth, because only few people will ask their victim to forgive the transgression. But **the opportunity is lost** if they fail to repent and ask forgiveness during the same life in which they transgressed against their fellow human beings. And they will then in the beyond be confronted with their transgressions, with their thoughtless, evil, wicked or criminal deeds. But by then it is usually too late to obtain the forgiveness of the victim, *even though the sinner may obtain the forgiveness of God.* (See Supplement I, p. 37:5).

Let us look at a few examples from life on Earth.

How many curses have not through the ages been pronounced by fathers and mothers against their degenerate sons and daughters who went astray and sank deeper and deeper into sin and Darkness? How many fathers and mothers have in their self-righteousness, bitterness and anger closed the door of their home to an errant son or daughter? How many sons and daughters have left their home despite the wishes and pleadings of their parents? And how many have remorsefully returned home *to ask the forgiveness of their father and mother?* They can easily be counted, **for they are few in number!** And how many fathers and mothers have during their lifetime called back their sons and daughters whom they have cursed, called them back *to forgive them and to bestow their blessing upon them before death ended their earthly life?* They are easily counted, **for also they are few in number!**

And how many married people have not separated in anger, spite and hatred? But how many have asked each other's forgiveness before their lives ended? They are still more easily counted, **for their number is appallingly small!**

Let us look at other examples from daily life.

If a person through lack of responsibility, recklessness, foolhardiness or the like causes one or more fellow human beings to become maimed, wounded or disfigured, does that person then ask forgiveness of the victims who have had to suffer? Only rarely does this happen; in most cases the matter is settled only in the courts through legal proceedings against the guilty party, who according to the judgment must then pay proper compensation to the injured parties; but it does not occur to him that he should also, or rather first of all, ask the forgiveness of his victims. And if he does consider this – possibly even for quite a long time – he shrinks from doing so, because he feels that it would be beneath his dignity to approach his victims with an apology for what he did. *But should he not do so,* **then the opportunity is lost.**

Or how many curses have not been uttered over men to whom the care of the funds and property of others has been entrusted, when they have betrayed this trust and have deceived and plundered both rich and poor, both widows and orphans? Have such men begged their victims to forgive them? No! Only very rarely has this happened. But by their conduct they have caused endless grief, despair, anger and hatred. And in many, many cases such men have killed themselves to avoid the condemnation and punishment of earthly justice. **Also these have lost the opportunity for remorse and forgiveness.**

Many further examples could be given from all possible walks of life in which human beings, instead of repenting in time, instead of seeking forgiveness while this is still possible, flee from their obligations, flee from judgment and punishment – or take their own lives. **But retribution in one form or another** will come to all these people in some future life.

It is to be hoped that human beings at some future time will fully understand *what the individual's* **responsibility** *means, and fully understand what* **timely repentance** *signifies.* **But there will then also be less spiritual and bodily suffering, less poverty, less misery, fewer accidents, fewer transgressions and fewer unlawful acts in earthly life.**

Let us hope *that the time when* **this will become a reality** *does not lie in the too distant future.*

29.

In "Toward the Light" it is written on page 306: "For it must be clear to all: no human being endures any greater spiritual or physical suffering than that brought upon himself or herself in previous lives". Can the awareness of these circumstances not serve to blunt the sympathy of human beings for their suffering brothers and sisters, or even to arouse reproach for their unknown sins of the past?

It should be out of the question that this could happen. Should not the sight of the sufferings of others rather increase the human being's sympathy and compassion? Would not most people reason thus: What have I myself transgressed in the past? What sins am I myself guilty of in my present life? I have possibly endured the same sufferings, the same sorrows myself – possibly shall I myself in some future life come to endure similar pain and misery. Would not these thoughts arouse compassion in the heart? And would not the sight of others' sufferings bring human beings *into closer contact with their conscience?* Awareness *that no human beings suffer more than they have brought upon themselves* should in any case cause everyone to reflect a little more than hitherto on the possible guilt in their own present lives, rather than speculate on their neighbours' possible transgressions in previous ones. But one thing is certain: that those who have themselves suffered on account of previous guilt of sin will feel the deepest compassion with the suffering and the grieving, because they have some faint memory *of the significance of grief and suffering for the development and education of humanity.*

But once the meaning for the individual of free will and responsibility has been fully understood, then human beings will exercise much greater care and vigilance in all aspects of life. *Then one will not wait for one's neighbour to better himself and then* **possibly follow his example. No, then one will begin by improving oneself, will seek to become an inspiring example for one's neighbour, and hope that he will follow the given lead.** Thus should it be, and thus will it be one day, **when human beings have fully assimilated the ethical and religious teaching that is given in "Toward the Light".**

30.

How do the efforts of mankind to prevent accidents and suffering and to improve the world affect the Law of Retribution? If the sum of all human suffering is reduced, can human beings then expect a lesser penance than would otherwise be their due?

Human beings – when they do not repent – will never escape with a lesser penance than is their due. **The scales of God never err,** *for the guilt of sin and the penance of atonement will always balance.* But if human beings grieve for themselves, repent fully of their guilt of sin, pray forgiveness of God and of their fellow human beings, *then atonement under the Law of Retribution is annulled;* **for then it is no longer necessary.**

Gradually, as human beings come better and better to understand the meaning of responsibility, as they become more considerate in thought, in word and in action, so that they more and more seldom become guilty of thoughtless, wicked or unlawful deeds, so will life on Earth become correspondingly brighter and better, not only for the individual but for all mankind. The guilt of sin will thus lessen *and the atonement will then be in proportion to the lesser guilt.*

When all the presently incarnated Eldest have been removed through physical death from life on Earth, humanity will no longer be as strongly influenced by Darkness as in the past, or even at the present time. But human beings will then – according to their spiritual development – receive less help through their conscience than has hitherto been the case; **for also in this respect will balance be maintained.**

Time and again during the 14,000 years[1] in which the Eldest ruled with almost absolute power over mankind, they drew huge accumulations of Darkness from encapsulation in the Light and gathered them closely about the Earth so as to strengthen their own position in the struggle against the influence of the Youngest upon earthly life. It was therefore necessary for the "conscience" always to be alert and ready to intervene, to lead and to guide the spirit that was bound to the human body. But once the reign of the Eldest on Earth has finally ceased it will no longer be possible to bring any "newly separated" Darkness to this globe, and – infinitely slowly – the separated accumulations of Darkness will be eliminated through the earthly lives of the Youngest and the human spirits, **and a new era in the history of human life will begin!** But during this period all should *be more careful in guarding themselves against the influence and temptations of Darkness.*

---

[1]) The incarnations of the Eldest began about 14,000 years ago.

Therefore: *once the reign of the Eldest on Earth has come to an end, human responsibility for self-purification will increase, and because of the self's inherent knowledge of evil, all individual human beings will more than ever have to strive away from the influence of Darkness, for only in especially difficult cases will the guardian spirit be permitted to offer help as a "strengthened conscience".* **But human beings should never forget that a prayer to God for help will always be heard if the prayer is deep and fervent.**

31.

The spirit assumes in the spheres the appearance that the human body had at the age of 30 to 40 years ("Toward the Light", page 191:4). Must this be understood to mean that the spirit-body suffers the same deficiencies and deformities that may have afflicted its human body?

When God promised some of His fallen children to take mankind into His care – *in other words to give each human being thought and will* – He also had to give these spiritually weak and undeveloped individualities an embodiment for their use during sojourn in the spheres between incarnations. God then formed from the Light a pliable and elastic substance with which He clothed these spiritual individualities, giving each single Light-body at the same time a plastic form. Just as the prototype of a blossom is hidden in the germ of the seed, *so does God conceal in this plastic form an ethereal principle that is more than a prototype for the true embodiment of the self,* a principle that first manifests itself visibly at the moment when the spiritual self is released for ever from earthly rebirth. This embodiment of thought and will has always preceded the entry of each "new spirit" into the earthly world. And each spirit therefore bears in its visible[1] body an invisible[1] ethereal prototype of its true form. **In this way God moulds in secret His child for eternal life in the Fatherly Home.**

On account of the pliability and elasticity of this Light-substance, and because of its plastic properties – or in other words its ability to reflect and conform to any shape and its ability to expand and contract – the spirit-body is able to assume the shape of the new-born human infant at each rebirth on Earth. This substance is also able – after the binding of the spirit to the human foetus – to assume a misty state as the development of the foetus advances. In other

---

[1]) "Visible" or "invisible" according to transcendental concepts.

words the spirit-body is prepared quite automatically to assume the shape and appearance of the little body at the moment of its birth. If the body of the new-born child is malformed in any way, *the spirit-body assumes the same malformed appearance down to the smallest detail.* By virtue of the Light-body's ability to expand, it conforms at all times to the human body as the latter grows and takes on greater dimensions. When the human body "dies" – regardless of the age at which it does so – the corresponding spirit-body will appear in every detail as an *exact copy* of the deceased body. It will thus either be old and bear the various signs of old age, or be young and supple with handsome, plain or unlovely features, or it will be deformed, as it was when the corresponding human body was born to life. If a child dies immediately after birth or in childhood, the spirit grows up[1] in the sphere where its home is located; and as the body assumes larger dimensions it is shaped and developed *according to the characteristics it received when the corresponding earthly body was born.*

If the human body during life on Earth is exposed to surgery, accidents, natural disasters, wars, and the like, and thereby loses part of a limb or loses arms, legs, the nose, an eye or an ear, and so on, and the person survives, then *the corresponding part of the spirit-body will fade and disappear.* The substance of which these parts are formed *does not dissolve but slowly retracts into the remaining undamaged substance.* However, if a person dies by sudden accident, for instance is struck by lightning, if the body is sundered by explosives or torn by wild animals, if the human body is crushed under heavy objects, destroyed by fire, or if a person expires immediately following surgery, or after an accident where the head, the arms or the legs have been severed from the body, if the body is lacerated by sharp blades or mutilated through a criminal act, if a person's death is caused through wounds inflicted by guns, bayonets or knives, or the like, then the spirit-body is automatically released – **no matter how extensively the human body is maimed** – *and thus it will not be permanently damaged, it will not be marked by the occurrence.* It therefore retains the appearance it had *before the fatal catastrophe.* (Regarding suicide see below).

Similarly, *the spirit-body will be released spontaneously* if the manner of death is decapitation, hanging or electrocution. But if these modes of death have been decreed through an earthly court of justice, **the spirit-body will be marked by the injury.** However, the head of the spiritual body of Light will not be missing, *but a crimson ring will be formed around the neck where the blow struck.* If the

---

[1]) See "Toward the Light", p. 190:3.

person killed was a victim of so-called judicial murder **the spirit-body will not be marked by the act of violence,** *but will appear in the shape it had before death of the physical body occurred.*

If people take their own lives, under whichever form[1] they may do this – and unless suicide was committed in delirium or while the person was unsound of mind – the spirit-body will be *clearly marked*[1] *by the wilful action.* If people commit suicide and destroy the body by using explosives or pour inflammable liquids over the body and ignite them so that the fire partly or completely consumes it, if people throw themselves before a train and are lacerated by the wheels, and so on, *then the spirit-body is released in the normal way at the moment of death, but it enters a black, misty state shortly after.* If suicide is committed by means of fire-arms and the discharge partly or completely shatters the head, the head of the spirit-body will to a greater or lesser extent assume **a black, misty appearance.** In all cases of suicide – except those committed in delirium – **the thought will unceasingly reflect on that which has happened.** And the state in which the spirit finds itself after the death of the human body *will continue until the hour that was appointed to be the last has been reached.* **The dreadful appearance** of a person who has committed suicide will also remain until that hour, and **is therefore often retained for many years.**

Thus: *any manner of death that is due to the will of the individual leaves its clear mark on the spirit-body.*

When the spirit is released at death from the human body, the guardian spirit[2] brings it to the home in the spheres where it regains consciousness after a longer or shorter period of sleep. The marks that the spiritual body carries from life on Earth *are thus retained until the spirit has rendered its account to God.* But even though the spirits who during life on Earth have been bound to blind, deaf, lame or retarded beings likewise retain the stamp of these afflictions until their accounts have been rendered, they are still able to *see, hear, talk, think and move about from place to place* in their home in the spheres. The reason for this is that God, in the plastic substance from which He created – and still creates – the spirit's body for its life in the worlds of the spheres, **has concealed the "ideal" of the spirit's true, eternal body.** And by the help of this ideal's psychic organs of vision, hearing, speech and its ability to move

---

[1]) If suicide is committed by any kind of toxic substance, the spirit-body will lie perfectly still in its home in the spheres. But the thought is "awake" and will unceasingly revolve around this action until the appointed hour of death for the human being has been reached – which may not be for many years.

[2]) See "Toward the Light", p. 186:1-3.

about, the former human beings that were defective in these respects can then as spirits *see, hear, talk, think and move about.*

When the account has been rendered, when the spirit has fully grieved over itself and fully repented of its errors, sins or transgressions, then the spirit-body assumes the appearance it had at the age of 30 to 40 years. If the human being dies at an earlier age the spirit-body retains the more youthful appearance. All the marks and blemishes that it acquired during the human being's life and work on Earth are *taken away and smoothed out by God.* Any lost limbs or organs *are drawn out and reconstituted by the power of God's Will,* and the spirit-body thus resumes **a normal appearance.** But those spirits whose human bodies were born – in accordance with the Law of Retribution – with a greater or lesser degree of malformation or paralysis, or with an imbecilic appearance, will retain – in accordance with the same Law – *a milder manifestation of these malformations or of that appearance.*

Those spirits who refuse for a long time to repent retain the earthly body's signs of old age, suffering and misery until remorse at last arises – perhaps not until they have spent many years in their home in the spheres. In those cases where the spirit demands an earlier incarnation than normal[1], this appearance is retained until the demand for a new incarnation can be accommodated. And also those spirits that committed suicide as human beings have their mutilated spirit-bodies restored in the same way as all others after the rendering of the account and after repentance in full. But in those cases where the whole spirit-body or parts of it have assumed a dark, misty consistency, God clothes the thought and the will once more *with new Light-substance,*[2] *from which a new spirit-body can be formed.* And the spirit is then bound immediately afterwards to a human foetus so as to live through another earthly life *parallel to the one that was abruptly terminated by the act of suicide.* Even though God clothes the thought and the will in new plastic Light-substance this does not mean *that the spiritual self must recommence its series of incarnations from the beginning.* It means only *that God enables the thought and the will – the spiritual self – to continue through earthly rebirth the development already begun.*

Thus: **all deformities and disfigurements that the spirit-body has acquired through the corresponding human body's life and work in the earthly world will be made straight and smoothed out, its missing**

---

[1]) See this Supplement, Question No. 8.
[2]) The "ethereal prototype" can never be destroyed, however dissolved the spirit-body may be. See also the Answer to Question No. 33 regarding the "ethereal prototype" – the true body of the spirit, or in other words, its eternal form.

limbs will be reconstituted and the body's signs of sickness and suffering will be replaced by its youthful appearance from the age of 30 to 40 years, or from an earlier age. This does not happen until the spirit has rendered its account, has grieved over itself and repented of its guilt of sin. But all the malformations of the spirit-body that it acquired from the birth of the corresponding human body – in accordance with the karma[1] of the spiritual self – are retained, although in a milder form, until a new incarnation is entered.

If the human body, in warfare, fire disaster or other form of accident *caused by one or more fellow human beings,* is disfigured or mutilated beyond recognition but survives – even as a totally deformed mass of flesh – *then the spirit-body is deformed in the same dreadful manner.* **But in such a case the love and the mercy of God intervene.** His deep compassion for the fate and sufferings of such wrecks of humanity cause Him to *suspend the existing laws for the destruction and reconstitution of the spirit-body, as well as for the incarnation of the human spirit.* And when death comes to these wretched beings the spirit is brought – in a sleep-like state – not to its home in the spheres, *but to be bound immediately to a human foetus so as to begin a new incarnation.* The spirit is then reborn in a home whose circumstances are such as to ensure the new-born human being **a life of light and happiness.** *A generous portion of the respective spirit's past guilt of sin will similarly be weighed against the bodily and spiritual sufferings it has endured.* When the spirit returns from this special incarnation, it must then render an account both of its life just ended and of its preceding life.

If a human being survives disfigurement or mutilation in an attempt under the Law of Retribution to save the life of a fellow human – or in an attempt made on that person's own initiative – then immediately after the death of the body the spirit will similarly *be reborn to a brighter and happier existence.*

Thus: **through the love, mercy and compassion of God these unfortunate beings will by rebirth immediately after the death of the body be removed so far from the bodily and spiritual sufferings they have endured that the spirit can review its previous life on Earth with greater calm.**

---

[1]) See Answer to Question No. 33.

32.

In the Answer to Question No. 31 it is stated that the human bodies that are malformed at birth will retain the malformed appearance in the spiritual world. Why does God not allow these beings a normal form of spirit-body once they have rendered their account?

1) The form or characteristic, which the plastic substance[1] of the spirit-body assumes at the birth of the corresponding human body, cannot be altered until a new rebirth, that is, a new incarnation, has taken place. Not until then can a change *both in the spiritual self and in the human body* take place. This change is brought about through the inheritance that the reborn spirit receives from its parents and their ancestors – bodily as well as spiritually.[2]

2) If God were to restore the "spirit-bodies" that were malformed from birth to normal characteristics, to a normal appearance, once these spirits had rendered their account, these beings would be *"strangers"* to themselves, just as relatives and friends from life on Earth *would be unable to recognize those on whom they had once bestowed their love, protection and tender care, when they meet once more in the beyond.*

3) Finally the Question should be viewed with regard to the Law of Retribution, since the deformity[3] is due to *a karma*[3] to which the individual is subjected.

Nursing homes are provided for such unfortunate beings in the various spheres. They remain there under the loving care of male and female attendants until they enter a new incarnation.

Therefore: *the spiritual and physical characteristics that a human spirit receives through earthly birth are retained both in its present life on Earth and in the spheres, until it enters a new incarnation whereby the spirit is endowed with new characteristics, both in a spiritual and in a physical sense.*

---

[1] See the Answer to Question No. 31.
[2] Through the astral brain.
[3] See the Answer to Question No. 33.

33.

Since the spirit that according to "Toward the Light" is bound to the human body enshrouds the body of the new-born child like a mantle, how then can the organs of the spirit-body assume the characteristics or shapes of the corresponding organs in the earthly body?

It must be remembered that the visible human body is of the earthly *three dimensions,* whereas the invisible spirit-body – created from a plastic Light-substance – is *four-dimensional.* Seen from the transcendental world the human body appears as a misty,[1] insubstantial figure. The astral spirit-body is moulded around this figure, but since the Light-substance is four-dimensional it also extends into the misty figure where, quite automatically, it shapes itself to both its inner and outer forms. The Light-substance will also quite automatically form *an insulation layer,* which separates the internal organs of the astral spirit-body from those of the human body. This layer is ejected and cast off at the death of the earthly body, but when the spirit is reincarnated it is replaced with a new substance that is added at the same time that the spirit is bound to the foetus. The moment the astral body has been shaped to conform to the inner and outer forms of the child's body, the parts that reproduce the *bone structure harden* and thus become as solid as the corresponding bone-structure of the physical body seen from the earthly world. But the system of vessels only *appears* to be carrying blood, in reality there is no fluid in the arteries. *The ability of the astral spirit-body to survive is therefore based on laws other than those of the physical body.* These laws cannot be explained. Concealed in the Light-substance rests the spirit's true **eternal body** created and formed by God, but since this is of a dimension unknown to human beings it has no space-filling properties in the four-dimensional astral world, and is therefore not affected by the various metamorphoses of the astral body. The inner structure of this truly spiritual body – which to avoid any misunderstanding could be called the *"ethereal body"* – is the same for all beings created by God and is identical with the spirit-body described in "Toward the Light", p. 187:4 to p. 188:4. When the Youngest have rendered the account of their earthly lives to God, the astral spirit-body in which their true self has been concealed during life on Earth is automatically cast off and dissolved. In their dwellings – in the last plane of the sixth sphere – they therefore appear in the "ethereal body" *which is their eternal form.* But when

---

[1]) Even more misty than the human body would appear on an X-ray photograph.

the Youngest work in the spheres – when they serve as tutors – they reduce the vibrations of the ethereal body by the power of their will and thus become visible to their charges. In those few cases where the human bodies of the Youngest have been malformed due to some form of karma, their misshapen bodies will also be cast off once the account to God has been rendered. This is possible because their ethereal bodies *have space-filling properties within the plane* of their homes *in the sixth sphere,* whereas the corresponding ethereal body of the human spirit *has no space-filling properties within the four-dimensional worlds of the spheres.* **The human spirit must therefore retain its deformity until the following incarnation will provide it with a new form.** *God can make use of this condition when human spirits must atone under the Law of Retribution.*

34.

Some people are of the opinion that it is justifiable to help fellow human beings to die when their sufferings are indeed very great and their death is in any case imminent. How are we to regard this problem? And though it may not be justifiable to help fellow human beings to die, to what extent is it permitted to relieve pain by analgesics, even though they may possibly shorten life?

According to the laws of God it is never permitted to take the life[1] *of a fellow human being,* not even at the wish and request of the person concerned. If a person suffers because of a painful disease, suffers following an operation or because of wounds or injuries due to accidents, or the like, the doctor may administer analgesics to any extent that is deemed necessary and justified. But in those cases where the patient's body is weaker than the doctors in all sincerity and *to the best of their judgment* had presumed, and the narcotics therefore precipitate death, the doctors in question will not be assigned any guilt. However, if they are aware that the ailing body cannot tolerate the precribed doses, *they will be regarded* **as murderers under God's laws.** The same applies to human beings who kill out of "compassion" to spare a relative or a friend the prolonged sufferings of an illness. And the person who through the "merciful help" of a fellow human being has been killed in order to escape human suffering **will be regarded as a suicide.** Such persons must then, like

---

[1] If the life a woman is endangered during pregnancy of birth, the life of the foetus must be sacrificed to save the mother's life. See the Appendix to Supplement I, p. 113:3.

others who kill themselves, endure in their home in the spheres the sufferings from which they fled, and suffer there until the moment arrives *when the earthly body should normally have died.* If the patient's life is terminated without his or her request, then of course that person bears no guilt. *In that case the responsibility rests only with the person who carried out the "mercy killing".*

35.

How should the use of alcohol, tobacco, coffee and other more or less harmful stimulants be regarded? Must this be taken into consideration when the human being after death renders its account of its life on Earth? What are the consequences if the human life is thereby shortened and the spirit thus returns to the spheres before the day appointed for the death of the body?

The entire course of one's earthly life must be accounted for after death – including any misuse of stimulants.

In the "Speech of Christ" ("Toward the Light", page 128:10) Christ says: "Be prudent with all strong drinks and dulling drugs; for you should know that you yourselves must bear the full responsibility for the foolish, evil and wicked deeds which you commit when you lose control of your senses and of your will through careless or evil habits". *Mankind is thus admonished to exercise care in the use of certain stimulants.* Their *use is not forbidden,* but it is said that they should be used in such a way that these stimulants *do not damage the health and do not form bad habits, nor cause the individual to lose self-control.*

As far as tobacco, tea and coffee are concerned these "poisons" are not harmful to the body when used in moderation. But if alcoholic beverages and other stimulants are used to excess, so that they destroy the health of the body and by this misuse cause the human spirit to return home earlier than it normally should, then this will not be regarded as suicide. Such cases are judged according to the law of God that states **that none shall treat their earthly body with carelessness.** And those who violate this provision of the law will be incarnated in circumstances *that will have an improving and educative effect, so that the corresponding human spirit may learn to guard against the excessive use of stimulants.*

36.

If the law against alcoholic beverages – "Prohibition" – is compared with the "Temperance" movement, would it be correct to regard Prohibition as rooted in Darkness, while Temperance is rooted in the Light?

Yes, it would be fully justifiable to express oneself in this way.

According to God's laws, no government has any authority to shackle the will of the people with so rigorous a statute as Prohibition. For a law that binds and constrains the initiative of the free will is of the evil, and will serve only to create an untenable situation, since all who will not be constrained will certainly find ways of obtaining what the law attempts to deny them. On the other hand, an effective campaign of enlightenment in respect of the misfortunes, sufferings and crimes that can result from the intemperate consumption of alcoholic drinks will always be appropriate, for it then becomes the concern of the individual to stay within the proper limits. The penalties for causing accidents and committing crimes under the influence of drink should likewise be significantly increased, since it is absolutely *no excuse* for the persons concerned that at the time of the accident, or while committing the crime, *they did not have full control of their mental faculties*[1] *or of their will.*

There can be no objection to weak-willed persons joining a temperance society if they can thereby find strength and support. But this must only be done at the individual's own wish, and not by the moral coercion of friends or relatives, nor by court decree or at the demand of an employer. Further reference should be made to the Speech of Christ in "Toward the Light", p. 128:10, and to the Speech of God's Servant in the same work, p. 137:1, which includes the following words: *"For Almighty God compels no one, and no one shall compel his neighbour. But pray you all to your Father to strengthen your will, that it may overcome the evil and lead you forward toward the Light!"*

---

[1]) Certain allowances must of course be made for mentally deficient persons. The above applies only to normal persons whose mental faculties are impaired by alcohol.

37.

How should one view the political principles of Liberalism versus those of Socialism?

Political strife must be resolved by human beings themselves. However, in this respect as in all other matters the individual will always be able to obtain the necessary guidance through the guardian spirit, the conscience. But it can be said with certainty from the transcendental world **that all political disputes are of the evil.** The governing and legislative authorities of the nations and the various communities have in the "Speech of Christ" ("Toward the Light", pp. 124 - 126:2) *received a guideline that clearly indicates the direction of God's wishes.* If the entire "Speech of Christ" in spirit and in truth became the guide for all in life on Earth, it would soon transpire *that all political factions and the incessant tug-of-war among the various party leaders* **were quite needless and caused nothing but harm.** *They are harmful, because they can in no way* **create calm and peaceful working conditions for those with whom the responsibility lies.**

38.

Why does "Toward the Light" supply the information that the thickness of the insulation layer is 1/8 millimetre? It would seem to be a superfluous and useless piece of information, since it cannot be observed and verified by human beings.

"Toward the Light" is a message *to all humanity,* and this would therefore include *the human spirits who inhabit the various spheres.* Thus, much apparently "useless" information can be found in this work, *useless to human beings, but of importance to human spirits.* One example is the information given that the measure for the thickness of the insulation layer is 1/8 millimetre. That this information is correct can never be verified by the earthly world. *But from the transcendental world it is very easy to verify that the measurement given corresponds to the actual fact.* This information may be of great value to a doubting human spirit, since the leaders of the various institutes of higher learning in the spheres can bring their students to the plane of the Earth to observe the dying of a human being. For after the death of the body *it is easy to examine the separated casing – the insulation layer – and verify the accuracy of the given measurement.* Similarly, for some years to come it will also be possible to demonstrate to human spirits that the thickness of the insulation layer of Darkness which the Eldest employed for their own incarnations also conforms to the given thickness of about 1/2 millimetre.[1]

Both human beings and human spirits who have doubts can thus find proof for the information which is given in "Toward the Light".

Besides, human beings have themselves inquired about the thickness of the insulation layer.

39.

Was there any special reason – for example the location of the Earth – why God chose this globe[2] as the future habitat for the beings of Light that He intended to create?

Yes, there were a great many very special reasons for this choice, but a more detailed explanation[3] will not be given here. Only this can be said: *the Earth's position in the universe was one of the main reasons.*

40.

Even though God's first children were created equal[4] they developed differently. Were they also able, each within their own field of spiritual endeavour, to be of benefit and enjoyment to each other – for example as scientists, poets and artists? And could they attain fame among their brothers and sisters as happens on Earth?

Before the advent of the great schism, the relationship among God's first-created children was perfectly ideal in every respect. They brought great enjoyment and enrichment to one another through their scientific or artistic achievements. They fully acknowledged one another's individual accomplishments without envy, *since envy was, and still is, an entirely unknown concept in God's Kingdom.* But fame as it is known among human beings did not exist among

---

[1]) See "Toward the Light", p. 199:7, and footnote 1 on p. 200.
[2]) See "Toward the Light", p. 6:5 to p. 7:2.
[3]) The reason why a more detailed explanation will not be given is that human beings themselves should be able to think of some of the reasons that formed the basis for choosing the Earth.
[4]) See "Toward the Light", p. 165:9 to p. 166:2.

these brothers and sisters. For a "famous" person on Earth has, as a rule, almost as many enviers as understanding friends and admirers; but as it has already been stated, *envy does not exist* in God's Kingdom.

41.

What was in fact the first sinful thought that made the Eldest vulnerable to the onslaughts of Darkness? And what exactly is the nature of sin?

The first influence of the accumulation of Darkness to which God – unknown to them[1] – exposed His children, after He had spoken[2] to them, evoked in those who were scientifically inclined **thoughts of self-admiration,** and subsequently **feelings of pride.** But at the same time arose **the lust for power,** or in other words, the conviction that their Father would give them dominion over, and leadership of, His contemplated and spiritually weakly-endowed beings of the Light, since *in their own estimation they were much superior* in knowledge and accomplishment *to their more artistically gifted brothers and sisters*. Since the others of God's children were not affected by the accumulation of Darkness that God had separated from its encapsulation in the Light, they were quite unable to understand the special attitude to this question adopted by their scientifically inclined brothers and sisters.

No exact explanation can be given of the nature of sin; only this much can be said: that wherever Darkness – and with Darkness sin – gains hold, there will arise the danger that all that is noble, good and beautiful in the thought may be distorted and destroyed, and that the will may be turned in the direction of evil. Darkness thus has a **distorting, dividing, disintegrating and destructive influence** upon thought and will. But the innermost core of thought and will, which both spring from God's own Being, **can never be destroyed by the powers of Darkness.** *There will thus always be a possibility that a personality destroyed by Darkness can, with the help of God and of the Light, restore and rebuild what has been debased and broken down.*

---

[1]) See the Answer to the following Question.
[2]) See "Toward the Light", p. 7:4.

42.

Why should the leadership of the as yet uncreated beings[1] on Earth have been such a tempting task for the Eldest that their desire for this brought them to defy God's warning and to risk subjugation to the power of Darkness?
Had they learnt nothing of the nature and the power of Darkness from God and His Servants in the course of the preceding millions of years?

The reason why God would give His first-created children the task of leading the immature beings in the process of their development was first and foremost *to provide an occasion for confronting them directly with the influence of Darkness.* He therefore said nothing about whom He would select for the task. Whether this task would be of any importance for them individually, from the intellectual and emotional point of view, God could not know on account of His self-imposed limitation. He had to leave it to them *to form their own thoughts and ideas about the task that He would give them. And He would have chosen those whose inclination lay in the direction of undertaking that work.* But there are various ways in which the individual's desire to lead others can manifest itself, just as the eagerness to undertake such a task can be expressed in very different ways. Had the scientifically inclined of God's children thought thus: that they would much like to be worthy of their Father's trust, that they greatly wished to undertake that work, that they longed to share their knowledge and their joy with immature beings, to open their eyes to beauty and splendour and to awaken their intellectual and emotional life, *then they would have acted rightly, then their thoughts and their wishes would have been pure and unsullied by Darkness.* But they did not think in this way. They did not beware of the Darkness that was upon them; and the first thought of the Eldest upon the problem put to them was thus **self-admiration,** which is the first step on the road to **arrogance** and to **lust for power.** Why it should have happened in this way cannot be explained; for it has its roots in the individual's thought and will, **whose innermost nature is inexplicable, and therefore incomprehensible to human beings.**

With deep and fervent grief God saw that Darkness had overcome some of His children – *and He warned them.* Thus began the great schism between the Eldest and the Youngest, thus began the power that Darkness wielded over the Eldest. And despite all God's warn-

---
[1]) See "Toward the Light", p. 7:4 to p. 8:4.

ings they let Darkness draw them further and further away from Him: deeper and deeper they fell, *more and more did Darkness distort and debase these once so radiantly bright, beautiful and perfected personalities.*

All God's first-created children had received instruction from God and His Servants on the nature and powers of Darkness, and had been given knowledge of the possibilities for evil that it contained. But the knowledge that they were given was not accompanied by experiment. For God did not wish to confront them directly with the influence of Darkness until the time had come that there was *in all probability a justified hope that they would all be capable – by the power of their thought and will – of recoiling from the radiations of Darkness, and thereby gaining the first victory over it.* And had they all emerged unscathed from this first encounter with Darkness and its possibilities for evil, God would then have exposed them little by little to the various radiations of this primal force and let them – under His guidance – experiment with its manifold powers and radiations, *so that they could become acquainted with all its manifestations.*

Although God had informed them that at some point in time – **unknown to them** – He would confront them directly with a separated accumulation of Darkness, the scientifically gifted among His children still let themselves be influenced by its radiations; they failed to resist the evil which met them. And despite God's warnings *not to concern themselves with evil, and not to be overcome by that which it would be unworthy for the self to heed, they did not seek to free themselves from the influence of Darkness.* **God's warnings had been in vain.**

And so it is in life on Earth. Human beings are warned time after time by their conscience, but again and again they follow their own ways, and time and again they succumb to the influence of Darkness, they fall prey to its temptations. Time after time human beings lose themselves *in self-admiration, in pride and in lust for power.* But this fall, these victories of Darkness, draw human beings ever deeper into its power and lead them ever further away from the ways of God. **And only deep-felt grief and remorse can free the fallen from the oppressive bonds and lead them onto the right path back to God.**

43.

How could the Eldest take such great pleasure in the newly-created world around the Earth that for extended periods of time they would absent themselves from God's Kingdom and the company of their brothers and sisters?
Was God's Kingdom not a more perfect habitat than this new world? Or had God's Kingdom become so familar to them that they became afflicted with boredom?

None of God's first-created children has ever felt boredom in the world of the Fatherly Home. *This concept is entirely unknown there.*

Even though the newly-created world around the Earth was like a pearl of great beauty, it could in no way be compared with the splendour of God's Kingdom. For that Kingdom is – in its form, in the variety of scenery, and in its richness of colour – of sublime perfection. But the true reason why the Eldest took such great pleasure in these sojourns was first and foremost that when they stayed in the Home of their Father they felt His grief stream toward them, they felt that their love for Him and for their artistically inclined brothers and sisters had been impaired, *they no longer felt at ease in the surroundings of their Home* and it was for this reason they were drawn toward the small, resplendent world around the Earth. **It became a refuge for them.** For by staying there *they avoided their Father's sorrowful countenance, they avoided the sorrowful reproaches of their brothers and sisters.* And their sojourns in this newly-created world became of longer and longer duration, even though it was slowly transformed by the Darkness[1] that was contained within their nature since their fall. Time and again God called to them and bade them return before Darkness gained complete power over them. But wilfulness bound them, *and thus for a time God had to accept the loss of some of His beloved children.*

---

[1]) Not until later, when the Eldest themselves sought to separate Darkness from its encapsulation in the Light so as to use it for "creation", was the Kingdom around the Earth completely darkened and destroyed. None of its former splendour remained.

44.

When God said to Ardor that if he created beings from Darkness it would enslave him and his helpers until their children had conceived pity for them, was this an arbitrary condition laid down by God for the redemption of the Eldest, or was it a necessary condition, imposed by the nature of Darkness itself, for the release of the Eldest from its bondage?

God knew that if the Eldest succeeded in creating viable beings from Darkness *they would be bound to these children by a life-giving bond*. And shortly before the time that God warned His fallen children against creating from Darkness, He saw that some of the Eldest had begun to yearn for the distant Fatherly Home. And He foresaw that if beings were created from Darkness these Eldest *would turn to Him for help* when they saw how imperfect their creatures were. And in the knowledge that He would at some future time grant this help by giving these creatures thought and will – that is, spiritual life – He warned Ardor *that Darkness would bind him and his fallen brothers and sisters until his creatures had learnt to take pity on them.*

It was therefore no arbitrary condition that God hereby imposed. Darkness by its very nature would bind the creator to his creatures with a bond – a bond that could be loosened only through grief and remorse, *arising either through the "creator's" awakening acknowledgement of the sinfulness of his action, or through the created being's feelings of compassion for the creator who had been overcome by Darkness*. And when God saw that Ardor's personal self at that time was so pervaded by Darkness that he would in all probability be unable to comprehend the enormity of the sinful action he had in mind, *He pointed with His words to a shorter road to grief and repentance for him and his fallen brothers and sisters,* a shorter road created through his own creatures' compassion for him, for his life in the deepest Darkness, in sin and in suffering. For every thought of compassion draws the Light to the person who is the subject of the thought, and the Light that embraces the individual *may then make it possible to break that person's defiance, and in this way awaken grief and remorse.*

45.

Is the significance of the prayer of intercession for the Eldest, which Christ and others of the Youngest were to attempt during their incarnations, due to the condition for Ardor's redemption mentioned in the previous question?

Are the Youngest regarded as Ardor's children when they are embodied as human beings, and was their prayer therefore of greater impact than if it had been said while they were disincarnated?

Ardor and the Eldest had through their fall by no means transgressed against their brothers and sisters, an act of intercession on their part could therefore *not free the Eldest from Darkness;* but it could call forth a help that in the Eldest might precipitate an understanding of their sin against God, and in this way awaken grief and remorse. (Regarding this help see "Toward the Light", page 10:5, and page 174:1).

When God called upon the Youngest to serve as leaders in human embodiment for the creatures of the Eldest – once He had inspirited the "shadows", had given them thought and will – He did this for three reasons: 1) Because He knew that the help the Youngest could offer mankind by being pioneers in every respect could shorten the journey of the human spirits to His Kingdom by several million years. 2) Because the Youngest through their lives on Earth would come to know Darkness in its many and varied forms and manifestations, would learn fully to counter its incursions *and fully to overcome it.* 3) Because once the Youngest were bound to the beings created by Ardor, *they would be equal to the human spirits in knowing pity, that is to say, in feeling compassion for the creator and creators of the human body.* And since all the Youngest without exception loved their fallen brothers and sisters and yearned fervently to win them back, the possibility arose, when they accepted the task assigned to them by God, that one or more of them during an earthly life would take pity on those who had fallen, and through a prayer of intercession call forth the necessary grief and remorse. Intercession would in this way come about at a much earlier time than would be conceivable for a human spirit to attain compassion for the fallen Eldest, and because of this compassion to *pray forgiveness of God for the creator and creators of the human body.* **God thus strove in every way to shorten the road to the Fatherly Home for all the fallen Eldest.**

46.

**Are we allowed any greater knowledge of, and information about, the life and work of our Father's Helpers, the twelve Servants, than has already been given in "Toward the Light"?
And what is the importance of their mighty intellect, their great spiritual knowledge and their love for the work of the Youngest for the development of the human spirits?**

All twelve Servants, or Helpers, of God are mighty personalities. *In appearance they are young and graceful, radiant and bright.* By nature they are *pure, loving, helpful and understanding.* For all time they were, and for all time they will continue to be, the helpers of the Youngest in their so very difficult task of serving as the pioneers of mankind. Time and again these radiant personalities have been the *guardian spirits* and *leaders* of the Youngest during their earthly incarnations, especially in those cases where *anything new within the fields of science, art or invention should be imparted to humanity.*

Before the great schism between the Eldest and the Youngest occurred, God's twelve Helpers served as *tutors* and *educators* for His first-created children, *who all loved them,* both for their kind, affectionate nature and for the knowledge and learning they received through their guidance.

When the great schism had taken place and the twelve beheld the profound, the infinite grief of their beloved Lord and Master, *they all went to the Kingdom around the Earth* in order, possibly through their influence, to call back the fallen children to the Father. But their words were in vain. **The power of Darkness was too great!** Time and again both before and after the creation of humanity they came to the fallen *to speak with them, to awaken their memory of the splendour, the joy and the life in their Father's Kingdom.* Were their words in vain, **they grieved as their beloved Master grieved.** But now and again, when their sorrowful words sounded to the Eldest, when their bright and radiant figures cast a blinding light over the abhorrent scenery of the "ravaged" Kingdom, they succeeded in calling forth the memory of the glorious Kingdom of God in the darkened minds and thoughts of the Eldest. **And then their joy was deep and fervent.** *And they brought back these remorseful, grief-stricken children* **to their Father's embrace.**

When the first multitude of human spirits had fully completed their earthly incarnations and fully released themselves from the power of earthly Darkness, they were brought by the twelve Helpers to one of the distant globes of the Light that God had chosen as their temporary habitat. The twelve Helpers then became by turns *their tutors and educators.* But since that time numerous human spirits – released from rebirth on Earth – have set out upon their journey from Light-world to Light-world toward their Father's Home *under their loving care and guidance.* The Eldest who are interned on distant globes *are also under the care and protection of the twelve Helpers.* Their task is now so great and so comprehensive that several of the disincarnated Youngest take part – between their incarnations – in this work of education, upbringing and protection. The task of the twelve Helpers is now indeed so great *that only one or two at a time can stay in the Home of their Lord, so that* **the burden of loneliness** *does not weigh too heavily upon Him in His vast and mighty Kingdom.*

47.

Since all God's children were created equal, how did Ardor among the Eldest and Christ among the Youngest become so much mightier than their brothers? Will this difference be preserved for all eternity?

Among the more scientifically inclined of God's children Ardor was the one *most advanced in knowledge,* while among the more artistically and emotionally gifted, it was he who is called the eldest of the Youngest *that was the most highly developed.* Influenced by the thoughts of their duals – thoughts of self-admiration and compassion respectively – these two therefore became the *leaders of their respective groups of God's children.* (See further "Toward the Light", p. 181).

The difference which then prevailed, and still prevails, will presumably – it cannot be said with certainty – be eliminated when God's first-created children are gathered with the human spirits in His Kingdom. **But individual differences will, of course, remain through all eternity.**

It is also likely that both the "Eldest" and the "Youngest", as well as the human spirits, *will preserve through all eternity their great love for the eldest of the Youngest, out of their memory of his deep, pure and faithful love for them all, out of the memory of his great patience, which could not be conquered by Darkness, of his great unselfishness,* **his never-failing trust in God's leadership** *and his inner strength and ability to help and sustain wherever his help was needed and desired.*

On the globes of the Light where they continue their development, all human spirits will at some time – millions of years in the future –

be confronted with Ardor and his dual, so that through long acquaintance *they may conceive a deep and fervent love for them both*. And when they have fully learnt to love these two, who were the first and direct cause of the creation of mankind, then they will be able easily and quickly to transfer this love to all the Eldest, even though they may not become acquainted with them until later, as they regain their lost personalities of Light. For long before the time arrives when all the Eldest will have restored their personalities, every human spirit will have fully understood that however hard it was for them to live through the sufferings, sorrows and struggles of their many lives in the earthly world of Darkness, nothing of what they had to endure could be *compared with the misery, sin and sufferings endured by the Eldest*. And on the basis of this understanding there will arise in their mind and thought – however slowly – **a rich, deep, fervent and lasting feeling for their elder brothers and sisters.**

48.

A major typographical error in the Answer to Question No. 48, in the original Danish language edition of Supplement I, was unfortunately not discovered until after publication. It was therefore decided to give the necessary correction at the corresponding point in Supplement II, which was to be published a few months later in February 1930.

This correction has, of course, now been incorporated in the English language edition of Supplement I, thus rendering superfluous any translation of the Danish text originally included at this point.

Translators' note.

49.

Since millions of years passed before the Youngest began to yearn for the Eldest, does this mean that they had become estranged from one another in God's Kingdom?

The love of the Youngest for their fallen brothers and sisters did not lessen because they had withdrawn from them. *They yearned deeply and sincerely for their absent brothers and sisters.* They saw their Father grieve, and they themselves grieved over that which had happened. But they did not understand the full extent of the schism.

And if such a seemingly long period of time elapsed before they turned to God's Servants in order to gain full knowledge of the absence of the Eldest, these millions of years should not be judged by earthly standards. For this number was given so as not to confuse the human understanding of the immense span of time that, seen with earthly eyes, preceded the creation of humanity after the fall of the Eldest – a time during which all earthly possibilities for life were transformed or completely destroyed by the Darkness that streamed in over the Earth. These millions of years must therefore be viewed according to the old adage: *One day is to the Lord as a thousand years, and a thousand years as one day.* However, human beings would be nearer the truth if instead of "a thousand years" they said: *millions of years.* The span of time referred to in "Toward the Light", p. 174:3, which to human perception is so incomprehensible, so immense, was in fact to the Youngest in God's Kingdom but a short period of time.

And what has otherwise been stated in Ardor's Account and in the Commentary – p. 9:14 to p. 10:6 and p. 174:3,4 – does in no way indicate that there *was any coolness* between the Youngest and the Eldest. Never was the love of the Youngest for their fallen sisters and brothers lessened. Not even the suffering of the many earthly lives the Youngest had to endure lessened their love, much rather did the suffering and grief deepen and strengthen it. For through their own pain and sorrow they gained a true understanding of the misery and dismal existence of the fallen brothers and sisters in Darkness and in horror, far away from their common Father. *Through their incarnations they reached an understanding of the life and actions of their brothers and sisters – an understanding* **that they could otherwise never have reached.**

But no human being can conceive of the grief the Youngest in God's Kingdom felt when they knew the truth about the disappearance into Darkness of their fallen, their beloved brothers and sisters, for there will always be one or more elements of selfishness in human grief over deceased, departed relatives and friends. For the Youngest this was not so; their feeling of grief was completely *unselfish, pure, sincere and profound.* Had the opposite been the case, they would never have had the courage – through their earthly incarnations – to engage in a struggle against Darkness in order *to vanquish it* **and to win their beloved, much-missed brothers and sisters back to their life in the Fatherly Home.**

50.

Can the transcendental world furnish a more detailed explanation toward an understanding of the different perceptions of the concept of time? When the Youngest, according to the preceding Answer, felt the absence of the Eldest to be only a short time, did the Eldest in the new world of Light around the Earth then experience this time as millions of years? Or does the perception of time depend on the nature of the intelligences rather than on their location?

The concept of time *is highly relative,* it is extremely different for the various beings and extremely different for **the time-rhythms** of the two primal forces – Light and Darkness. The transcendental world may possibly elucidate this question to a very limited extent, but an exact explanation cannot be given, since even the most gifted among human beings *will be unable to fathom the innermost core of the problem:* **the different time-rhythms of Light and Darkness.**

1) *The two primal forces, Light and Darkness, are each of a different nature,* since the ethereal, spiritual and material oscillations of the Light are based on a very high frequency, whereas the corresponding oscillations of Darkness are based on very low frequencies in comparison with those of the Light. If Darkness is enclosed in the Light, it is drawn forward with the circulation of the Light through God's flaming Being, but it can never keep pace with the strong forward thrust of the Light. Thus it becomes a slowly moving undercurrent in the swift forward surge of the Light-ether. Time for the movements of the ether of Darkness is therefore exceedingly slow compared to that of the Light-ether.

2) *If the Darkness has been separated from encapsulation in the Light-ether,* its movement, its forward thrust becomes slower still, even though the oscillations of polarized Darkness on average are faster than those of depolarized Darkness.

3) *Since God's Kingdom is formed and created from the ethereal-material radiations of the Light,* the concept of "time" in His Kingdom is based on a rhythm which is very different from that of earthly time.

4) *Earthly life is primordially based on the material or molecular oscillations of Darkness,* the concept of time in the earthly world must for this reason become an expression of the slow time-rhythm of this primal force. This must necessarily cause a very significant difference in the perception of time in God's Kingdom and the corresponding concept in the earthly world.

5) *Since the astral worlds around the Earth are based partly on the*

oscillations of astral Darkness and partly, in the case of the higher spheres, upon the oscillations of astral-material Light, there will similarly be differences in the concept of time for the beings who inhabit these transcendental worlds. But none of these time-concepts can be measured against the rhythm of time in God's Kingdom.

6) *The spiritual disposition of the various intelligences must also be taken into account.* The higher the intelligence, the faster is the rhythm of time; so that differences in the perception of time can also arise for this reason. In God's Kingdom such differences were predominant between God and His Servants, and between His Servants and God's first-created children, so that the time-rhythm increased in speed upwards from God's children to God Himself.

7) *Similar differences in respect of the relativity of time apply also in the earthly world.* To a certain extent this is due to the higher or lower levels of intelligence of the beings who live in that world, but there are also other causes.

Let us consider a few examples:

For a young, normal child a "day" is a vast period of time, but a day seems very short for an adult or aged person. If a person is highly gifted and his or her day is occupied, for example, by scientific research or artistic creativity, then the day seems much shorter than it seems to a less gifted person or to an "idler". For a healthy and happy person a day can pass as if it were an hour, while an hour can seem like a whole day for a spiritually or bodily suffering human being.

Relativity must therefore always be taken into account, whether in connection with fixed or non-fixed concepts and determinations of time.

8) *Life in God's Kingdom was splendid, glorious and happy.* The rhythm of time was therefore *swift and fleeting* for God's children.

When the Eldest departed in significant numbers in order to settle in the Kingdom around the Earth, while the Youngest continued to live in the familiar surroundings and environment of God's Kingdom, *the rhythm of time became slower for the Youngest because of their grief for the beloved brothers and sisters who had disappeared.* But they did not understand the reason for this. For the millions of years that elapsed, in terms of earthly time, before they turned to God's Servants to inquire about those who were absent, were experienced by them **as but a short span of time.**

9) *For the Eldest in the Kingdom around the Earth, the rhythm of time slowly changed as Darkness destroyed more and more of their Kingdom.* But since the Eldest were engrossed in restoring their once splendid home they did not become aware of the full extent of

this change in the rhythm of time. Not until they descended to the Earth to investigate the ravage caused by Darkness there did they understand **that the time-rhythm of Darkness was quite different from that of the Light.** And when they had created mankind and become bound to their creatures through the bond of Darkness, they became subject in every way to earthly conditions and concepts of time. **And time became infinitely long for all of them.**

10) *So that the Youngest could more or less accustom themselves to earthly concepts of time,* God was obliged to remove them from His Kingdom and give them dwellings in the sixth sphere around the Earth. And as long as their leadership of mankind's journeying toward the Light continues, so long must they remain there between their human incarnations. An exception is made, however, for the visits they make from time to time to the Fatherly Home, in order to rest and *renew their strength and courage through discourse with God and through His strong and intense radiations of Light.*

No further explanation of this matter can be given from the transcendental world.

51.

In the Answer to Question No. 32 in Supplement I it is stated that human beings must themselves solve the problem of the nebulae. But since the latest astronomical theories suggest that nebulae are extremely distant galactic systems, and therefore cannot belong to the system in which the Earth is situated, cannot some further explanation be given? It is, of course, stated in "Toward the Light" that the nebulae belong to the galactic system in which the Earth is located.

Since the theory that the distant nebulae are galactic systems separate from that of the Earth *is mistaken,* we have obtained permission to answer this Question and to present the facts of the matter.

Huge accumulations of Darkness exist at several places in the ether around the galactic system of the Earth. These accumulations of Darkness were separated by the fallen Eldest at the dawn of earthly time from encapsulation in the ether. *And radiation-images of the star-globes within the region of the accumulations or of the nebulae are caught and reflected in these accumulations.* Just as a raindrop in the earthly world can capture and reflect a "picture" of the sun, so can "pictures" of star-globes be caught and reflected by the accumulation of Darkness surrounding the respective globes, which are few in number in relation to the enormous numbers which the nebulae display in the telescope. **The nebulae are therefore an optical illusion.**

52.

a) In "Toward the Light", page 322, and in the first Supplement, page 23, it is stated that those of the Eldest who still live on Earth will be removed from the globe to astral habitats in one of the other three star universes. Will this transfer take place at the death of the physical body, is it agreed to by the Eldest through their free will, or is it a "compulsory transfer"? They have in the past been unwilling to leave the earthly scene. How can they now agree to be banished immediately after physical death? Or is compulsion resorted to in certain cases?

The removal from the Earth immediately after death of the physical bodies of the Eldest[1] who are still incarnated is definitely not a "compulsory transfer". On the contrary, it is a help which God extends both to the Eldest and to humanity.

When God annihilated the "ravaged Kingdom" (in other words, Hell[2]) at the time of the return to the spheres of the earthbound spirits, all the Eldest were left without a home. God had therefore created dwellings on the distant globes of the Light for both the disincarnated and the incarnated Eldest before He destroyed the Hell-sphere. *Those of the Eldest who, together with the earthbound human spirits, in the year 1911 heeded God's calling were immediately brought to these new habitats, where they may rest in quiet and peace until they enter their earthly incarnations of atonement. When this will take place is not yet known.* These homes that God provided for His unhappy fallen children are bright and splendid compared to the dismal and grim ruins they inhabited in the Hell-sphere. All of them were therefore only too happy to leave the harrowing and oppressive Darkness of the "ravaged Kingdom", which had been their home for millions of years. *There was therefore absolutely no question of exerting pressure upon these beings.* **It was a gift, a help ex-**

---

[1] Incarnated by Ardor. They should not be mistaken for *those* of the Eldest who are incarnated under the Law of Retribution.

[2] See "Toward the Light", p. 100:8 to p. 101:10.

tended by God, and as such it was understood by these Eldest. However, since it is likely that this information will cause some to pose another question, namely, why the Eldest could not be allowed to stay in one of the spheres around the Earth, we shall take this opportunity to explain the reason why this was not possible. Between their incarnations the self-incarnated Eldest stayed partly in the Hellsphere and partly on the astral plane of the Earth, but not in the spheres created by God as habitats for the human spirits during their time of rest and learning. However, *those* among the Eldest[1] who through grief and remorse had bitterly regretted their wilful incarnations, and asked their Father for help and forgiveness, were in the course of time provided with dwellings in the spheres when they returned from their first incarnation of atonement. In other words, *those* of the Eldest who had subjected themselves *voluntarily to the Law of Retribution* were, and still are, considered equal to human spirits, since they must restore their personalities through numerous incarnations. But since *the* Eldest who responded to God's calling in the year 1911 were so numerous that it was impossible to incarnate all of them simultaneously, God provided them with these beautiful, bright and peaceful habitats in order to uplift and to sustain them during their difficult time of self-searching before they could be incarnated under His leadership. (Many of those who have fallen the deepest repose there in peaceful sleep. This is also a help from their Father, since these wretched beings through a long, restful sleep are removed so far from their earthly existence that upon awakening they can with greater calm look back upon their numerous unlawful incarnations, for which they must account to God).

When Ardor had returned, *God reinstated the laws* that He had given for the development of the human spirit, *and which Ardor had upset in order to hinder this gradual progress.* Among these laws was also the so-called *"Law of Sleep".*[2] The remaining Eldest - incarnated by Ardor - will therefore, like the human spirits, fall asleep at the moment of death when their earthly, human bodies cease to function, whereupon they are brought to the dwellings that await them on the distant globes of the Light. And when they awaken from their *"sleep of death",* they will only feel gratitude to find themselves in these bright and pure surroundings. *All the Eldest who are incarnated by Ardor know of this provision*[3] *and none of them has had cause to raise any objections.* And why should they object to

---

[1]) See "Toward the Light", p. 321:5.
[2]) See "Toward the Light", p. 204:4 to p. 205:3.
[3]) They were informed of this during one of their nocturnal sleep releases.

living in light and gracious surroundings rather than in the deep Darkness, impurity and hideousness of the ravaged Kingdom? For it should be remembered *that the Eldest began their unlawful incarnations because their life in the Hell-sphere had become quite unendurable.*

b) How can the Eldest thus be barred from the outer world? They were once able to travel great distances in space, for example from God's Kingdom to the Kingdom around the Earth.

Since the Eldest have been, and still are, brought *to globes of the Light,* and since their thought and their will have for millions upon millions of years *been able to control only the powers of Darkness* and **not those of the Light,** they cannot by the power of their thought and will penetrate the Light-ether surrounding their habitats, even though they were able to move through the Light-ether a long time ago. Nor do they in fact contemplate making any such attempt. By this arrangement – by transferring the Eldest to globes of the Light – God helps both the Eldest and humanity. For since these Eldest cannot reach the Earth, *mankind need never fear an unwelcome invasion of the Eldest that are interned in these worlds of the Light.*

But can this help that God has given both to these Eldest and to mankind be called **compulsion?** *Does not this arrangement that God has made spring rather from His boundless love, both for His fallen children and for the children who strive in the earthly Darkness toward His Kingdom? None of the Eldest, neither the disincarnated nor the incarnated, has raised the slightest objection to this procedure,* and neither should any human being have any complaint against it.

53.

If God does not create further human spirits after the death of the incarnated Eldest, what will happen to the human foetus of the most primitive races, to whom a previously created spirit[1] is not to be bound?

Several of the most primitive races have long ago died out, and others are about to do so. For as "civilization" spreads, many races

---

[1]) Nothing is written in "Toward the Light" to the effect *that an already existing human spirit may not be bound* to a foetus of the most primitive races. On page 313:6 of that work, it is stated that newly-created and young spirits are *mostly* incarnated among the primitive or fairly primitive peoples. There is thus *no compelling* reason for creating new human spirits when the Eldest are no longer bound to their creatures.

that cannot assimilate the benefits of civilization, *but only its evils, will gradually become extinct.* The most primitive of the existing races will therefore not suddenly disappear, but their fertility will gradually diminish, fewer and fewer children will be born to these doomed races, and they will finally die out when God has no further use for them.

In the first sphere there are multitudes of human spirits who have undergone only one or two lives on Earth. *In times to come God can employ these spirits for the binding of a spiritual self to the human foetus of the dying races.*

54.

Will the number of spirits be finally determined with the death of the last of the Eldest, or is it possible that God will continue His creation of new beings in the future?

After the death of the last of the presently incarnated Eldest the number of human spirits will not be increased. The number that will have been attained at that time will then **be the final number of human spirits.**

It is not known whether God may possibly create new beings at some time in the eternal future.

55.

In "Toward the Light" it is written on page 31:8 that "God walked among them, and He spoke to each one". Are the bodily forms of God and the Youngest of the same size as those of human beings on Earth, or must this expression be understood in a figurative manner?

The expression should not be interpreted figuratively but should be taken quite literally.

God walked among His children and He spoke to them.

The figures of God and His first-created children are somewhat taller than the normal height of men and women. When human spirits are released from life on Earth, their ethereal figures will be of the same size as the ethereal bodies of the Eldest and the Youngest.

56.

The mystery of the uncreated is beyond the comprehension of human beings. Does this mean that the question "where does everything come from?" which human thought has asked again and again is unwarranted, because this question does not exist for the more highly developed intelligences, or did not exist for primal Thought?

As it has been stated in "Toward the Light", p. 160:4, there is a possibility that one of the Youngest at some time in the future will in an earthly existence undertake the mission of attempting to explain the riddle of eternity and the mystery of the uncreated. But nothing can be said of the time when this may happen; it could possibly happen in a hundred years, or perhaps thousands of years from now, for it depends on how soon mankind will be guided by the truth that is given in "Toward the Light".

However, one should not say that the question "where...from?" is unwarranted, for humanity is perfectly justified in asking this question. But so long as human beings have not progressed further in their spiritual development, it will be impossible to impart to them any true understanding of this "mystery".

In His state of "primal Thought", God was also confronted with the problems of *eternal life and the uncreated,* and He solved them from the inner knowledge of primal Thought. God's Servants and His first-created children are all fully acquainted with the answers to these questions. But as it has already been stated, it is at present impossible to clarify this to even the most gifted of human beings. Furthermore it should be taken into consideration that there is a limit to what the human brain can register without disrupting the self. It would for this reason be impossible to answer such complex questions through the physical brain of our earthly helper, even if it served merely as a "passage" for the thought-messages received from outside spiritual intelligences. And if we cannot impart to our intermediary even a very partial understanding of the problem, it is of no use giving answers that cannot pass the physical brain, because the individual, the medium who must receive them will be incapable of translating the given thought-answers into words that can be understood by human beings. *The brain of our intermediary has a limited scope.*

The only way in which humanity may receive the solutions to these riddles is for one of the Youngest in a coming incarnation to undertake this task, endowed by God in such a way that the individual from the inner knowledge and with the help of the guardian spirit will be able to explain these problems to others. But until the time comes when this can be done, *human beings must patiently await the solutions to the riddle of eternity and the mystery of the uncreated.*

57.

Before primal Thought and primal Will reacted to the radiations of Darkness was the Thought conscious of itself, so that it reflected the cosmos within itself and conceived thoughts about itself and the surrounding world – Light, Darkness and Will?

Primal Thought and primal Will can each to some extent be regarded as *a conglomerate* – a collection of heterogeneous components. *But their innermost cores cannot be defined.*

Before the time arrived that primal Thought and primal Will reacted to the radiations of Darkness, which contained all possibilities for evil (see "Toward the Light", p. 3:8), *the Thought was not conscious of itself.* But when Thought and Will simultaneously reached the latent poles of the Light they awoke – as also described in "Toward the Light" – *to fully conscious and willed activity.* In the inactive state both primal Thought and primal Will contained "complexes" that could be influenced respectively by the radiations of the Light or by those of Darkness. The Thought thus contained complexes **for the good and for the evil – for a good, splendid, light and harmonious cosmos, and for an evil, hideous, dark and discordant cosmos.**

When the Thought reached one of the poles of the Light, with which it fused, it became fully conscious of itself. It knew **that it contained complexes for the good and for the evil,** it knew **that the evil should be overcome, separated and eliminated, and that the good should be preserved, developed and strengthened.** *It knew* **that it had to strive to achieve a perfect union with its "Will".** When primal Will reached the other pole of the Light, with which it fused, it became pervaded by the radiations of the Light, which purged and eliminated the complexes that were susceptible to the influence of Darkness. But Darkness thereby lost all possible influence over it. And it then became the task of the Will, by virtue of its inherent power of attraction, **to guide and sustain the Thought in its self-purification, and in its struggle out of and away from Darkness.** Each time that the Thought – fully consciously – had eliminated some of its complexes that were susceptible to Darkness, and had thereby drawn nearer to the Will, a reaction occurred – a state of rest – accompanied by an intense desire to cease the struggle. But the ever stronger and ever approaching influence of the Light-Will imparted to the Thought new strength, new courage; and the Thought continued its struggle, continued its self-purification until all complexes that could be influenced by Darkness had been cleansed and eliminated.

In this way primal Thought was purified, in this way it gained knowledge of its own self, gained knowledge of all the various forms and manifestations of evil, in this way it gained knowledge of the impermanence of Darkness and of the existence of the Light through all eternity. And the moment the Thought – infused with, and purified by, the concentrated radiations of the Light – met with the Will, they became united in a harmony of perfect beauty, they became one, an entity, indissoluble for all eternity, an entity which no outside force could break or destroy. (Regarding this question see "Toward the Light" p. 259:3 to p. 260:1).

Thus: *Through all eternity primal Thought and primal Will contained complexes that could be called to life through the radiations either of Darkness or of the Light. But the first reaction to the effect of Darkness caused them to drift, infinitely slowly, further and further away from its influence. And under the influence of the ever-increasing power and radiance of the Light, after its union with the one pole of the Light, primal Thought began its long struggle against Darkness, it cleansed and eliminated the complexes that could be influenced by its radiations.* **In this way Thought overcame Darkness, in this way complete victory was gained over the evil.**

It is not feasible for the transcendental world – through a human being – to give a more detailed explanation of the concepts of *primal Thought and primal Will,* since it will always be very difficult, if not impossible, in an earthly language to find adequate words, expressions or images that are in full accordance with, or that fully cover, these complex questions, abstractions or concepts.

Thus it is not possible in an earthly language to give a more detailed answer to this Question, or to provide a more exact explanation than the one given here.

58.

In the Answer to Question No. 57 it is stated that primal Will led primal Thought out of and away from Darkness. How should this be understood? Primal Thought and primal Will had at that time moved into the Light and become united with its two poles, which leads one to assume that both were beyond the reach of the radiations of Darkness.

In "Toward the Light", p. 159:3, it is stated: *"Between the two primal forces, on the boundary between Light and Darkness, rested the Thought and the Will"*. With this passage as a point of departure we shall attempt partially to elucidate this Question.

The primordial power called the Light rested as a faintly luminous globe[1] in the surrounding Darkness. The shape of the globe was perfectly circular. In this globe of Light rested the two latent "cores of the poles". If one imagines this globe projected as a circle with primal Thought as a tangent at the left, and primal Will as a tangent at the right of the circumference of the circle, *a line can be drawn from the Thought through the core of one pole to the centre of the circle, and from there through the core of the other pole to the Will*. Both cores of the poles in the projected drawing should *lie one third of the distance along the bisecting line – the diameter –* from the Thought and the Will respectively. When primal Thought and primal Will simultaneously responded to the radiations of the surrounding Darkness, their movement into the Light and toward each other[2] began. But at the same time the powers of both Light and Darkness awoke slowly to an ever rising activity. The radiance of both primal forces automatically increased in strength and intensity of energy manifestation each time Thought and Will moved further into the Light. One should therefore visualize how the Darkness that encompassed the globe of Light would, from time to time encroach upon the area of this Light-globe *like gigantic "tentacles"*. These tentacles sent out rays of Darkness over the Thought and the Will in order to draw both of them back, and into the Darkness. When Thought and Will each reached the core of their respective poles with which they became united, these poles awoke from their latent state, became vitalized and were transformed from a "polar core" to a male (positive) and a female (negative) pole, respectively. At the union of

---

[1]) Like the core in the illustrating image of primal cosmos given in the first Supplement, Question No. 22 on p. 46.
[2]) At that moment the Thought and the Will were compared to the seeds in the core, that is to say, the globe of Light. See the same reference as for footnote 1.

primal Will with the core of its pole, it acquired so much strength and energy *that it was able to repel the radiations of Darkness from the right-hand side of the globe of Light.* This primal force thus withdrew its tentacles from the Light and retracted them into itself. But since the Will was still far away from the female pole, it was impossible for it to repel the radiations of Darkness that penetrated the globe of Light from the opposite side of its area. *The tentacles and radiations of Darkness thus pursued the Thought on its way inward the centre of the Light and forward toward the Will.* **And in this way Darkness impeded the self-purification of the Thought.** But sustained by the power of attraction of the ever-nearer approaching pole of the Will, the Thought moved – with longer or shorter pauses[1] – continually forward until its full self-purification was accomplished. (This must be visualized as having occurred in the immediate proximity of the centre). The poles of Thought and Will then moved simultaneously into the centre of the globe of Light – *their union was complete,* **and God arose as a personal Being, as the centre of the universe.**

No further information on this subject can be given from the transcendental world.

59.

Are we in the opinion of the higher intelligences justified in asking why we and the world exist? If so, is it conceivable that primal Thought during its struggle against Darkness asked itself questions concerning the purpose and value of existence?

This question is of course justified, both in the opinion of the higher intelligences and from the human point of view.

When primal Thought was confronted with the possibility of a struggle against Darkness, it asked itself the following questions over and over again: 1) Whether the purpose, the object, of its existence was a union with primal Will, a personal existence – a bodily self within a surrounding world of Light, an eternal life in wisdom, omnipotence, love,[2] beauty, peace and harmony; or 2) a continued

---

[1] See "Toward the Light", p. 160:1,2.
[2] In the event that primal Thought – as an embodied personal being – should create beings predestined for eternal life.

existence as Thought without Will and without embodiment; or 3) an absolute extinction called forth through a life lived in a cosmos of Darkness, in which the powers of Darkness would ultimately cause disintegration and annihilation[1] of primal Thought and primal Will.

Primal Thought weighed the opposing arguments in these questions, it sought to clarify for itself whether *a battle against Darkness was worth fighting in order to achieve eternal life in a sublime and eternal world of Light.* It pondered deeply and to the full on the value of eternal life, and when it had considered all the arguments, for and against, **it resolved to take up the struggle** against Darkness. And from its inner conviction that the goal *of eternal life in wisdom, omnipotence, beauty, peace and harmony* **was truly worth the struggle,** *it continued to strive against Darkness until victory was won.*

Since the spiritual human being *has its origin in God's own Being,* it is *natural* that human beings should also ask themselves questions concerning *the purpose and value of existence.* The purpose of the existence of the human spirit in a "world of Darkness" is fully explained in "Toward the Light". The Eldest – God's fallen children – were responsible for the fact that God did not create beings of Light on the globe He had chosen – the Earth – as had been His thought and purpose. It is also explained in "Toward the Light" why God gave human beings – the imperfect creatures of the Eldest – a spark of His own Being, gave them thought and will, clad thought and will with a spiritual body, and gave the human spirit the gift of eternal life. God did all this to help His beloved fallen children gain victory over the Darkness that in their pride and wilfulness they had drawn forth from encapsulation in the Light. God did all this in the hope that all human spirits would assist Him – by the strength of the thought and the will they had been given – in overcoming a part of the Darkness of earthly life and thereby eliminating it. *And He gave the human spirit the gift of eternal life, that it should have a goal at which to aim, a goal for which to strive,* **a goal for whose attainment to yearn.** But whether this gift is of value to the individual human spirit, must each alone decide. Every human spirit is therefore confronted – when it is mature enough to draw its own conclusions – with the choice: **an eternal life in God's Kingdom or eternal extinction.** The human spirit must then itself decide whether eternal life in God's Kingdom can outweigh the struggle against Darkness, its temptations, its sin and its evil. The decision must be the spirit's own whether to continue in numerous earthly lives – interrupted by the

---

[1]) See Supplement I, Question No. 64, p. 87:3.

death of the earthly body – *to strive against Darkness, overcome it and journey victoriously on the road to God's Kingdom,* **or whether to be extinguished by God for ever.** Human spirits during their sojourn in the spheres have again and again been confronted with this choice, and again and again in the future will they be given the same choice. For the choice is not made once and for all; the possibility always remains open to human spirits – when they have chosen to continue – that after a completed life on Earth they may choose complete extinction. **God compels no one to continue the journey;** *each spirit can therefore always decide for itself whether the cup of suffering has become so full that eternal life in God's Kingdom* **can no longer counterbalance the suffering and misery of earthly life.** But God always extends His help to those spirits who are in doubt regarding this decision, those who are weighed down by the burden of their struggle, weighed down by the temptations, evil, sin and suffering of Darkness. He calls forth before them images[1] of the splendour of His Kingdom.[1] He shows them the life and existence of the first-created children in the Fatherly Home before the great schism between the Eldest and the Youngest. He explains to them what they will gain by striving through Darkness to the Light, and what they will lose if they cease the struggle. **And no human spirit has yet chosen eternal extinction, all have decided to continue their journey until victory over Darkness can be gained.**

60.

Can one say that it would have been better for God and all His children if primal Darkness had never existed so that the cosmos had been entirely a world of Light? Or should one agree with Leibnitz that evil in fact emphasizes the harmony of existence in the same manner that the shadow sets off the light in a painting? Can it be said that Darkness was necessary in order for the spiritual beings in this way to attain a deeper and richer development, and in order for their joy to be more perfect after a victorious struggle against Darkness than it would otherwise have been?

The inquirer has in fact answered these questions.
The example given – the shadow that sets off the light in a painting – is especially well chosen. For a painting without shadow, even if

---

[1]) However, the richness of colour and the radiance of such images are always subdued, since the human spirit would otherwise be unable to perceive them.

executed in pure, bright and beautiful colours, would still remain flat, lifeless and uninteresting to the viewer. Also the old saying that happiness becomes greater against a background of sorrow is perfectly true.

Darkness was necessary in order for a harmonious and perfected personal Being to arise from primal Thought and primal Will. And when God thought to create His first children, He knew that one day he would have to confront them with Darkness, so that through this direct acquaintance they could learn to repudiate its powers and possibilities for evil. For if He did not do this, they would for all eternity be dependent, protected children.[1] They would then never have become fully developed, perfected personal beings, they would never have attained the sublime development of their intellectual and emotional life.

If a human being during life on Earth is able to overcome a difficulty, if the individual can ward off the temptations of Darkness, can overcome a vice or the desire to hurt, sadden or ruin a fellow human being, then the victory - be it ever so small - will always bring joy to the mind, and this gladness will then become a contributing factor to a richer, deeper and more harmonious emotional life. It should not be necessary to provide any examples of this, since most people have experienced such feelings of joy or gladness in their everyday life. Most people have also experienced the feeling of grief and shame when the evil, the Darkness, in life has gained victory over them. But a feeling of grief and shame can also contribute to the development of the human personality; for if these feelings are deep and true, the individual will become more mindful, become more careful in thought, word and action. And if people later succeed in gaining a victory where they formerly failed or were defeated, *then the joy of the victory gained will be greater and richer.* The will for the good and the true grows stronger, the thought and the mind become brighter, the feelings toward others grow more friendly, kind and loving, and individual human beings become **more understanding, more forgiving of the errors, failures, sufferings and sorrows of their fellow human beings.**

Therefore: *Darkness serves to develop that which is good, true, beautiful, loving and harmonious within the spiritual self. The darker and more painful the background for the victory gained, the purer, the brighter, the more harmonious, the more understanding will be the personality of the individual who gained the victory.*

---

[1]) See "Toward the Light", p. 164:1-3.

The heartfelt joy that God's first-created children experienced when they lived in God's Kingdom under His care, attention and leadership can best be compared to the spontaneous feelings of a small human child. Their joy was perfect and sincere, but absolute jubilant elation, the sublime feeling beyond all human conception was unknown to them. The Youngest came to know this feeling the moment they learned *that Ardor, their beloved lost brother, had been redeemed* through *God's forgiving love,* had been delivered through their struggle against Darkness, delivered through *their* victories over the evil and hideousness of Darkness.

Every one of the Eldest and every human spirit will be held fast by this jubilant, sublime feeling *when they enter God's Kingdom* – the Eldest because they have returned to their Fatherly Home, and the human spirits because they have reached the goal of their struggle, the goal of their journeys under the Law of Retribution.

And when all God's children are gathered together in the Fatherly Home, *the faint memory of the horror, suffering, evil and grief of their life in Darkness will for all eternity* **be the background, the shadow that brings out the perfect harmony, the peaceful beauty and the joy of eternal life.**

61.

How can God experience everything – including the future – in the present ("Toward the Light", page 271:2), when, because of the free will of human beings, not even He can know what will happen – as has so often been stated?

The passage to which the Question refers concerns first and foremost *the retrospection of the human spirit within its memory upon the struggle out of Darkness and toward the Light.* In the same paragraph it is also written: *"But to God it is not retrospection* **but experience in the present".** It is thus a review of the past and not a preview of the future that is experienced in the present. Furthermore, it is also written as follows:"...for as He carries all time – finite as well as infinite – in His all-embracing Thought, the concept of time does not exist for Him". Neither *in this passage* is there any question of *a prescience* that depends upon God's knowledge of a progressive series of events. It gives in fact an explanation of the preceding passage: *that the concept of time does not exist for God, so that all recollection of the past is for Him experience in the present.* If it had been the intention to state that God knew in every detail *the* *events* both of the heavenly and of the earthly *future*, this would have been stated more explicitly, for example as follows: and just as God can experience the past in the present, so can He also in the present experience what is to come. But no such statement can be made, for it would contradict reality and be in conflict with the truth. **For the free will of all God's children limits His foreknowledge of all that the future may bring.** The expression "His all-embracing Thought" thus means *that God's Thought encompasses all that was and all that is, but it does not encompass* **that which does not exist,** *and neither does it embrace* **the events that through the future enter into existence, enter into the present.** Because of His children's free will, God is only able *to deduce the events of the future from those of the present.* Yet He carries all time – the finite as well as the infinite – within His Thought; *for He has only given the concept of "time" for the use of all created beings.* Human free will is thus not **a fiction** but **an absolute reality,** *as so often has been emphasized from the transcendental world.* The questioner must therefore have overlooked: 1) that there is nothing in the relevant passage to indicate *that God experiences the future in the present,* as one must suppose from the manner in which the Question was formulated. 2) The following passage must presumably also have been overlooked, the passage in which it is explicitly stated that: *"The concepts of time and space are given by God for the use of all created beings."*[1] **God Himself is thus completely independent of time and space.**

God lives in the present with all His children. From *their* thoughts, *their* deeds and *their* conduct He can see what the near future holds in the earthly sense for the individual, or for nations as a whole. For God cannot know beforehand whether the individual human being will choose for the good or for the evil.[2] Not until the choice has been made – in each individual case – is God able to deduce the earthly future from the earthly present. And then He lays His plans, but again and again His plans and determinations are nullified by the free will of humanity. Thus it is, and thus will it continue to be, **until human beings have learnt to unite their will with the Will of God, have learnt to unite their thought with God's Thought.**

Thus: *the earthly future is known to God only from the conduct of human beings, from their thoughts, their deeds and their choices,* **because He has given every human being – every human spirit – a free**

---

[1] God's Servants are also to some extent dependent on the concepts of time and space. (See "Toward the Light", page 271).

[2] This refers to Ardor's future-images. The images can be read by clairvoyants, so that it might appear that the future has been determined by God.

will. God has thus for a time limited His omniscience and thereby limited His prescience, His omnipotence.

62.

Does the spiritual element of Light originating from the Eldest contain only the possibility of thought, of bringing order? Or does the element of Light also contain the corresponding possibility of will?

The faint current[1] of spiritual Light that during their attempts at creation flowed from the Eldest into the astral counterparts of their creatures – the shadows – did not contain the least suggestion of thought or will. It served only *to bind* the particles of astral Darkness together, *and thereby prevented the dissolution of the counterpart when it was released at the death of the corresponding human body.*

63.

According to "Toward the Light,"[2] God united a spark of His own flaming Being with the astral counterparts – the shadows – of the first human beings. Did this spark contain thought and will, and was it conveyed to the shadows through the stream of Light which binds humanity to God?
And at what time during pregnancy does the binding of the newly-created spirit take place?

The spark of His own flaming Being which God united with each single shadow was thought and will. It was conveyed to them directly, independently of the stream of Light. Some time after God had endowed the shadows with thought and will, He clothed each shadow in a plastic substance of Light,[3] whereupon they were each bound to a human foetus so as to enter the earthly world as beings gifted with spiritual life, that is to say, with thought and will.

Each newly-created spirit is also clothed in a plastic substance of

---

[1]) See "Toward the Light", p. 13:8. No distinction is made in Ardor's Account between spiritual and astral Darkness.
[2]) See "Toward the Light", p. 18:3.
[3]) Regarding this substance of Light see the first and second paragraph of the Answer to Question No. 31 in Supplement II.

Light before it is brought to the Earth to be incarnated. The binding[1] to the foetus takes place during the same period of pregnancy in which all spirits of Light are bound to the human foetus, that is to say, *a period from the beginning of the fourth month to the end of the fifth month.*

64.

Since God created His children after He had arisen as a personal Being, and since He thus created them at a point in time when His Thought and Will no longer contained any complexes of Darkness, the spark of thought and will which He bestowed upon each of His children – the Eldest, the Youngest, and the human spirits – would therefore necessarily be all Light, with no complexes of Darkness. How then could Darkness in any way influence these thoughts and wills of Light?

That portion of the thought and will of the Light that God bestowed upon each of His created beings contained from the first beginning *absolutely no complexes of Darkness.* But in order to explain why these portions of the thought and will of the Light could nevertheless be influenced by Darkness, we must first explain *in what form and under which conditions these portions of the thought and will of the Light were bestowed upon God's children.*

Since God wished to create His children as duals, that is to say, as single beings belonging together in pairs who were destined to fulfil and supplement each other's spiritual being as an expression of the male and female principle of primal Thought and primal Will, but yet endowed each with personal thought and personal will, He had to approach His work of creation according to a plan carefully considered in advance. The portions of thought and will with which God would endow His children, and by whose help they would become independent personal beings, therefore had to be separated from each other, so as to represent one portion of thought and one portion of will extracted from His own firmly and harmoniously merged

---

[1]) During the work of producing "Toward the Light", no direct questions were asked regarding the embodiment of thought and will, or regarding the binding of the newly-created spirit to the foetus. A more detailed account could therefore not be given than the one presented in "Toward the Light", p. 189:3, of the first appearance through earthly birth of a newly-created spirit. However, direct questions were asked as to how the Youngest and the more highly developed human spirits were bound to the foetus; these questions were answered in "Toward the Light", p. 189:4 and p. 201:1. It was left to human beings themselves to form their own conception of the absent link between these two sections. Thus, the information on p. 189:3 pertains mainly to the absorption of the Light-element into the astral counterpart.

primal Thought and primal Will. For if God, at the creation of His children as spiritual individualities, had endowed each individuality with a spark of His own firmly merged primal Thought and primal Will, His children would in a spiritual sense have become *both male and female beings as Himself and His Servants,* and their personalities of Light would for all eternity *have been impervious to the influence of the radiations of Darkness.* But then they would also have remained immature creatures through all eternity, with no prospect whatsoever of fully developing into intelligences of firm will and independent thought, because they would have no knowledge of the radiations, properties and powers of Darkness, as did God's Servants. For as thoughts within God's Thought and wills within God's Will they had experienced and taken part in His struggle out of Darkness. And God therefore gave all His children – both those first-created, as well as the later created human spirits – an absolute free thought and an absolute free will, in other words: the portions of the integrated and fused primal Thought and primal Will that God bestowed upon His children became *separated* while He created them and were **given as one portion of thought and one portion of will.** In the male dual part the element of will was *greater* than the element of thought, and vice versa for the female dual part. But so that none of His children should in the course of time lose their thought or will, God joined these elements with a bond of Light that can never be disrupted, no matter how far they should be separated from each other through the possible influence of the radiations of Darkness. And so as to form an unbreakable union between the male and the female duals God likewise created a bond between each complementary pair. These bonds between thought and will, between the male and the female dual, are spun from the spiritual-ethereal substance of the Light and are therefore invisible, not only in the earthly world, but also in the spheres and in the perfect spiritual worlds of the Light.

Thus equipped and thus protected, *God's children* were created, and for a short time will still be created, *for a life of independence and development continued for all eternity. And even though there is no limit set to the possibilities for development of God's Children* – **they will never be able to attain God's fulness of love, His knowledge or His omnipotence** – *their given portions of thought and will can never achieve so firm, harmonious and united a whole as was formed by primal Thought and primal Will when God arose as a personal Being.* That the union of the individual thought and will of God's children can never exhibit the same harmony as can the nature of God and of His Servants is primarily due to the fact that *the* *male dual's portion of will is greater than his portion of thought, and vice versa for the female dual part.* But through a progressive development, and by virtue of the innate tendency of thought and will to merge with each other, each single individuality must reach a point of culmination *in which the individual's thought and will fuse together to form* **an entity.** And when this has taken place, **the individual is impervious to the radiations of Darkness.** At the moment of merging of thought and will, *the bond between them is eliminated.*

But apart from this merging of each individual spirit's portions of thought and will, the complementary dual pairs will through a gradual development similarly achieve a perfect balancing of each other's lives of thought and will. In other words, since the male dual represents the primal principle of Will and the female dual represents the primal principle of Thought, these two spiritually complementary beings must develop into *exact mirror images of each other.* **Thought and will must be balanced – but they must not fuse;** for if they should do this their bodily personalities must also fuse to form a single personality, whose spiritual nature would be both male and female, in the same way as the spiritual nature of God and of His Servants.

The foregoing explains for what purpose and in what manner God gave separate portions of thought and will to His children; in the following it will be explained how these pristine portions of the thought and the will of the Light could be influenced by the radiations of Darkness.

The reason that God, in creating His children, gave each a separate portion of thought and will was this: *that the innate properties of absorption, attraction and repulsion of the primal Thought and primal Will that fused in God's Being passed at the moment of merging into a latent state –* **a state of rest.** If portions of this firmly merged Thought and Will were bestowed without separation upon created beings, they would therefore remain latent, that is to say, **be impervious to Darkness.** They had therefore to be separated, so that the properties of absorption, attraction and repulsion of each portion of thought and each portion of will *could once more awaken to activity.*

The portion of thought and will that God binds to each newly-created spirit *has its own permanent but hidden centre in the psychic brain of the spirit.* But the portions of thought and will that were given to the first-created children – the Eldest and the Youngest – were much greater than the corresponding portions that were given to the later-created human spirits.

A life of beauty, love and joy was God's gift to His first-created children. But in order that they should become personalities of independent thought and will the hour had to come when they should be confronted with Darkness. And that had to happen before each individuality's thought and will had reached – through its spiritual development – its point of culmination, *the moment of fusion.*

In "Toward the Light" it is written on page 166 that: "After God's children through countless aeons had lived a life of beauty, splendour and joy in their Father's Kingdom, He saw that they had advanced so far in their understanding of the mastery of Will over Thought, and in their understanding of the need to limit the desires of the thought according to the ability of the will to make fruitful and implement, that there was a possibility for them all to emerge with victory from a confrontation with Darkness. He then decided to set them a difficult task – ...". Thus God's children were far advanced in their knowledge of the relationship of thought and will to each other, but each individuality's thought and will had not yet become united. And when God confronted all His first-created children with the influence of Darkness some fell prey to its influence – *because of the distinctive character of each single individuality* – while others remained unaffected by this first attempt. In other words, those individualities who did not recoil from the radiations of the approaching Darkness let their thought and will "absorb" its rays without resistance. But complexes of Darkness were thereby formed in their thought and will, complexes that came into contact with Darkness and *thus formed active areas for the degrading, destructive and divisive properties of that primal force.*

At that time, when God confronted his first-created children with Darkness, the dual pairs had not yet become perfect reflections of each other's nature. In other words each single pair, regarded in the case of the male part as **"will"** and in the case of the female part as **"thought"**, had not yet become fully balanced. But the moment that some of the female duals had succumbed to the thought of Darkness *that their knowledge entitled them to claim leadership of the as yet uncreated beings of the Light,* and their male duals joined in this dark thought, *the balancing between them was completed.* And the moment that God – at a much later time – approached the other children who had not succumbed to Darkness with a request for their help in the leadership of the human beings – the creatures of His fallen children – and the female dual of the eldest of the Youngest, through her desire *to bring this help,* influenced the eldest of the Youngest to step forward with his offer,[1] *the balance between*

---

[1] See "Toward the Light", p.15:11 to p. 16:1 and p. 180:5 to p. 181:2.

them was attained. When all the other Youngest then joined these two, the same balancing of their nature took place. The balancing of the spiritual nature of these male and female duals – both the Eldest and the Youngest – can never be undone through all eternity: **they are and will for ever be a reflection of each other's life of thought and will.** And the moment that the balancing took place – for both the Youngest and the Eldest – *the bond that bound the dual pairs together was dissolved.*

Thus, the balancing of the dual nature of God's first-created children took place long before the elements of thought and will of each individual had fused into an entity.

When God began to create spiritual beings who were destined to become united with the creatures of the Eldest – the human beings – He employed the same method by which He had created the Eldest and the Youngest. But since these beings from the outset were to begin their life in a world of Darkness, God had to endow them with a much smaller portion of thought and will than the first-created children had been given. This was done so that the radiations of Darkness should not have unduly large areas for their influence and activity. However, the given elements of thought and will from the first beginning were, and still are, nothing but **Light.**

Thus God sent, and still sends, the newly-created spirit to its first human embodiment as a perfectly "pure" creature of the Light, **as a true child of God's own Self.** But these pure spiritual beings are bound to impure[1] bodies of Darkness. And since the human body from the hand of its creator is formed and brought to life from a double substance – *astral and molecular Darkness* – and since the spirit that is bound to the body is *connected directly*[2] to both the astral and physical (i.e., molecular) brain of this body, the spirit – the self – can be influenced both from the "inside" and the "outside" through the "life-giving cord".[3] *From within,* that is to say, through the astral brain, the psychic brain of the self – the thought and the will – is influenced by the accumulated and summated matter of Light or Darkness within the human automatic retention, which is **the spiritual inheritance.** From the outside, in other words, through the physical, molecular brain, the self is influenced by the accumulations of Darkness or streams of Light that exist wherever the human being happens to be. But so that God's creatures of the Light are not left to fend for themselves on their ar-

---

[1] In a spiritual sense.
[2] See "Toward the Light", p. 282:3 to p. 288:2.
[3] See "Toward the Light", p. 189:4 and p. 278:4.

duous journeys in the human world, the child, as so often explained, is accompanied by a guardian spirit, which is the human conscience. With love, gentleness, patience and care the guardian spirit watches over its charge and seeks in all ways to sustain, guide and correct the child's faltering, uncertain foot-steps in the earthly world of Darkness. If the human being – as a spiritual personality – from the very beginning and at all times in the various circumstances of life would not only listen to *but also follow the guidance of the conscience,* the spirit bound to the human body would after the ending of each incarnation return to the home in the spheres **as pure in thought, in mind and in will as when it was sent to its first incarnation.** But the newly-created spirit's portions of thought and will are each as but a faintly glowing ember compared with God's "blazing" Thought and Will. And instead of heeding the promptings of its ever-alert conscience, the self allows itself to be influenced by the impulses of Darkness and the fantasies and images of thought coming both from within – from the astral brain – and from the outside – through the physical brain. Through the "life-giving cord" the spirit absorbs in its thought and will the inner and the outer Darkness, *which is then deposited there as* **complexes of Darkness.** But through the complexes of Darkness received in this way the thought and the will of the self are separated from one another, *the bond between them is slackened.* And with the help of these absorbed complexes of Darkness, active areas are also created in the human spirit for the debasing, distorting, divisive and destructive abilities, radiations and forces of Darkness. *The will becomes ready to draw the thought toward sin, evil, wickedness and misdeeds, and the thought lets itself be drawn in* **the direction determined by the will.**

Should God's creatures during their human existence never have the strength of their thought and will increased through a direct infusion[1] of Light from God, the spiritual self – because of the continually repeated incarnations – would soon be completely abandoned to the powers of Darkness; it would succumb to sin, evil and misdeed, for the spiritual armament of the self would then be too weak to offer an effective resistance. The spirit bound to the human body therefore receives additional Light from God at each rebirth. This infusion of Light strengthens the thought and the will, that is to say, *it awakens the ability and the desire to offer resistance,* so that the thought and the will become more and more capable of repelling the Darkness coming from both within and from without. Gradually, as

---

[1]) See "Toward the Light", p. 188:5 and p. 322:2.

the successive incarnations increase this capacity, desire and strength to resist, an active reaction against the Darkness will be created. The will awakens to an active movement toward the Light, and slowly the thought is influenced to follow the direction given by the will – the purification of the self begins, that is to say, *the absorbed complexes of Darkness are eliminated, as the self gradually overcomes the evil, the wicked and the sinful in its nature.* And through the continually progressing earthly lives, the moment will eventually arrive when the forward movement of both thought and will toward each other **will result in a union.** As a rule, the incarnation in which this occurs will be the last for that particular spirit. For once all complexes of Darkness have been eliminated, so that thought and will form **a solid entity, Darkness will have nothing on which to work its influence.** *But not all human spirits have succeeded in expiating their karmas to the full when this point of culmination in the life of thought and will within the self has been reached. Their karmas must then be expiated in one following incarnation, or in a few following incarnations,* **whereupon Christ releases the spirit from all future life on Earth.**

Cleansed and purified, the released spirit enters its further development on the globes of the Light. The duals will accompany each other during this development. Two and two the human spirits progress from Light-world to Light-world toward their Father's Home and Kingdom. The one, the male – whose nature represents **"will"** – and the other, the female – who represents **"thought"** – must in this close relationship attain a perfect reflection of each other's life in thought and will.

The lives of the human spirits in the glorious worlds of the Light correspond to the lives of the Eldest and the Youngest during their first many millions of years in God's Kingdom. The duals will come nearer each other's life with respect to thought, feeling and will. Gradually, the duals attain a purer and clearer reflection of each other's nature, *while retaining their own thought and will, which have become firmly merged through their lives on Earth. And when the perfect balance of the duals has been reached, the bond between them is dissolved* – **they enter God's Kingdom, and their Father will then receive His children and bid them welcome out of His deep and His rich Fatherly love.**

At the time when all the Youngest promised their Father to become the pioneers of mankind, the nature of these male and female duals was – as already stated – balanced, *but their individual thought and will had not yet merged into* **an entity.** This union therefore had to be attained during their earthly incarnations while they worked for humanity. As human beings they were thus to gain knowledge of Darkness, were to learn to struggle against its temptations, against its influence in all aspects of life, in order to conquer it *and become perfected personalities.* But at the same time they should lead the human beings forward spiritually and in every way seek to counteract the influence of the Eldest on the earthly, the human situation. **An exeedingly difficult task!** But the Youngest were for this reason very often of a *divided* nature and *unsure* in their conduct, which must be attributed to the struggle of their incompletely merged thought and will against the Darkness within the self, as well as that in the earthly environment. For they must dispel – as must the human spirits – through numerous incarnations all the complexes of Darkness that during their first many earthly lives were formed in the individual thought and will of the incarnated Youngest, *until the point of culmination has been reached when the individual thought and will form* **a merged entity.** Numerous of the Youngest have in the course of time attained this union of thought and will, *but they will continue their incarnations for as long as their Father has need of their help.*

When the Eldest succumbed to the onslaughts of Darkness, the nature of the male and female duals – as has already been stated – was also balanced the moment the fall took place. *But the individual thought and will of these beings, like those of the Youngest, had not merged at that stage of their existence.* And the complexes of Darkness which at the fall were formed in their thought and will were continually increased through the subsequent deeper and deeper falls – **especially through their arbitrary and unlawful incarnations.** Those of the Eldest who returned[1] to their Father sooner than the others and who had not taken part in the unlawful[2] incarnations regained – under God's care and protection – their personalities of Light, which had been distorted and destroyed under the influence of Darkness. This purification of the self took place in the habitats that God had provided for them, and as the purification and elimination of the absorbed Darkness progressed, *the thought and will of these Eldest drew closer and closer to each other. And when the complete purification had been attained, their individual thought and will* **became one.**

But those of the Eldest who were guilty of the unlawful self-incarnations must all – *under the Law of Retribution and under the guidance of God* – struggle out of Darkness through numerous earthly rebirths and thus regain their lost personality of Light. In

---

[1] See "Toward the Light", p. 14:12 to p. 15:5.
[2] See "Toward the Light", p. 23:8 to p. 25:14.

other words *the struggle will continue until the point of culmination is reached when the individual thought and will* **form a solid entity.**

God thus created, and will for a short time continue to create, all His children as duals, the male part **being an expression of the primal principle of Will,** *and the female part* **an expression of the primal principle of Thought.** *These duals are mutually bound by a spiritual-ethereal bond,*[1] **which is dissolved at the moment the dual parts exhibit a perfect balance between each other's lives of thought and will.** *God gives all His children* **an individual thought and will** *at their creation – in the case of the first-created He gave* **a larger,** *and in the case of the human spirits He gives* **a smaller spark** *of His own firmly and harmoniously merged primal Thought and primal Will. But so that His children can become independently thought-creating personal beings with an independent will, God separates the given portion of the Thought-Will that is fused in His own Being, so that the gift* **takes the form of one independent and free portion of thought and one independent and free portion of will.** *These parts are, however, linked together by a spiritual-ethereal bond,* **which acts as a correlating channel.** *Every one of God's children, under the influence* **of Darkness** *and through struggle* **against Darkness,** *must attain a certain point of culmination* **at which individual thought and will merge and form an entity.** *When this point of culmination is reached,* **the bond between the thought and the will is dissolved, and the child emerges as a personality that is in all respects strong in the Light, and that for all eternity will remain impervious to the radiations and manifold powers of Darkness.**

When explanations must be given from the transcendental world of such difficult and important problems as those raised by the foregoing Question, it is not always easy – in earthly language – to separate *abstractions from realities* in a complete and fully understandable manner. The words, expressions and images employed will therefore not always be capable of precisely defining the reality and truth of the matter to be explained. It is stated in this dissertation, for example, that in order for His children not to lose the portions of thought and will that were given to the psychic brain of the self, God linked these portions with *a bond*. No one should imagine that the thought, or possibly the will, could therefore disappear in some mys-

---

[1]) These spiritual-ethereal bonds are based on various ethereal oscillations, whose frequencies are varied in such a way that the bonds never collide with one another.

terious way from the psychic brain of the self, *for example* through *elimination by Darkness;* **for such can never happen!** These words are intended to illustrate that in order to help His children, and to facilitate the mutual attraction and interchange between the individual thought and will, God bound them together, or in other words, *reinforced their capacity for mutual attraction.* But even though this can only be comprehended by human beings as an abstraction, it is nevertheless a reality. The bond between thought and will – like the bond between the duals – *is an absolute reality, seen from the standpoint and with the knowledge of God and His Servants.*

The answer to this Question thus cannot come any closer to the reality than has been attempted here, **for behind all apparent abstractions lie absolute realities.** But that which should be the main endeavour of human beings – even though they cannot fully understand the explanations given – is this: **to strive toward the goal of becoming personalities of the Light,** *or in other words, to strive in all the circumstances of life to direct the thought and the will toward the Light, toward truth, love and compassion. They must endeavour in spirit and in truth to be God's children,* **to become expressions –** *albeit as pale reflections –* **of His pure, loving and exalted Being.**

65.

Does the faint spark of thought and will that the newly-created human spirit receives from God have the inherent strength to grow spiritually? Or is it augmented at each new incarnation with new portions of God's Thought and Will? When did our God and Father implant the seed[1] of love in the human mind?

That spark of thought and will that God gives to each newly-created spirit must be developed through the many incarnations under the influence of the two primal forces of Light and Darkness. The portion of God's Thought and Will once given is not augmented through new additions, but the stream[2] of Light that binds humanity to God strengthens the faint spark of thought and will at each new incarnation, in other words, *it reinforces the ability of the human spirit to recoil from the influence of Darkness;* and it thereby becomes easier and easier for the will to offer resistance to the various phases of the radiations of Darkness, and to overcome its influence.

---

[1]) See "Doctrine of Atonement and the Shorter Road", p. 38.
[2]) See "Toward the Light", p. 188:5, and p. 322:2.

The seed of love – the ability to express love – is given simultaneously with thought and will. **It is implanted as a basis for the emotional life of the human spirit,** which is an infinitely faint reflection of God's own emotional life. (No further explanation can be given).

66.

a) Life on Earth and in its spheres is apparently more burdensome than life in the worlds of Light where, for example, there is no suffering due to separation and death. But a longer succession of incarnations would seem to indicate that the human beings who are presently on Earth and in the spheres must be subjected to the so often very difficult earthly conditions for a longer period than were the generations previously released from the Earth. Thus, the human beings who were released in the past seem to have had an easier lot than those of the present. How can this be explained?

As sin and atonement will always be properly balanced, it should be obvious that the human spirits who during their earthly lives have sinned to a lesser degree *also have less to atone for,* whereas the human spirits who *continually oppose the promptings of their conscience* during life on Earth must clearly have more to atone for than those who only *occasionally* act against their conscience. Furthermore, it should be remembered that the generations[1] of the distant past lived under far more difficult conditions than did the later generations. They also endured temptation, grief and suffering, as have all succeeding generations up to the present day. *Consequently, neither in this case is there any injustice whatsoever on the part of God.*

b) The Youngest would for the same reason seem to live under far more burdensome conditions than any human being, inasmuch as the Youngest are "condemned" to remain bound to the plane of the Earth for millions upon millions of years, while many of the human race have long since been transferred to globes of the Light. Also in this case does there appear to be inequality, not to say injustice.

Neither in this case is there the least injustice.
It is stated in the Question that the Youngest are "condemned" to

---

[1] All the spirits who have been released from the Earth underwent their earthly development during the period of time between the first incarnations of the Youngest and the unlawful incarnations of the Eldest.

remain bound to the plane of the Earth for millions upon millions of years! How can the term "condemned" be applied in this case? Who has "condemned" the Youngest to carry out their task? *Certainly not God!* Is it not clearly explained in "Toward the Light"[1] that the Youngest of their own free will promised their Father to lead humanity to His Home and Kingdom? Is it not understandable that by undertaking this work they had to live their earthly lives *under the Law of Retribution,* the law under which the development of the human spirit takes place? The Youngest submitted *to the Law of Retribution* **of their own free will,** that is to say, that if they transgress against the human beings they are to lead, or if they sin against their Father or the divine within the self, *like all other beings created by God they must of course atone for what they have sinned.* **Is there any injustice in this?** Do not ever forget *that we, the Youngest, have promised our Father to help His immature children find the way to their rightful Home; we have promised to ease, in many and various ways, the journeying of our immature earthly brothers and sisters. And we shall continue to be of help to our Father, shall continue to be of help to mankind so long as our help is needed, so long as it is necessary* – **even if this help causes us grief, disappointment and suffering.** But no one has "condemned" us to undertake this work of love and compassion. And if we had been "condemned" to carry it out, *what value would our work have for humanity or for ourselves?* **All our efforts would be utterly worthless!** For only the actions *that spring from an absolute desire within the self to help and sustain, only the deeds that spring from the deepest love and compassion* **can be of everlasting value to the helper and to those who receive the help.**

c) One can also consider those of the Eldest who have never been and never will be incarnated. They also seem to achieve their development in an easier and less demanding manner than either the Youngest or the human beings. How can it be said that an exact and just balancing of the length and difficulty of the journey has taken place in all these cases?

How can *any injustice whatsoever on the part of God* be found in these circumstances? On the contrary, would it not be an inconceivable injustice *if God had treated all the fallen Eldest alike? Those* of the Eldest[2] who in response to God's call returned from the

---

[1]) See "Toward the Light", p. 15:6 to p. 16:4.
[2]) See "Toward the Light", p. 14:16 to p. 15:5.

"ravaged Kingdom" long, long before the others began with grief and remorse to think of their evil deeds, these Eldest, who never broke their Father's Law of Incarnation, never took part in the wilful incarnations of the others, if they should be judged by God alike with the more deeply fallen Eldest, *then would God in truth be unjust!* **But God is not unjust!** And for this reason those of the Eldest who returned to God when He called, before the arbitrary incarnations began, were not incarnated and never will be. They have long since rendered their account to their Father, their guilt of sin has been forgiven and obliterated, since they themselves – but with their Father's help – had dispelled and overcome the Darkness and sin that had broken down their personalities. And so as to atone for their previous evil deeds against humanity, they offered[1] their Father of their own free will to participate in the education of the human spirits in the spheres, and to assist the Youngest by acting as guardian spirits. God accepted this offer long ago and assigned them various tasks within these areas, *so that these Eldest have now become assistants of the Youngest.*

The length and difficulty of the path of development **depends fully upon the individual's own free choice.** But can God be blamed if many of His children choose, spiritually speaking, to make long and arduous detours on the road to His Kingdom? Can God be blamed that His children cast themselves into the chasms and bottomless pits of Darkness? Can He be blamed that they blindly, carelessly, thoughtlessly and heedless of the voice of conscience leap over ditches and fences into the clinging mire of impassable marshes? Can God be blamed that His children cast themselves into the maelstroms of earthly life, or seek to clamber over steep rocks and mountains instead of keeping to life's beaten path?[2] No indeed, no one has the right to reproach Him, for in this He is blameless. For it must be remembered *that He has given every single child a free will,* **freedom to do good or to do evil.** It is thus self-evident that those who voluntarily – despite the guidance of their conscience[3] – *choose the longer road to the Fatherly Home must face a longer and more difficult journey to their destination than those who travel directly toward the goal.*

But why constantly assume *that everything that is given in "Toward the Light" concerning the acts of God and His laws is based on* **injustice?** For it is incomparably easier to understand that

---

[1]) See "Toward the Light", p. 318:6.
[2]) Refers to the conscience.
[3]) God was the "conscience" of the Eldest until – because of the Darkness – they could no longer hear His voice.

work *if trust in God's absolute justice is taken as the basis for all the information that is given there. And if everyone should act in this way, there would be no question of any prejudice causing everything to be judged and criticised from a mistaken point of view.* **If God's justice** *were made the firm, unshakable foundation for the judgment of "Toward the Light", it would soon transpire that* **no human being nor any spiritual being has ever been, or ever will be, confronted with an unjust action or an unjust disposition on the part of God.**

67.

It has been said that material causality and the laws of the conservation of energy and matter would render impossible God's intervention in earthly life or in the world order in general. It is written in "Toward the Light" that God has ample means at His disposal. Can this be explained in more detail?

Since God is both the Creator and the Keeper of the world order, and since He gave the laws both for material and for immaterial life, He must self-evidently be able – by virtue of His knowledge of these laws – fully and at all times to govern them and to observe these laws without breaking them.

When the Eldest[1] in the past drew enormous masses of Darkness out of encapsulation in the ether, this Darkness streamed over the Earth, whose germinating and budding life was subject to the laws given by God for its growth and continued existence. But even though Darkness ravaged, coarsened and made ugly all life called forth by God, *it was still not powerful enough to annul completely the laws[2] that He had established for life on Earth.* And through these laws God was, and still is, connected with the matter visible to human beings. Infinitely slowly and almost imperceptibly – through millions of years – a steadily increasing order has been called forth under these laws in the purely material conditions on Earth.

However, concerning material causality and the conservation of energy and matter, human beings do not yet have full knowledge of *the true reason[3] for cause, effect and continued existence.* **For the energy of the Light is eternal,** *whereas the energy of Darkness is*

---

[1] See "Toward the Light", p. 9:6-12.
[2] Regarding the Corona of Light see "Toward the Light", pp. 261:1 to 263 – 265:3 – 266:2 – 269:1 – 272:3 – 272:4 – 273:3 – 295:5 to 296:1.
[3] The true cause can be learnt for the first time in "Toward the Light", in the information given about the Light-corona.

transient. And if Darkness – when it streamed in over the globe at the fall of the Eldest – had been powerful enough to annul completely the laws which God had given for the then existing life of the material Light on Earth, *that life would have ceased[1] long ago*. For only through the eternal energy[2] of the material Light is earthly matter constantly supplied with new energy[3] *as replenishment for the loss of energy suffered*. The cause of the continuity and energy of earthly-material life **must therefore be sought in the law of the eternal energy of the Light.** *This is one way in which God maintains a connection with, and influence upon, earthly-material life and earthly conditions.*

But the most important connection goes through the energy of *spiritual Light that is also eternal.* God can, if He so desires, intervene by His Thought wherever His help is needed or desired. But all takes place under the laws of the Light that in many ways intervene, or may intervene, in temporary earthly-material life. Even though human beings refuse to acknowledge God's supremacy over all life – be it spiritual, Dark-material or Light-material – **His Power is still undisputed and everlasting.** And not until human beings include God and His laws in their considerations will they be able to achieve a clear view of either the world structure or the world order, *and not until then will they be able to reach the true core of* **cause, effect, their interrelation, energy and continued existence.** But it must be clear to all that it is impossible from the transcendental world to provide any survey of the laws that for a time bind the earthly-material Darkness to the material Light, and through this to the eternal energy of the Light and to God. *Human beings must be satisfied with the clear explanations regarding these matters given in "Toward the Light", and with this as a basis continue their search.*

68.

The view has also been presented that the doctrine of a free will would be in conflict with the theory of energy in the field of physiology. Does this present a problem and, if so, how can it be solved?

A great many things on which people base their points of view must be changed before they enter into a true relationship to reality. **For not all theories are irrefutable truths.**

---

[1]) See "Toward the Light", p. 266:3 to p. 267:1.
[2]) Dependent on the ethereal Light-corona.
[3]) See "Toward the Light", p. 273:3 to p. 274.

The only answer to the foregoing Question is that not only human will, but also human thought[1] is completely free and individual. All the previously given information and the information in this Supplement on the absolute freedom of individual thought and will, and also the information on the spiritual and physical heredity[2] of the individual, should enable qualified people – on the basis of this work – to reach the right conclusions. The problem that this question might present must therefore be solved by human beings themselves.

69.

Some people believe that God is so exalted, so "hallowed" and so remote that human beings cannot make contact with Him and that consequently the concept of "The Father" cannot be rightfully applied to Him. Is there an answer to this?

"Toward the Light" is presented to humanity so that all can know the relationship that the true God – *and not a divinity formed by human thought* – has to each human being and to life on Earth.

Whatever concepts human beings formed in older times, or still form in the present, regarding God and His nature, *the concepts held* by the individual will always characterize the individual's *own spiritual level*. The various levels of development possessed by human spirits determine that human beings themselves are at widely differing stages of maturity in their spiritual development. The greater the spiritual maturity expressed by the individual in its nature, its thoughts, feelings and its actions, the better will it be able in its religious life to comprehend God as *the Father,* as *the Creator of the spiritual self*. But if the individual has only advanced to a relatively low stage of spiritual development, as is the case with most human beings, then God will appear so remote, so unapproachable, that the individual can perceive nothing of His rich, deep and boundless Fatherly love. *God is then surrounded by a translucent halo of mystery and holiness.* He becomes arbitrary in His actions, indefinable and unpredictable in His hidden and incomprehensible nature; His personal Being is dissolved into nothing and replaced by a vague unreality – in short, **the individual human being cannot comprehend Him.** And this results in the fear of God in its worst

---

[1] See Question No. 64 in this Supplement.
[2] Concerning the relationship of the three brains to the psychic and the physical areas, see "Toward the Light", p. 274:4 to p. 289:4.

form – **servility.** Or else the feelings of the self in religious respects become stunted, and it becomes indifferent to the thought, the idea of the existence or non-existence of God.

For when God in His relationship to humanity apparently fails to evince justice, and lets, for example, *"mercy"* or *"choice"* determine whether the individual shall be blessed with an eternal life in beauty, splendour and joy, or whether it shall be abandoned to Darkness and suffering, then many will clearly become indifferent in their relationship to God, since they can of course do nothing themselves to alter such predeterminations. For the one who – *like the potter's vessel unto honour* – is destined to be good, **is good,** and the one who – *like the potter's vessel unto dishonour* – is destined to be evil and wicked, **is evil and wicked in life.** And why should individual human beings then seek to better themselves, seek to cleanse themselves of sin and evil? Individuals *are and will remain* wicked and sinful, *because they were created as* **vessels unto dishonour!!** But to many people "belief" in the death of atonement of Christ then appears as *the only possible means of salvation.* Through belief in Christ *as "Saviour",* through belief in *the "Mystery of the Cross",* through trust in the mercy of *God, a door is opened to the Kingdom of Heaven* to those who would otherwise *be denied admission,* a door which the faithful *can now slip through.* **Foolish thoughts!** *Expressions of the timidity of spiritually primitive human beings before God, expressions of their dark conception of His Being, expressions of a* **"heathen" way of thought.** But those individualities, whose spiritual maturity and development greatly exceed that of the spiritually primitive, have thus assumed *a grave responsibility* by leading the spiritually immature into these misconceptions and misunderstandings of God and of His nature. For from their inner knowledge, from their sense of logic, **they must know** that the concept of God in the Christian teachings does not accord with the truth, does not accord with the nature of God. And with the knowledge that many of the more highly developed intelligences possess of the "heathen" religions they must know that much of Christianity derives from heathen conceptions, **they must know** that the dogmas of Christianity *are influenced by the thoughts of heathen times and thus cannot be and indeed* **are not in contact with the truth.** But so long as those who should be the leaders of the immature do not purify the teachings of Christianity and do not give the spiritually young a clear and truthful summary of *what is proclaimed in* **"Toward the Light"** *about God, His nature and His relationship to humanity,* so long will the fear of God, servility and indifference not be changed into *true love for God, true submission to His care, with trust in His just* *guidance, or into true yearning for Him and for life in His Kingdom.* And before this happens the immature cannot achieve a true understanding that every individual human being – **with the help of God** – *must cleanse the self of sin and Darkness.*

But even though all should at some future time attain some understanding of God's nature, and be able to comprehend His Fatherliness, His love, care and justice, this does not mean *that individuals should place themselves on a level with God.* For even though He fully participates in the sorrows, sufferings and joys of human beings, *He is and remains the pure divinity, exalted over all that is of the Earth.* He is and will remain the distant Father of mankind – **though near in thought and in prayer** – to whose Home and Kingdom *the journey's road is long and arduous.* Therefore shall none *abuse God's exalted Being,* neither in thought nor in word, *none shall trail His love, gentleness, compassion and justice in the dust.* For though God is Fatherly, gentle and loving in His nature, **He is also firm and masterful in His demands.** He demands *that His children should live a life in truth, in mutual peace, love and purity, that is to say, purity of thought, of mind and of feeling.* He demands *that each individual human being, by virtue of the thought and the will that He gave it, shall cleanse the self of sin, of evil and of the impurities of Darkness.* And no human being has therefore the right to speak of the *"small holy flock"* nor of the *"Communion of Saints",*[1] nor to consider himself or herself *included in any such designation or concept.*

"Hallowed be thy name!" *Thus sounds to human beings the ancient prayer Jesus taught his disciples. Jesus himself loved God as his Heavenly Father, yet he clearly felt God's purity and exaltation over everything pertaining to the Earth, and this feeling was translated in the human thoughts and words of Jesus into the wish* **that the expression, the name**[2] **of God should be "hallowed" to human beings.** *That is to say, no one should take God's name in vain, and no one should ever curse or swear in His name.* **And indeed so it should be – or so it should become – for each and every human being.**

---

[1]) Refers to the article of faith.

[2]) It should also be noted here that in certain of the more ancient religions, the name of the divinity was too "sacrosanct", too hallowed to be spoken. As a result it was replaced with various other forms of expression.

70.

Can one rightfully call "Toward the Light" a religious system like all other religious systems, even though this is the most perfect one of the kind?

If a comparison is drawn between "Toward the Light" and all other existing religions, one problem will immediately present itself to any truly thoughtful person, and it will be quite inconceivable to that person if he or she does not accept the explanation given in "Toward the Light" of the way in which this work was produced and brought into the earthly world. The problem is that the entire Message, including the two Supplements and "The Doctrine of Atonement and the Shorter Road" is presented in an exceptionally beautiful, clear, logical and ethically irreproachable form. How is it possible for one single human being – *even if that person were a genius* – to create from the self a religious system so perfect in every respect? This is the point at which most people stop! And since they do not *wish* to trust the explanation of the way in which "Toward the Light" has come to be produced, they dissociate themselves from it, for they will not search to the depth of its truths. And for this reason one receives such answers as *"it is a religious system like all others"*, or *"it stems from the subconscious"*. This is the easiest, the quickest way – such is their hope – in which to dispose of this highly bothersome work. *For regarded as just another work by human beings it means nothing to the common populace.*

But let us examine more closely the question of "Toward the Light" compared with other religions.[1]

No existing religion, even the most primitive, has ever entered into human life in its completed form. They all have a first, a definite source;[1] they are born as vague, often indefinable, random thoughts, ideas and feelings that grow stronger, become ordered – as far as this is possible – gradually cease further development and emerge as definite religious views, dogmas, acts and ceremonies. The person who within each religion or the various religious sects was the first to bring new thoughts, new ideas in these areas was normally able to give only a more or less schematic outline of the teachings that form the foundation for the emergent religion.[2] After the death

---

[1]) i.e., all older religions. Since the more modern so-called religions are all more or less derivatives of the older ones, these "sects" are not considered here.

[2]) This does not refer to the "sages", who during their human existence in one nation or another expressed to their fellow humans their own conception of the world and their views on life and its phenomena. Even though certain truths or glimpses of the truth exist in profound writings of this kind, they also suffer from shortcomings and misconceptions. These sages cannot be regarded as religious founders in the full meaning of the word.

of the founder his disciples usually continued to develop and promote this system of thought according to their own perceptions. Some sought to adapt their heritage in some direction of their own choice, others forgot what their teacher had said on certain subjects and spoke from their own thoughts and opinions. Yet others laid quite new – often erroneous – interpretations upon the teachings of the founder. After the passage of a certain time – often the passing of one or more generations – the adherents[1] began to write down what had hitherto been passed on by oral tradition. Again new formulations were devised, new additions and alterations made in various directions and within various areas of the particular religious system. In other words, religions[2] were slowly evolved according to the needs and desires of successive generations until they hardened into dogmatic formulas, postulates and doctrines. Each individual religion thus became a system that was sacrosanct to its adherents. Even in the most complete and consistent systems there were many changes and additions in the course of time.

But "Toward the Light" did not come about in the manner described above, *for this work was compiled from the direct questions of human beings,* and these questions *were answered directly by purely spiritual intelligences – by disincarnated individualities.* They have been answered **according to God's wish, at His direction and under His guidance,** *for which reason the answers given must be in accordance with the existing order.* **And since God is Logos itself,** *it goes without saying that there must be order, sense, clarity and logic, in short –***system***– in the answers to the Questions that have been asked.* But this Work is not a religious system like all other religious systems, inasmuch as it has not evolved from generation to generation. In its present form this Work *has been given over a certain number of years by transcendental individualities through the co-operation of an intuitively gifted human being.* **That which has been given is the truth, the absolute truth that can never be changed, nor will it ever be changed by the transcendental world,** *even though human beings refuse to accept this Work, refuse to acknowledge it as being an expression of the truth. Indeed, even if people "invent" new systems which – in their opinion – are more in agreement with their conceptions of the divine, of the religious, of the ethical life and the world order,* **it still does not alter the existing**

---

[1]) Only rarely – in the case of the older religions – has the founder personally expressed his thoughts and religious opinions through the written word.

[2]) The quite primitive religions, such as those of the savages, have been passed on only by word of mouth through the shaman and medicine man of the tribe. But also in these cases have there been additions and changes in the course of time.

state. But although "Toward the Light" and the related works are expressions of eternal truths, God will never – *by decree* – compel human beings to acknowledge that which has been given, or to comply with it. For no individual can grasp more than the spiritual self, according to its development, *is capable of comprehending.* What God does ask of human beings in this respect is *that those of His incarnated emissaries who understand this Work from their inner knowledge and who recognize its truths must also fully acknowledge these truths to the world and share them in full with their fellow human beings, so that also regarding this question do they become* **pioneers** *for those whose thoughts are too weak, too immature to recognize* **that they are confronted with a work presented to them as a gift, a gift that God has given to all His children.**

Thus, "Toward the Light" is not a religious system created by human thought, human opinions and human conclusions. It is a work *that presents many eternal truths, a work that offers far, far more than all the religious systems together can bring humanity.* The answers enter into areas which hitherto have been unknown to human beings. Mysteries that occupied the human mind and remained unsolved for thousands of years have now been explained. Pointers are given in widely different directions in which clear-thinking and gifted people may continue to search – *if they so desire.* Answers are given to questions on the origin of mankind, on conditions upon the Earth, on the relationship to God and on the relationship to evil in the world. Reasons are given for the endless suffering and grief in human existence. Indeed, answers are given on numerous subjects; *human beings themselves must study the messages of this Work –* **must make their own comparisons, must judge for themselves!**

But is it conceivable that one single human being – be that person the greatest genius – could be so lucid, logical and concise in answering all these questions without the least contradiction? **Must it not be divine thought – Logos itself, God – that is behind that which is given?** *Could the intelligence of one single human being penetrate and illuminate the dark mystery of human existence with such clarity?* **We must ask** – *we, the individualities from the spiritual world who have answered the questions and produced this disputed work through our answers* – **could any human being have created all this?**

We ask – human beings themselves must answer!

71.

When mention is made of the way in which "Toward the Light" was produced, the statement is often made that it stems from the "subconscious". What is the subconscious and what is the supraconscious?

Human mental life exists *on three levels:* 1) **The supraconscious, 2) the conscious, and 3) the subconscious.**

1) **The supraconscious** comprises all that is contained **in the brain of the spirit bound** to the human body – *the large nerve-centre* – and of which human beings *know nothing during their earthly existence,* that is to say, the individual is not aware of the matter withheld in those areas of the psychic brain *that lie* **outside** *the contact areas of the life-giving cord.* For human personality, as it appears in life on Earth, normally[1] represents only a fraction of the knowledge that *conjointly characterizes the true personality* of the disincarnated or fully released spirit; for the knowledge, learning and experience that has been acquired by the spirit through the numerous, varied and progressive incarnations is retained by, and comes into the permanent possession of, the psychic brain. When a spirit is to be incarnated, the transcendental world gives due consideration to the impending life on Earth, and this is done in the following manner: the life-giving cord, which is the correlating channel between the three brains of a human being[2] – namely the psychic, the astral and the physical – is woven into *those* centres of the psychic brain that will be needed by the spirit during its earthly existence. All that is retained in this manner in the psychic brain thus lies **above** *the ordinary consciousness of the human personality.* And this supraconscious knowledge will not normally be able to pass through the channel to the astral and physical brains that is formed by the life-giving cord. But exceptionally, for example under intense mental pressure – when the individual does not allow itself sufficient rest but works all hours of the day and night – or during times of profound grief and worry, the fine fibres extending from the life-giving cord that are interwoven with areas of the psychic brain can rupture. The ruptures may be of greater or lesser extent and may manifest themselves in various ways in the nature and conduct of the individual's visible personality. For example, if the broken fibres are displaced and thus come

---
[1]) The psychic brain of the newly created spirit and of the very young spirits will, of course, have no areas withheld from their conscious mental life.
[2]) Regarding these brains see "Toward the Light", p. 274:4 to p. 288:2.

into contact with the contents of other areas of the psychic brain – with the knowledge, experience and memory of the respective spirit's *previous incarnations* – then the individual can feel as though it were two or more personalities, a state that can lead to insanity. Such splitting of the personality[1] can also arise through lesions in the "casing", for the surrounding Darkness can in very rare cases cause destruction of the insulation layer and of the fibres of the life-giving cord. These ruptures can furthermore be brought about by the individual's engagement in spiritualistic trance séances. When the spirit is released during trance from its dormant body, the fine fibres can be damaged to a greater or lesser extent through the continually repeated releases. And as stated above, if these loose fibres move across otherwise excluded psychic areas, the spirit may – through the life-giving cord that connects it to the physical brain of the quiescent body – be capable of giving information and answers to questions that it could not have given in the normal state of its body. But it is self-evident that these repeated trances must have a destructive effect upon the normal consciousness of the individual.

2) All who desire information on the normal **consciousness** of the human being may read of this and everything in connection with the psychic and astral brain in "Toward the Light", p. 274:4 to p. 288:2. However, the following additional information is given here because the questioner assumes that with the help of the "subconscious" one may, for example, awake from one's nightly sleep at a specified time if, before going to sleep, one impresses upon the mind the intention of waking at a particular hour. This "phenomenon" has absolutely nothing to do with the so-called subconscious, but must be referred to the area of activity of the normal consciousness. If the individual impresses upon the mind the intention of waking precisely at 7 o'clock for example, this "command" is conveyed to the psychic brain of the spiritual self and is "recorded" in a centre there. *The self thus knows that it must be alert at the specified time.* When the hour comes the thought and the will begin jointly to send "vibrations" through the life-giving cord to the physical brain of the sleeping individual, and these vibrations awaken the individual's brain to consciousness – *the person awakes at the predetermined hour.* But sometimes the brain of the sleeping body must be "called" repeatedly before it reacts – so that one awakes *shortly* or *long after* the specified time. But by no means all human beings can rely upon perfect contact between the sleeping body and the vigilant spiritual self. For if the individual is in deep sleep the transmitted vibrations

---

[1]) See "Toward the Light", p. 312:6 to p. 313:2 regarding split personality.

cannot call with sufficient insistence, even though they may be repeated again and again; the individual will not awake until the body is fully rested, unless some external means is employed, for example an alarm clock!

3) **The subconscious,** or in other words, all that lies below *the threshold* or *frontier* of the normal consciousness, but whose presence both in the psychic and the astral retention is due to the human being's knowledge and experience accumulated *in the present incarnation,* must be divided into *two classes:* a) the **purely "nonconscious"**, which is the content of the astral brain, whether the accumulated material in this retention is due to inheritance, conscious thought, or to the "thoughtless" recording of what is seen, experienced, heard or read. That which is received during the individual's earthly life rests inertly in the retention of the astral brain and can be *reproduced into the physical brain* in response to some internal or external prompting. As a rule it emerges exactly as it was received and retained, *without any additions of any kind whatsoever.* The reproduction thus takes place completely **automatically** – without the least involvement of any *thought process.* (See "Toward the Light", p. 274:5 to p. 285:3 regarding this retention and reproduction). But in advanced age, when the cells and centres of the human brain slacken or harden, the reproduction is often deficient, for then the vibrations of the astral brain, *which are quite automatic,* cannot awaken and activate the cells of the "lethargic" physical brain, and for this reason the memories emerging from the astral brain *either cannot be reproduced at all, or are reproduced with a greater or lesser number of "voids".* The astral brain can at other times function in a quite abnormal way, so that it continually reproduces matter that should remain dormant. The same sentence, the same motto, date, musical notes or poetic stanza, the same melody or image may thus be repeated endlessly and at all hours. This irritating condition is quite abnormal and is caused by *a nervous disorder.* Since the human astral counterpart – that includes the astral brain – is interwoven with the cells of the physical body, the nervous system of this brain is very easily stimulated by the nervous system of the physical brain to produce some meaningless, disturbing and endless repetitions. The individual should seek to control this disturbing nervous disorder through the power of will – *or the nervous system must be calmed by other means.*

b) **The "psychic subconscious"** is all that the self retains in the psychic brain *that is due to the life and activity of the individual's normal conscious personality* **during the present incarnation.** All events from the earliest childhood, all learning acquired at schools, universities or elsewhere during the spirit's human existence will rest as well-defined centres in the psychic brain, **but all lies within the fibre-area of the life-giving cord.** All carefully considered thoughts are likewise retained there, but all lies dormant unless the individual has a need for this accrued matter in daily life. If the automatically acting astral brain for some reason does not respond to an outside stimulus through the physical brain such as sight, hearing and so on, *the "thought" must search for the desired subject matter in the psychic brain.* The apparently "forgotten" matter can then through a *persistent thought process* be revived and – through the life-giving cord – move forward into the astral brain, where it activates the corresponding memory-centres, and from there it passes into the physical brain to the individual's consciousness, but usually in fragments, because the psychic memory-centres become "stunted"[1] through lengthy periods of dormancy. *Loss of memory is therefore not only due to a weakening of the physical brain tissue.* If a person for some reason wishes to come into contact with the matter retained in the psychic brain, a thought process is therefore initiated. The psychic brain-areas must be "awakened" from their state of dormancy. Every one has surely experienced this probing of the memory for details of some past event, this searching for a name, a word, a date or a quotation with which the person was formerly acquainted. *(It is assumed that the astral automatic retention for some reason is unable to react and respond automatically.)* The intense probing apparently does not succeed – *the person gives up!* But suddenly the forgotten matter presents itself – perhaps at a moment when "the thoughts" are far away from that for which they previously searched within the memory. But the reason for this unexpected reappearance of the previously acquired matter that emerges belatedly is due to the fact *that the many thought-vibrations* – initiated by the probing thoughts – *will continue to prod the "dormant" centres in the psychic brain and the corresponding cells or centres in the astral brain,* even though the initial thought has left the subject for which it searched. The vibrations will therefore continue their probing until they have caused sufficient activity to awaken the "dormant centres". But a certain time elapses from this awakening until the matter can be dispatched through the channel – the life-giving cord – to "awaken" the corresponding astral cells to an automatically supportive function before it passes through to the physical brain. The subject matter one has been seeking therefore often emerges at a

---

[1] When the spirit at the death of the body returns to its home in the spheres, the memory-centres or areas of the psychic brain quite automatically awaken to full activity.

moment when the physical brain is occupied with other activities. And if it fails to respond immediately, the vibrations will continue to call for attention, that is, they will continue to vibrate until the physical cells respond, *and the subject will then appear clearly in that person's consciousness* – **but only if the psychic brain-centres have not become disabled.**

When science speaks of *repressed complexes* in the "subconscious", the word "repressed" already implies that some *"effort"* has taken place. This implies that the individual has wilfully repressed the thought, the memories – *in the psychic brain* – of for example a sinister, sad or harrowing experience. Or the individual has wilfully repressed the memory of a vice, of obscene images or actions that once beset the "thoughts". All this appears to lie dormant below the threshold of the conscious mind. *But this is only apparently so,* since these experiences, events and memories *have merely been repressed through an act of will but have not been eliminated by the thought,* so that from time to time they will emerge in the normal *conscious mind.* The person has not eliminated – that is to say, removed – that which is causing agony or uneasiness of the mind through a serious and penetrating thought process. But this remarkable, and to many people so incomprehensible, emergence of the repressed or – in rare cases – truly "forgotten" matter, forgotten by the consciousness of the self, can also emerge during sleep. It will then appear as veiled, confused dreams *but with a core of reality,* and these dreams can then at times be clearly recalled by the individual upon awakening. But this emergence of repressed complexes – either in dreams or when the person is awake – *is always brought about through a process of thought.* The thought is disturbed by the "Darkness" radiated from these complexes, it wishes to be rid of these areas of disturbance, it reacts to the uneasiness and calls for attention through the channel to the individual's astral and physical brain. But the will is vigilant and forces the advancing disturbance back under the threshold of the normal consciousness. But at an unguarded moment, when the will is occupied with other work, the suppressed disturbance breaks through into the channel and advances upon the physical brain. Again the will must force it back into obscurity if the individual does not then seek to analyse the matter, and *through intense concentration rid the "thought" of the complexes that radiate Darkness.* Once this has happened peace of mind is restored, the centres of the psychic brain are brought to rest until the self calls them to life once more by an act of will, or until the spirit – the self – after the death of the body must render its account of the completed life on Earth. But when Darkness – *during earthly life* – has been cleansed from the once repressed complexes, *these will not cause the individual any sorrow, pain or shame when the account must be rendered unto God.* **For then nothing will remain but a calm introspective recollection.**

The supraconscious *is* thus *the knowledge and the experience that the spirit has acquired during its numerous incarnations –* **but which are outside the fibre-area of the life-giving cord.**

The subconscious *is: a) The astral retention that during the formation of the foetus receives and retains the "spiritual inheritance"*[1] *of the family, and in which all the individual's experiences and impressions from the present life on Earth are recorded and preserved. All is reproduced fully automatically to the physical brain, either through external influence or through vibrations – set in motion by the "thought" – from the corresponding areas and centres of the psychic brain, since these vibrations can awaken the astral retention to perform its automatic function. b) The* **"psychic subconscious"** *is all that is received and acquired during the individual's present life on Earth through conscious thought, but which lies dormant in the psychic brain because the individual has no use for it or does not "think" about it. But if anything is suppressed by an act of will, forced back below the threshold of the normal consciousness, then areas of "unease" are formed in the psychic brain. All this is called forth through* **a thought process** *and can –* **likewise through a thought process** *– be despatched through the life-giving cord, both to the astral and to the physical brain.*

No further details can be given in this manner. Though it must be added that those scientifically trained persons who seek in various ways to explore the psychic life of human beings will not be able to obtain any true results unless they take account of the **three brain-factors** of the individual personality: *the psychic, the astral and the physical brains.*[1] It is similarly impossible to explain the "subconscious" life in detail unless **two classifications** are considered: *the automatically functioning retention and the psychic subconscious,* which "apparently" rest "forgotten" below the threshold of the normal consciousness.

Since the manner in which "Toward the Light" was produced has

---

[1]) See "Toward the Light", p. 274:4 to p. 278:1 regarding family inheritance.
[2]) See "Toward the Light", p. 274:4 to p. 288:2, regarding these brains and their mutual correlation.

been explained sufficiently often, it is left to human beings themselves to decide whether the two categories of the "subconscious" that have been discussed and explained here *can have played any part in the production of this work in the earthly world.*

72.

How will the future shape itself for humanity when all of the Eldest incarnated by Ardor have at their death been removed from the Earth? Will the line of development interrupted by the wilful incarnations of the Eldest now be resumed, so that the intelligence of the incarnated Youngest will in the future be only a few degrees above that of human beings?

We cannot answer this Question in full, *for our Father has not yet determined which course He will follow in times to come.* But we know that our God and Father at present bides His time; He waits to see what attitude the leaders of the Danish people in the theological and literary areas will in the near future take to "Toward the Light" and its associated works. **And thereafter He will determine the future line of development for humanity.**

But there is much to indicate that *the earlier line of development that was interrupted by the arbitrary incarnations of the Eldest must now be continued along the same path.* For in recent decades a multitude of God's emissaries – the incarnated Youngest – have taken a strange attitude toward the human beings whose spiritual development they were to lead during their life on Earth. For rather than lead others, they allow themselves to be led by the dominant contemporary "mainstreams" in their evaluation of religious sects and of the various forms of art, literature and, in a few cases, science. These "trends" of the present – this contemporary "culture", or whatever one may choose to call it – *are due partly to the decadent leadership of the Eldest incarnated by Ardor, and partly to advanced, incarnated human spirits who in their earthly existence consider themselves capable of bringing new life to the numerous art forms or religions, and in this way seek to impress upon the "spirit of the times"* **the individual characteristic and stamp of their personal spiritual level.** It goes without saying that if the incarnated Youngest are unable to impart to their fellow human beings the full understanding that contemporary taste, numerous forms of contemporary entertainment and the culture of the times, as well as the teachings of the Church, bear the stamp of decadence, *their leadership is then of little value.* It goes without saying that if the leaders fall into step with the common people and take cover behind their broad backs, if the leaders relinquish their leadership to those of spiritual mediocrity, or to those whose intelligence is below average, *then God has no use for His emissaries,* **for then they are of no value for the work they were to carry out.** For the leadership of the Youngest should aim far beyond today, far beyond the boundary of contemporary life. *Their leadership must spring from their own desire to share with their fellow human beings an appreciation for, an understanding of, the best, the most beautiful, the noblest and the most true in all spiritual life, in all forms of art, in all science as well as in the area of religion.* **The aim of their leadership should be for eternity – never for the present time.** But if the human "spirit" and the "spirit" of the Eldest have brought to heel and bound the spiritual courage of these leaders and annihilated their trust in the invisible Father who sent them to the Darkness of the Earth, if they court public opinion, public acclaim and popularity, they are no longer useful in any way. If therefore the human "spirit" and the "spirit" of the Eldest will also in the near future continue to mould the majority of the incarnated Youngest, it is possible that as the present emissaries return from earthly life, our God and Father will replace them with new emissaries, whose spiritual level, whose intelligence is only a few degrees above that of the human spirit. And humanity at large must then slowly work its way out of and above the present earthly chaos, until normal conditions and normal relationships have been attained. Infinitely slowly – through numerous generations – human beings must assimilate that which has already been presented by the geniuses in the various arts and sciences, and that which has been given within the various areas of technology and of invention by *those* of the Youngest who were, and still are, able to assert themselves as the unique personal beings that they truly are. However, we could envisage one area in which the standard would remain very high, *namely in the area of medicine.*

But if "Toward the Light" and its supplementary works are accepted *as the firm, broad and unshakeable foundation upon which all present and future generations on Earth can meet in good will and understanding under the leadership of God's present and coming emissaries, it is likely that our Father will let the human intelligence of His emissaries continue to be several or many degrees above that of the human spirit.* However, our Father has not yet decided, has not yet spoken to us about this problem. He could possibly choose other ways, *ways of which we as yet have no knowledge.* **No one knows – only the future can tell!**

73.

May we receive more comprehensive and more concrete knowledge of the appearance and personal characteristics of our God and Father than we are able to imagine on the basis of the information given in "Toward the Light" and Supplements I & II? And how are we to understand the expression "God's flaming Being"?

No exact, detailed description of God, our Father's appearance and personal presence can be given, for earthly languages lack the words, none of them possess expressions that can describe *the appearance of this exalted, pure and glorious figure.* And no earthly artist can with brush and palette conjure forth even the faintest suggestion of the form of His body or His countenance.

A flaming Being is God! *For the ethereal rays of the Light issue from His body and they glorify its radiant beauty.* **Youth, purity and beauty in their most sublime form are expressions of His personal presence. His countenance bespeaks infinite but sorrowful love. Grief and pain dwell in the depth of His unfathomable look, for He carries the suffering and grief of all creation in His mind.** *With yearning, with sorrow and with pain He gazes into the vastness of space, His eyes seek the Earth, He beholds suffering and struggling humanity. His Thought follows the much-missed and so distant beings,* **who are His beloved children.** *And when He sees that they go in the ways of Darkness, when He hears their disputes, when He sees their unworthy conduct in mutual intolerance, in strife, anger and hatred,* **then His eye is veiled with shame and sorrow** *for the children to whom He gave eternal spiritual life, to whom He gave thought and will, and whose mind He endowed with a spark of the purity, love and beauty of His own Being. But when He sees that some of His children follow the ways that He indicated for the journeying of their earthly life,* **then He fervently rejoices and a loving smile dawns over His sorrowful and solemn countenance.**

If you human beings knew how your Father grieves over you, if you knew the depth of His agonizing sorrow for you, if you knew the anguish of His mind called forth by your unworthy conduct, by your evil, wicked, hideous and illicit thoughts and actions, **then you would be ashamed!** If you knew the horror and revulsion that fill His Being on observing your conduct, *when with weapons at hand, with explosive substances and with poisons you war with one another, destroy peoples, realms and nations, subverting all that is splendid, pure and good both in your own minds and in the minds of others,* **then you would be yet more ashamed!** Then you would grieve over yourselves, then you would turn in mind and in thought toward your distant Father, who is yet so near, then you would answer Him when He calls, then you would beseech Him to lead you in the ways and paths that lead to Him, that lead to His Kingdom. Yea, then you would fully show your Father *that you love Him, that you are worthy of His love and care.* **And your Father would then rejoice over you!** *The anguish, the suffering, the grief that now impress His countenance, and oppress His mind would vanish, and from His deep and boundless love He would bless you, He would in spirit and in truth be your Father, God, Protector and Supreme Leader, both in your earthly life and the worlds of the spheres, yea, wherever you should walk.*

Our God and Father calls upon you – day and night – at all times His calling voice sounds to you!
Human beings, give Him your answer!
Do you not hear Him?

———————

CONCLUDING REMARKS

The last part of our work of supplementing "Toward the Light" is now complete. The questions that our Father desired that we should call forth in the thoughts of people suited to that purpose have now been evoked and answered in accordance with the truth. But in addition to those questions that we had undertaken to elicit, we have received many others that, seen from our world, it should strictly speaking have been superfluous to ask; but since many others than the respective questioners will have difficulty in abandoning old beliefs and accepting new ones, we – the spiritual leaders of humanity – have included some of these apparently unnecessary questions. We have done this in the hope that also these answers can have significance for human beings and awaken understanding also among those who otherwise find it hard to comprehend philosophical and scientific matters.

When we were engaged upon the production several years ago of "Toward the Light", the questions were posed by a small and specific circle of people, so that we were able to arrange the answers in such a manner (in the Commentary) that the questions themselves could be omitted and the answers formed into a coherent whole, thus avoiding repetitions. But since the questions that have been included and answered in the two Supplements stemmed from many different people, each of whom quite properly wished to obtain a direct answer, we were obliged to accommodate these quite justifiable wishes. The questions were therefore included as chapter headings and the answers addressed to each individual questioner. But since some questions touch upon others, though without being identical and not proceeding from common premises, we have not been able to avoid repetition in the answers. However, such repetitions can in our view also be justified, since many people have difficulty in projecting conclusions from one context to another.

The questions that were raised have been arranged in such a sequence that each Supplement possesses *a certain continuity,* which thus facilitates reading and also makes it easier for the reader to draw the proper conclusions from the given text.

Before ending our task we, *those* of the Youngest who in various ways have contributed to the presentation of these works in the earthly world, wish to make the following statement to humanity concerning our work and concerning the gifts our God and Father with our help bestowed upon His earthly children.

Thus we ask all of you who know these writings, and those who in the course of time will become acquainted with them, to do everything within your power to understand in spirit and in truth **the precious gift that our God and Father has bestowed upon you.** Seek to understand *that what has taken place is* **unparalleled in the history of humanity,** seek to understand *that any re-occurence at a future time is precluded.* Seek to understand *that had we failed to complete it, we who in manifold ways have taken part in this work, we should have been incarnated among you so that in the normal way - each within a different field - we could bring you that which has now been gathered in these books.* Seek to understand *that had this been the case, all would have come to light in fragments, would have been given in many different places throughout the civilized world, and at long intervals.* Numerous incarnations should we then have had to endure in order to bring you all this, and the absolute continuity of the present texts would have been impossible to achieve during our earthly lives. For then the necessary contact between us would no longer have existed, *the close contact with one another that we have in our disincarnated existence* **under the direct and supreme leadership of our Father.** But so that our task might be successfully completed, as has now been done, we needed an earthly helper whom we could fully trust, just as we needed to be assured that this intermediary would not abandon her part of the work after a brief while. For since such close and fervent co-operation between a human being and transcendental intelligences *was hitherto unknown in the earthly world,* our intermediary would probably come to feel distressed because of the numerous attacks, misunderstandings and ridicule that could ensue from uncomprehending people, and for this reason be so influenced by the opinion of her contemporaries and the judgment of the world *that the earthly part of our work would become stranded.* For if a person works *solely* for her fellow human beings and is continually met with opposition, ridicule, coolness or silence, then it is human - *though in fact unjustifiable* - to become so influenced by the criticism and opinions of others as to say: *"When you will not understand, when your only response to the work that is carried out on your behalf is silence or foolish denunciation, it is of* *no use for me to continue – I will no more!"* But also this our Father had foreseen and considered, for which reason He spoke the following words to our earthly helper, when He asked her to take part in the production of "Toward the Light"[1] and its supplementary works: *"Do not ever heed the* **opinion of others,** *do not ever heed* **their opposition,** *their possible* **silence, ridicule or foolish denunciation of your work,** *but seek always to abide by the one thought:* **that your spiritually kindred brothers and sisters need your help,** *for should you fail, then your spiritual kin must through many and difficult incarnations, fragment by fragment, impart to humanity that which* **through your help they can now bring as a completed whole.** *Always let My words shine before you,* **let them be the guiding star,** *that leads you during life on Earth. For if that guiding star is quenched,* **you would become unsuited to the task** *with which I hereby entrust you. And do not ever forget* **that I, your Father, am behind all that is given,** *do not ever forget* **that you work on My behalf and on behalf of your spiritual kin!"** Our Father's words became the shining star that gave guidance and strength to our earthly interpreter in her difficult and often wearisome task. *The acknowledgement of our Father and our own gratitude have long since outweighed for her the lack of human understanding.* But when the time comes for these gifts to be received in the way they should be received, *you must never place our earthly helper* **in a position other than the one assigned to her by our Father.** *For no part of that which has been given was born in her mind and thought, for no human being, not even the spiritually most highly developed, could have brought you what you have now received.* **If you feel the need to give thanks, you should thank our Father, respond to His fervent love for you by making these works the foundation of your future lives; then will His blessing be with you!**

To the foregoing words of my spiritual guide I wish to add the following:

Since my task as intermediary, translator, interpreter and secretary for the spiritual intelligences is now ended, I would hereby like to thank all the sympathetic friends I have gained through my work. *I thank each of you for the support that you have given both to my husband and to me in so many ways.*

---

[1]) See Supplement I, Question No. 11.

And to all present and coming generations I should like to say: If you wish to give thanks for the gifts that have been presented to mankind through my help, *you should thank our common Father, who constantly guided me in my work and who encouraged me to continue, when my human self reacted to the lack of understanding on the part of my fellow human beings.* **Offer your thanksgiving where it rightfully belongs – with our Heavenly Father.**

Johanne Agerskov
née
Malling-Hansen